CHASING THE DREAM

LIFE IN THE AMERICAN HOCKEY LEAGUE

TED STARKEY

796.962

WITHDRAWN

444-6053

Copyright © Ted Starkey, 2016

Published by ECW Press
665 Gerrard Street East
Toronto, Ontario, Canada, M4M 1Y2
416-694-3348 / info@ecwpress.com

Editor for the press: Michael Holmes
Cover design: Scott Barrie, Cyanotype
Author photo: Chris Gordon
Cover images: Jerry D'Amigo © Micheline
Veluvolu / Rochester Americans; Toronto
skyline © Roland Shainidze / Shutterstock;
Syracuse armory © Kenneth Sponsler
/ Shutterstock; Map of NYC © Andrei
Tudoran / Shutterstock; Interstate 94 in
Chicago © Henryk Sadura / Shutterstock;
City bus in blizzard © Paul Vasarhelyi /
Shutterstock; Welcome to New York ©
Katherine Welles / Shutterstock

Purchase the print edition
and receive the eBook free!
For details, go to ecwpress.com/eBook.

LIBRARY AND ARCHIVES CANADA
CATALOGUING IN PUBLICATION

Starkey, Ted, author
Chasing the dream : life in the American
Hockey League / Ted Starkey.

Issued in print and electronic formats.
ISBN 978-1-77041-298-9
also issued as: 978-1-77090-915-1 (pdf);
978-1-77090-914-4 (epub)

1. American Hockey League.
2. Hockey–United States.
3. Hockey players–United States. I. Title.

GV847.8.A4S73 2016   796.962'640973
C2016-902393-1   C2016-902394-X

PRINTED AND BOUND IN CANADA
PRINTING: NORECOB   5   4   3   2   1

MIX
Paper from
responsible sources
FSC
www.fsc.org   FSC® C103560

DEDICATED TO PAM, TO TORI,
AND TO THE PLAYERS, COACHES AND STAFF
CHASING THEIR DREAMS IN THE AHL.

INTRODUCTION

On a bitterly cold afternoon, the Pocono Mountains are glistening white, the hills more vibrant than the menacing grey clouds hanging on the horizon. And a bus is barreling down the highway, through the bleak landscape. Winter has taken its grip on this part of the country.

While this spot on the Pennsylvania Turnpike's Northeast Extension is around 100 miles from the closest National Hockey League arena — less than two hours by interstate — the bus, carrying a hockey team, isn't headed there, but to an arena that lies in the shadows of the professional hockey world.

The game may not be as important to the reporters and analysts as those being played in the NHL, but for the athletes on this bus, this contest could be a life-changer. It's a chance to earn a ticket to the show, a chance to skate on the big stage — and live out their childhood dream.

Young players don't dream of playing for the Toronto Marlies, the Syracuse Crunch or the Rochester Americans. But they do imagine wearing the uniforms of the Toronto Maple Leafs, Tampa Bay Lightning or Buffalo Sabres. And being able to put on a Marlies, Crunch or Amerks sweater means they're just one step away from fulfilling that ambition.

The NHL team's logo on the shoulder of their American Hockey League uniforms reminds them of what they hope to achieve — and where they hope to skate. In the meantime, they vie for the illustrious Calder Cup. The lessons a player learns going through the four grueling playoff rounds to win the trophy in a two-month span are a test of endurance, luck and skill — lessons they hope to bring to the NHL.

Welcome to life in the American Hockey League, where rookies, depth players, prospects and veterans of National Hockey League teams chase the dream of the NHL. While the top 700 professional hockey players plying their trade in North America call one of the 30 NHL teams home, the next level of the continent's top professional talent plays here — just waiting for their chance to join the sport's elite.

A simple phone call — the result of an injury, a trade made between clubs opening up a roster spot or even a struggling team looking for a sparkplug — can change a player's life dramatically. A wave from the coach during practice means you skate off the ice, head to the locker room — making sure to wave to your now-former teammates — and quickly pack your belongings for a hurried trip to catch a flight to prove you're good enough for the next level.

A recall means getting a chance to skate with the world's best in front of sold-out crowds and television audiences around the world. It means going from long bus rides or commercial plane delays to chartered jets, luxury hotels and never having to haul your equipment to the bus after games. Instead of stopping at highway rest stops for fast food, you're exploring some of the continent's top restaurants. Those playing on two-way contracts, deals where they might play either in the NHL or in the minors, will receive a scaled salary that could bring as much as a tenfold increase in earnings.

And many do make that leap to the top level. Over its 80 years, the American Hockey League has created an impressive list of alumni. In fact, on opening night of the 2015–16 NHL season, 84 percent of the players had played at least one game in the AHL.

Players know they have a good chance of fulfilling that NHL dream if they play in the AHL. But even if you're an elite prospect who was drafted high, there are no guarantees of success. If you don't work hard to improve your game and play through the grind to deliver a consistent performance, you may never get a chance to move up. Some players are prospects whose NHL dreams have faded over time, but are still looking to prove they have the skill to make the next step and earn the attention of the scouts that sometimes outnumber the media in an AHL press box. And there are the veterans who are there mostly to help teach the new skaters about life on and off the ice, provide leadership and bring some spark onto the ice. Many of them are just happy to be able to make a decent wage playing a game they love.

The AHL is a league that's been built on dreams and hard work, and it has evolved along with the sport. During the Original Six era, with only the top 120 players or so skating in the NHL, AHL rosters were stocked with talent that could easily match many of the NHL's teams. The 1967 expansion of the NHL meant the AHL expanded as well, and began to develop into the league that is more familiar to today's fans. The cornerstone AHL city of Pittsburgh joined the NHL in 1967, and Buffalo wasn't far behind in 1970. But towns and cities like Hershey, Rochester, Springfield and Providence remained the bedrock of the AHL league.

The creation of the World Hockey Association in 1972 lured players who might have called the AHL home, offering much larger paychecks and a more lavish — and what turned out to be financially unstable — league. The WHA also moved into some AHL towns, such as Quebec City and Cincinnati. The WHA eventually went bust in 1979, but four of those rebel teams were absorbed into the NHL, growing the league to 21 clubs. All of these newer teams needed farm teams. Some were created in the AHL, which had 10 teams in the 1979–80 season, all in the northeast from Hershey, Pennsylvania, to Moncton, New Brunswick. And some NHL teams decided to affiliate and send their prospects to the International Hockey League out west.

In the late 1980s, the International Hockey League, following in the WHA's footsteps, aggressively moved into larger markets to directly compete with the NHL in cities like Chicago, Detroit and Los Angeles. Rather than focusing on player development, the IHL sought to provide stellar entertainment at lower prices, billing itself as a cheaper alternative to the NHL. As a result, IHL teams were eager to sign veteran skaters and offered larger salaries than the AHL could offer. This meant players who had seen the doors to the NHL close could make a good living skating for an IHL club. But by 2001, the IHL's ambitious plans collapsed under the weight of financial strain. Six IHL teams joined the AHL, bringing in distant cities of Chicago, Milwaukee, Grand Rapids, Houston and Salt Lake City.

In a dozen years, the AHL had nearly doubled in size. After the merger of 2001–02, it had 27 clubs (up from 14 in the 1989–90 season) and it had increased its footprint across North America, splitting the league into distinct parts.

The eastern region is made up of cities that remain from the AHL's old footprint, with Hershey and Rochester having been part of the league through most of its 80-year history, joining a solid core of teams playing across Pennsylvania, New York, New England and the Maritimes. Thanks to the big-market goals of the IHL's teams that eventually entered the AHL, the presence of Chicago and Milwaukee also helped attract larger markets such as Toronto, San Antonio and Charlotte. In 2015, another distinct group of AHL teams emerged in California, as five teams in the NHL's Western Conference moved their AHL teams west to the Golden State to form the new Pacific Division. With that addition, the AHL now spans some 4,200 miles — from San Diego, California, to St. John's, Newfoundland — and occupies some of North America's larger hockey markets.

This means that an AHL player's experience can be dramatically different, dependent on which team he plays for. Northeastern teams are shuttled across the familiar thoroughfares of the New York State Thruway, Massachusetts Turnpike and other interstates and highways to play a compressed, weekend-heavy schedule. Players rarely stay overnight in a hotel; instead, they ride back and forth in the "iron lung." Western teams mostly pile into commercial planes — sometimes not even riding with their teammates — and have to deal with the pitfalls of modern air travel. They don't play quite as compressed a schedule as their eastern counterparts but spend more time on the road, as more extensive travel is required.

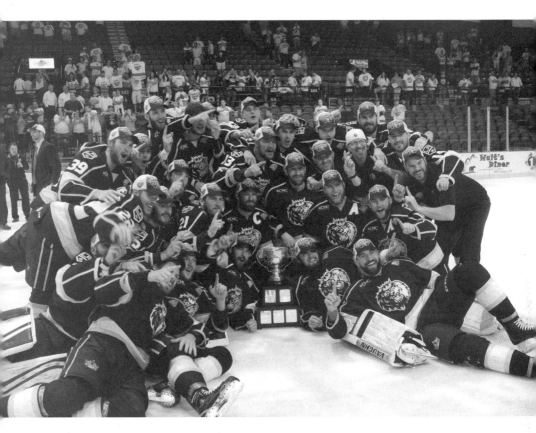

American Hockey League teams differ on philosophies on how to properly develop players for the National Hockey League, with the Los Angeles Kings being one of the teams that looks to teach winning in the minors, as the Manchester Monarchs did in 2015. (COURTESY AHL)

Philosophies on winning and development vary from AHL club to AHL club. Some teams look to teach young players through winning — adding valuable veterans to provide leadership in the locker room and to help earn the club a long playoff run. While it costs more money for NHL teams to supply their AHL affiliates with veterans, these seasoned athletes are considered to be key figures in the development of young players.

Other clubs let their young players take on major roles, win or lose. These teams aren't actively shopping for veterans, and a potential playoff run isn't quite as important as making sure players get the ice time they need. Sometimes that philosophy carries growing pains that don't always translate to AHL success.

And some teams adopt a hybrid system — mixing young players and veterans — that coaches hope not only earns players the chance to win the Calder Cup, but a chance to develop. While they want players to learn how to win, they also want them to do so without losing ice time to players who really don't figure in an NHL team's long-term plans.

It's a 30-team patchwork quilt of cities, players and histories; goals and aspirations; players and coaches — and one with a long and storied tale that most NHL players have experienced at least once in their careers.

And the players aren't the only ones working tirelessly to reach their goals. In the arenas, behind the benches and in the broadcast booths, the public relations personnel, coaches and broadcasters also have their eyes on someday reaching the bright lights of the National Hockey League — at much longer odds than the players.

They ride the same buses as the players, put in the same long hours, go through the same grind and watch as some players — and other colleagues — reach their goals. While a player's NHL dream usually happens in an instant with the rapid change of rosters, front office personnel have to be more patient; there is a slower job turnover up top. While there are 690 roster spots in the NHL, there are only 30 head coaching jobs and 30 play-by-play broadcasting jobs, and a limited amount of space in media departments. With fewer jobs available, most of those working in the front offices of the AHL patiently wait to see if they will be able to fulfill their own dreams.

As the bus on the interstate highway fades into the distance, the hopes and dreams of the players, coaches and team personnel roll on, with many miles to go. This book chronicles the hurdles they face and immense effort they put into every game — the very things that make the AHL the exhilarating league that it is.

CHAPTER ONE

THE *SLAP SHOT* LEGACY

When many people think of the minor leagues, they think of the iconic film that hit the silver screen on February 25, 1977. The story of Reggie Dunlop (played by Paul Newman), an aging player and coach who is trying to lead a hapless hockey team to victory (and rein in the sparring Hanson brothers), has long resonated with hockey lovers. Nearly 40 years later, *Slap Shot* is part of the game's lexicon, a cult classic that fans around the world regularly quote. Clips from the movie are still staples at arenas around the globe, and what was originally issued as a VHS tape has been reissued several times on DVD to introduce younger generations to the movie.

The tale of the Charlestown Chiefs, a team playing in the Federal League, is in fact fictional — it's a loose adaptation of the actual North American Hockey League that played from 1973 to 1977. The NAHL played in several cities AHL clubs call home today — Syracuse, Utica and Binghamton — and not surprisingly, two of the rinks used in the filming of the motion picture are now home to American League teams.

The Chiefs were based on Johnstown's NAHL club, the Jets, and the city's Cambria County War Memorial Arena served as the filming location for Chiefs home games. But several memorable scenes were shot in Syracuse's Oncenter War Memorial Arena and Utica's Memorial Auditorium, now the homes for the AHL's Crunch and Comets, respectively.

To this day, taking a walk around both buildings offers glimpses of film history. War Memorial Arena in Syracuse played the home of the Hyannisport Presidents. The arena was the setting for the legendary scene in which a set of keys thrown from the stands at Jeff Hanson after a Charlestown goal sparks the Hanson brothers to climb into the stands to fight the crowd. Jeff Hanson was played by Johnstown Jets player Jeff Carlson, who wasn't exactly a popular player with fans of the NAHL's Syracuse Blazers. In the movie, this real-life villain in Syracuse was established as Hyannisport's Public Enemy No. 1 and placed under arrest.

While the War Memorial has had many modern touches added to its early '50s frame since America's bicentennial summer — the red scoreboard with the movie marquee–type lettering shown in the film, for instance, has been replaced with a modern video board — you can still easily see the arena's open stage at one end where, in the film, the Chiefs rush into the stands. And under those seats — now blue instead of the red in the film — in the hallway leading to the Crunch locker room from the ice, there's a blue door. There isn't anything seemingly remarkable about this door, it's simply decorated with the words "SYRACUSE CRUNCH HOCKEY CLUB" in white letters with the team's logo. But if you've seen *Slap Shot*, you know this door. And you've seen the room behind the door, too. This door is the same one Paul Newman answered when the cops came knocking, and it leads to what was once the Chiefs' yellow-tiled locker room.

The black rotary phone where Newman's character, Reg Dunlop, called sportswriter Dickie Dunn is long gone, and the minimalist blue benches have been replaced with a modern hockey locker room remodeled for the Crunch, featuring wooden lockers for each of the players, with blue carpet featuring the team's logo and blue paint with silver trim adorning the room.

But the door remains, the film's "NO ADMITTANCE" replaced with metal trim and the AHL team's logo.

Sitting high above the rink in the press box one night, Crunch broadcaster Dan D'Uva said he always points the famous doorway out to new players and visitors.

"My line is, 'You've seen *Slap Shot*, right?'

"'Oh yeah,' they say.

"'Remember Paul Newman? See this door? This is the door where the cops come to get the Hanson brothers. See this hallway right here? This is where Paul Newman goes to pick up the phone. This is our locker room — where the Hanson brothers are arrested after climbing into the stands.'"

The team embraces the film's history in the building. "Historically, it's the first movie we watch on our first road trip of the year," said Jim Sarosy, the Crunch's chief operating officer. They show the locker room to recruits and tell them: this is where you're going to dress all year. "It's an iconic movie for hockey, and it has that cool factor."

Part of the film was also shot in the arena's press box, up a flight of very steep stairs and literally hanging above the crowd. It's where actor Paul Dooley, playing Hyannisport's announcer, uttered the now-famous lines: "The fans are standing up to them. The security guards are standing up to them. The peanut vendors are standing up to them. And by God, if I could get down there, I'd be standing up to them."

Lehigh Valley Phantoms broadcaster Bob Rotruck thinks of that scene whenever he visits. "I think I'm almost in the exact same spot where that announcer is," he said.

D'Uva said the club found a connection with a famous Syracuse alum who spent time broadcasting the team's games after finding film from the Blazers era and a microphone manufactured in 1973. "Bob Costas very may have well used that microphone to broadcast the Blazers championship the next year. More and more you get to know the connections. The announcers in the film are as much a part of it as the players. And there are some broadcasters in the American Hockey League who would fit perfectly in the film."

The Crunch even raised a No. 7 Chiefs banner after Newman's death in 2008, keeping it in the arena's rafters for a season. "After the news about Paul Newman's death, we raised a banner in honor to him for the role he played and being part of that movie. It's something as an organization we embrace for sure," said Sarosy.

An hour's drive east of Syracuse, Utica's Memorial Auditorium, then the home of the NAHL's Mohawk Valley Comets, played Peterborough's home where, in the film, the Chiefs get into a pre-game brawl with the Patriots.

"The Aud," as the building is known locally, was blue with red and yellow trim back then, featuring white banners hanging from the roof to the walls and from the ceiling over the stage at one end of the ice. The building now follows the blue-and-green color scheme used by the current occupants, the AHL's Comets — based on its NHL parent club, Vancouver — and the plain banners have been replaced with advertisements. Sitting in the arena today, it's easy to see the circular seating pattern from the movie, despite the building's modernization.

The skaters used in the film were mostly drawn from the Johnstown Jets, Syracuse Blazers and other NAHL teams, but there's also one who turned into a prominent NHL figure.

Bruce Boudreau, now coaching in the NHL after spending years in the American League as a player and coach, makes a brief appearance. A much younger Boudreau, with a full head of hair, can be seen in the film's opening minutes, wearing a No. 7 green Presidents jersey. Boudreau is first seen screening Charlestown net-minder Denis Lemieux in the movie's first game sequence, then later celebrating Hyannisport's first goal, carrying the puck behind the net, scoring the Presidents' second goal and skating in front of the cage on the third tally.

Boudreau played for Johnstown just before the movie's filming, and the apartment he shared with Dave Hanson served as the model for Reggie Dunlop's home, reportedly because it was messy — exactly what the producers were looking for.

John Walton, who spent time with Boudreau as Hershey's broadcaster, said the coach would make sure everyone saw his cameo appearances during the team's bus trips. "I can say that I've been on a bus with Bruce when *Slap Shot* goes on. And in the old days of VHS tapes, he'd pause it and say 'Look, here's me. I'm right there.' That's an experience — once."

Manchester Monarchs broadcaster Ken Cail, who spent time with then-coach Boudreau riding the bus from 2001 to 2004, recalled the same story. "We've seen *Slap Shot* a number of times because he's in the movie. . . . That's probably his all-time favorite movie, for sure."

The game of hockey has changed a great deal since *Slap Shot* was in the theaters, but as broadcaster Bob Rotruck says, there's something iconic about the film. "It's goofy. The mix of personalities in the film, I think that's what is always going to be true with a minor-league sports team — I've been around minor-league baseball as well — you have this different combining of characters all together. That never changes," he said. "The fighting is not the same as what it once was, but you still have some. I don't know if you have guys put bounties on other guys' heads anymore or things of that nature, but you go back to the guys that lived that stuff in the 1970s and they'll tell you, 'Yeah, that was pretty much [how it] went, as crazy as that stuff sounds.'"

Joe Beninati, a television broadcaster for the Capitals, well remembers the wild style of play in his AHL days. "If you're referring to the shenanigans on the ice, there [were] some terrific line brawls. I did the American Hockey League from 1989 to 1993, and in that window, there were some incredibly tough games. The thing is, you were playing a rival 10 times a season, maybe a dozen times. Just think about the hatred, the animosity that would build up. So, you had some terrific nights where there were tons upon tons of penalty minutes."

Beninati also recalled a moment in 1988 when a now-prominent NHL analyst and former Mariners coach went into the crowd during an AHL game after the organist played a not-so-flattering tune whenever Mariners player Steve Tsujiura was hit or took a penalty. "I was a studio host when Mike Milbury went into the crowd at Palais des Sports in Sherbrooke [Quebec]. He was trying to get to an organist who had just irritated the you-know-what out of him. I remember our announcer at the time was Scott Wykoff, and he said, 'Mike Milbury is headed into the crowd.' I said, 'What, Scott, what?' I remember it like it was today."

A common thread throughout *Slap Shot* is the bus, and for most AHL players — particularly in the Eastern Conference — for better or for worse, the bus is still a big part of life at this level.

Beninati jokingly said he wanted to recreate one of the movie's famous bus scenes. "There was never anyone who took a sledge-hammer to the bus to say, 'Make it look mean.' But there were times when I wanted to hit the bus because I didn't want to be on it."

Walton said watching the film on the team bus was an experience: "There's a certain feel when you watch *Slap Shot* on a bus. I've probably seen *Slap Shot* on a bus at least 50 times. Back in the day when you needed the entertainment and you didn't always have it readily available, *Slap Shot* was a go-to."

But he said that in the modern American Hockey League, the players' attitudes are more professional, as they chase the dream of a National Hockey League roster spot. "It's not *Slap Shot* anymore. I saw a transitional period when I was in Cincinnati [in the 1990s] with games against Kentucky where sometimes it was just a fight night and craziness, and I saw plenty of that," Walton said. "By the time I got to Hershey [in 2002] — not that you couldn't have the wild rivalry games with Wilkes-Barre/Scranton on occasion — but what the modern game is today, a lot of draft picks have a chance to make it to the NHL, and there's more mutual respect among players.

"From the college game to the AHL to [the NHL], there's a businesslike attitude. It's a career; it's a livelihood. I think in the 1970s, for guys in the minors it was something to do, and not have to do another job. It's not that way anymore. It's a very professional atmosphere, and it continues to be more so. It doesn't mean you don't earn [a spot in the NHL] with the 3-in-3s and the other stuff that you don't have to do [in the NHL], but I don't think it's as much [like the movie] as the people think."

Sarosy, who joined the Crunch in 1995, agreed that there have been changes in how the game is played. "I remember the early years. It was a little bit like what I think people would think the movies were like. Win or lose, hooting and hollering, watching movies, having fun, and it's changed throughout the years. Personally, I think it's the amount of money that is available to these athletes. And the players who come here now — with all due respect to those who came before — from day one, they're chiseled and in phenomenal shape. It's basically become a year-round occupation for them, because they have such a short window earning-wise."

While *Slap Shot* featured players at the end of their careers, most of today's AHL players are just beginning theirs. "You have some guys who are 20 years old, and it's like a high school kid going off to college. When the season's over, you're going back home," said D'Uva. "The players who come here, they're doing it not only because they love the sport but [because they] have a legitimate chance at reaching the National Hockey League. In *Slap Shot*, they're playing to get by. They're playing because they can, and someone will give them a check to do it, and there's few scouts."

In the movie, they talk about scouts, but can you imagine any of the guys in *Slap Shot* getting to the NHL? "It doesn't feel that close. *This* is close. *This* is a heartbeat or a sprained ankle away from the NHL," D'Uva said, adding that the AHL is no longer the traveling circus portrayed in the movie. "It's a legitimate developmental league where winning is a premium and almost any player in an American League game could play in the NHL. It's the consistency and ability to adapt between those who get there and those stuck here, but anyone in this league would be serviceable for a game or two in the NHL. I don't think you'd be able to say that about the minor league teams in *Slap Shot*."

Dave Starman, who was a Baltimore Skipjacks radio analyst in the early 1990s, said the game has changed with roster spots at stake. "I think everyone thinks the minor leagues are still *Slap Shot*, and it is the furthest thing from that. This is not a culture where players are going out every night and getting hammered, because it's a different world now," said Starman. "Teams are investing millions of dollars in these athletes, and they're assets. These players know there is huge money to be made at the next level, as opposed to years ago where there was just good money to be made at the next level. A lot of these kids know if they stick with it, that eventually they're going to find their spot."

One aspect of AHL life that is still similar to the movie is the tightness of the group. The compressed schedule and travel required in the modern American Hockey League means the players need to be around each other and often form stronger bonds than their NHL counterparts.

In the National Hockey League, there's more free time available for players, who normally just come to practices, morning skates and games, and when traveling, it's a ride to the airport and a charter flight to their road games. With the minimum salary being $575,000 for an NHL player during the 2015–16 season, players can afford to live on their own. And, usually being a bit older, NHL players are more likely to have a spouse and family than those starting out their careers in the minors, and more commitments outside the rink.

But in the American Hockey League, players are generally a few years out of junior or college, and with a minimum salary of $44,000 in 2015–16, you're more likely to need a roommate to get by. Even for those who make the top-end salaries in the AHL — players not on one-way NHL contracts, who are spending time in the league and are paid the same amount in either league — earnings max out around $400,000 per year.

Troy Brouwer, who started his career in the AHL, smiled when asked about his time there. "For me, I lived in a house with four guys, and it was a pretty much a mess. Nobody cooked, nobody cleaned, and it was pretty much what you'd think a fraternity would be like," Brouwer said. "We played video games, drank a few beers here and there, and were generally just enjoying ourselves. We were all just 21, 22, 23 years old, living on our own for the first time, and trying to get by."

Steve Oleksy, Brouwer's former NHL teammate, agreed. "When you wake up, you're at the rink with these guys, you eat together, you live together, you're around each other 24 [hours]."

Brian Willsie, who spent three years in Hershey before playing in the NHL, talked about the bond of a young group of players looking to make the next level. "There was a group of us — Rick Berry, Brad Larsen, Dan Hinote, Scott Parker, David Aebischer and Ville Nieminen — who eventually all made it to the NHL. We were all in Hershey, young single guys, and Hershey is a nice family town; we're all 20 and 21 and playing hockey, but there wasn't much else going on, so we came back and played poker every afternoon.

"We all get called up and we spent a week and a half in Denver, and I think it's arguably one of the best cities in the U.S., or right up there. I'm not knocking Hershey at all, but when you're comparing the two, you're like 'wow.' The Avs had just won the Cup in 1996 and were on their way to another one in 2001, and with those Hall of Famers, and that just fueled us.

"One of your best buddies would go up for a game and he'd come back and have stories about how he did this in Denver, ate here and played the game with these guys. We had so much incentive to get up there. One year, three of them went up, and the rest of us made it the next year, so the seven of us made the big club.

"It was a little bit of pushing each other, and you don't want to get left behind, but we really pushed each other and wanted to get to the bright lights and big city of Denver. . . . You're all thrown together, rode in together every day, hung out every day on the bus, and formed a friendship that lasts a lifetime."

AHL president and CEO Dave Andrews described the players' experience as going through a rite of passage. "You're coming out of junior hockey or college hockey and now this is your first freedom, and you're a pro. You're getting paid to do it full time and you have all these experiences you've never had before," said Andrews. "I think they do make great friendships and they never forget them."

It isn't an easy journey, said longtime AHL veteran Eric Neilson, but the travel and relative lack of amenities also help teammates bond: "We call it the jungle. That's what we call it down here. We're eating pizza and chicken fingers, and you get called up to the show, they're having sea bass and steak and flying for an hour-and-a-half and we're riding on a bus for three or four hours. You definitely have to love the game. It's a grind during the year, but at the same time, I think that brings a team closer together. All that time on the bus — and in the back of the bus playing cards."

Some players feel that the bond among AHL players may in fact be stronger than those in the NHL. "There's a camaraderie outside the ice, teams are tighter. I will say the players [in the AHL] are not quite as businesslike as players in the NHL. There's less individuality," said J.P. Côté, Neilson's longtime teammate. "At this level, we're trying to make everybody feel as good and be the best person they can be, so they're feeling good. There may be players who enter the team who are quiet and shy, and we really try to group everybody together."

Barry Trotz, who started his pro coaching career in the AHL, says the strong bond exists between players and coaches as well. "If you played in the minors, there's a special bond. And I don't think you see that as much in the NHL," he said. "I think with minor league teams, almost every player you coach in the minors you still have a relationship with, and they will call you. I think just riding the buses, it just brings it out — it's almost like college, it really is. You have those roommates and those friends in college, and there's that special bond. I think the minor league is sort of like that. . . . It's not the greatest or most glamorous life, but it is fun."

The unique circumstances of the AHL give the games an interesting dynamic. Players, knowing that scouts are watching and evaluating their every shift, want to bring their best every night to try and earn a promotion. Some nights, teammates are battling teammates for the chance to get a spot in the NHL, and it makes it a challenge to worry not only about your own game but the team's game as well.

"You want to go out and have your fun, but at the same time, you can't be satisfied. Your ultimate goal is to make the NHL and there's a lot of competitiveness on teams — and within teams. Not that you want to see the other guys fail, but you want to be the guy who gets called up. You want to be the guy who gets to the next level," said Brouwer. "For that reason, I think it created a lot of good battles and that makes everybody better, because they always want to improve their games and stand out. We had good teams, and a lot of the guys I played with in the minors, we all moved up to Chicago at the same time."

The veterans AHL teams sign have to be a kind of guide to the younger players, to help teach that while individual success is important, the team — and parent club's success — trumps all. With a lot of young prospects looking to battle for an NHL roster spot, it's a matter of keeping them on the same page — all while they're looking to prove their own worth, on and off the ice.

Côté says for AHL vets, it can be a grind to keep their place in that league. "The AHL is definitely something that, every night, you can't take anything for granted. I am going to be 33 soon. I'm one step from the NHL. . . . You can't take a shift off," he said. "You know you're going to get hit one second later than you would get hit in the NHL, but guys have something to prove. There are guys here who are just as fast as the fastest in the NHL, but they're just missing some other skills. And there are guys who are tougher than the guys in the NHL, but they're just missing something. That makes a league that's very explosive."

Oleksy knows it's difficult for players. "It's obviously very demanding. Especially the style of hockey down here, players are trying to move up to the next level. It's balls to the wall every night — there are no off nights. The thing with that, all four lines, all six defensemen are hitting, just trying to make an impression," Oleksy said. "There are no off nights, and that puts the 3-in-3s in perspective. That's why it's important to know and understand your game, and be consistent every night. Don't try to do too much, because what happens as the 3-in-3 goes, your body's tired and it takes a toll, so it's definitely a different element that you learn over the course of your career."

Neilson also mentioned how the scouting and evaluations can be mentally taxing. "It's a toll on the body and the mind, . . . being away for weeks at a time. The 3-in-3s. The NHL doesn't have that. You play Friday, Saturday and Sunday afternoon. And the thing is, every time the guys get on the ice, they're getting judged, they're getting watched and there are scouts. At the NHL level, those guys making millions can take a night off. Guys here, they're trying to get there, so every time the guys get on the ice, they're being watched and judged and trying hard all the time," he said. "Not everyone can play in this league."

The golden ticket to the NHL usually goes to those who don't really worry about a promotion, but rather those who do their job well at the level they're at. Looking up at the bright lights of the NHL instead of worrying about your day-to-day job in the AHL isn't usually a road to success. In fact, players who have spent more time worrying about reaching the NHL than doing their job in the minors rarely get there.

As Trotz says, it's far better to focus on the job at hand. "I think players that just worry about the day-to-day in the minors, and just enjoy where they are, and play as hard as they can, those [are] the guys that always make it. The guys that don't make it are the ones who think, 'I'm better than this league, I should be up there,' and they keep looking up instead of looking forward right in front of them. Those are the guys who never make it. That's what I've always found."

Rob Zettler, who coached the Syracuse Crunch, uses the NHL jump as a motivational tool for his players. "One of the best parts about coaching in the AHL is you walk in the room, if you look at everyone in the eye, everyone thinks they have a chance to play in the NHL. That's a fun thing. My job and our staff's job is to convince them if you do what's right at this level, you will have a chance to get to the next level. If you focus on what's going on in the NHL and not worry about your job, you're not going to get there. It's what you do on the ice with the players. The skill level you show on the ice with the players on a day-to-day basis will get an invite to the NHL," he said. "Frankly, at this level, play can get sloppy at times. Guys can run around because they're young, energetic, want to prove themselves, but you go to an NHL [game], it's a lot of control, a lot of skill and a lot of doing things the right way, and the details of hockey done that way. It's our job to teach the kids that and get them ready for the next level."

Bill Peters, who coached Rockford in the AHL before taking over the NHL's Hurricanes, noted how different it was coaching the IceHogs compared to juniors or the NHL. "When you're coaching juniors, they want to be in juniors so they can turn pro. When you're coaching in the National Hockey League, they want to be there and they want to stay. When you're coaching in the American League, they don't really want to be there. They want to get to the National Hockey League. The guys who have figured out you put your time in, put your work in, and it's a process, you're in the American League for development. As a coach you have to keep one eye on the standings, but another on the development process and making sure you get guys ready as quickly as possible."

And keeping players focused on the task at hand can be your primary role as a coach. "That's the biggest challenge at our level, making sure the players are *here* while they're here. And that's just making sure they're developing at this level — making sure you're the best player you can become here and investing in your team and your own development," said Chadd Cassidy, a former Rochester coach. "Because once you start looking forward, where you think you should be or [are] going to be, you miss a lot of learning. That's the one thing we do here: commit to the guys being here, making sure their focus is on what they're doing now."

Martin Biron, who played in Rochester before starting his NHL career, recalled that he made sure he kept his focus on the American League. "You don't really think about the NHL as much. You think American League, you read about the American League, you prepare for the American League. You're thinking that's your whole world right now and that's what you focus on. Yeah, you keep an eye out, but you can't always be about the NHL because you'll forget what you have to do in the AHL."

Despite how much things have changed over the past 40 years — how professional the game has been become, and how high the stakes now are — one aspect has remained the same. You have to give it your all every game. As coach Reggie Dunlop tells the Hanson brothers in *Slap Shot*, "OK guys. Show us what you got."

CHAPTER TWO

THE SYRACUSE CRUNCH

In the winter months, the hills alongside the Interstate 81 are usually snow covered. Heading north, an hour past Binghamton, you come upon the U.S. 11 exit for the Onondaga Indian Reservation. And as you reach the top of the hill, the city of Syracuse appears on the horizon. The white, puffy roof of Syracuse University's signature building, the Carrier Dome, is prominent, and to the left, the skyline of New York State's fifth-largest city.

SU, known for its basketball, football and lacrosse programs, dominates the city's sports landscape, but that doesn't mean hockey doesn't have a long history in this town. The first-ever Calder Cup champions, the 1936–37 Syracuse Stars, called the city home — and that was even before the actual trophy was made.

When the Hamilton Canucks moved to Syracuse in 1994 and became the Crunch, many wondered if the team would survive in the Orange's shadow (the basketball, football and lacrosse teams are all called "Orange"). But the Crunch has not only survived — they're just one of six AHL teams that have operated continuously since the mid-1990s — they've enjoyed a strong wave of success, both on and off the ice.

With a great deal of innovation, not to mention financial risk, the Crunch has worked hard to deliver a major league experience to its fan base. It certainly hasn't been easy, but that just drives the team to try new things, some of which don't work, but others resonate throughout the entire league.

In Syracuse's downtown core, a coating of snow covers the sidewalks. There's sun overhead, but dark clouds streaming off Lake Ontario loom in the distance. The clouds are a reminder of the bands of lake-effect snow that push southward all winter long, and put this city into contention for the "Golden Snowball Award" — an annual honor given to the snowiest city in America. The snowfalls leave the hills and the city below white, giving it a very hockey-like feel, and one of the city's attractions is the Clinton Square rink where skaters glide outside under the buildings and trees, despite the sometimes bitter conditions that winter brings.

A few blocks south of the rink sits the Oncenter War Memorial Arena, an old-school hockey arena built in 1951. One of the oldest arenas still housing professional hockey in the United States, the War Memorial Arena still features an old-fashioned illuminated movie marquee with "SYRACUSE CRUNCH" spelled out in red letters with the team's upcoming home games, just like a theater would have advertised feature films in a bygone age.

The words "SPORTS MUSIC ARTS SCIENCE" are emblazoned on the grey, square building, as are the names of various battles fought long ago, such as "IWO JIMA" and "PEARL HARBOR." Inside the arena, a postwar-era style still dominates, with turquoise walls and lots of steel and mirrors.

It's game day in Syracuse.

Tonight's opponent, the Lehigh Valley Phantoms, bused up a day early to avoid a winter storm that dumped a half-foot in Pennsylvania, and they have arrived at the arena for their relocated morning skate.

Inside, the arena feels like a hockey barn. Eight hours before puck drop, the hum of the lights is audible. At one end there is an open stage with the words "IN MEMORY OF OUR SERVICE VETERANS" emblazoned above it. The metallic roof above resembles an airplane hangar. The blue seats below are right on top of the action — and hanging directly above them is a press box that is literally suspended above the lower deck.

The building is more than 60 years old, but as Jim Sarosy, the team's chief operating officer, says, the team embraces the historic aspect of this building. "It's a unique building," he says. "It's cool place to play. It's our version — the American Hockey League version — of Wrigley Field."

According to Sarosy, the building's history plays a part in the game. "It's in the air. It's almost like the ghosts of the War Memorial. Our players — in between periods, to get to our medical room — they have to walk through a hallway that the fans have access to," he said. "For us, every building we go to, we pull up on a bus, we go to a door, right to a locker room. There's no interaction at all, and you're kind of secluded. Here, it's the opposite: you're on top of everyone and in the hallways."

For all the team's embrace of history, its marketing approach is thoroughly modern. When the team first arrived, the owners and managers knew they'd be up against a well-established university that dominated the local media. And they knew they would have to be creative to survive.

Team owner Howard Dolgon, who has made a nice career of being a promoter, is a driving force behind the aggressive marketing plan that has seen the team make a name for itself. Dolgon, the longest-serving individual owner in the AHL, knew the team would have to be unique.

"We knew when we came to town [Syracuse University was] there, and it's the white elephant in the room," he said. "We knew we had to be different and more creative, and it kind of drove us to do what we did, to create our own brand. We established one right away almost of irreverence, of 'what are these guys going to do?'"

Syracuse hosted the AHL's first outdoor game in 2010 — on a rink built at a race track at the nearby New York State Fairgrounds. And in 2014, it put a rink in the Carrier Dome. "It was always like the Crunch was on that edge, whether it was signing Gordie Howe to play in his seventh decade, whether it was bringing in Riddick Bowe [who had an ownership stake]. What it did for our brand, it made local fans be able to tell their friends from out of state that they were Crunch fans, because they knew the out-of-state fans had heard of us," said Dolgon. "They didn't know who the Springfield Falcons were in L.A., they didn't know the Albany River Rats, but they'd heard of us because of the stuff we did. We were in TMZ, in USA Today. We branded ourselves nationally, and it was as important for us to do that right away as it was to brand ourselves locally."

The team doesn't even shy away from scheduling home games when the Orange host football or basketball games a short distance away at the Carrier Dome. "I think what we did was became stubborn right off the bat. We don't ignore it, but we don't do any scheduling around their games. Some people think we're silly, but we're very proud of our product, and we take care of what we can control. And it's been like that since day one," said Jim Sarosy, the Crunch's chief operating officer. "We're proud of the niche we've been able to carve out. We've done that in many different ways, from a corporate area where we're very strong. SU [football and basketball] prices are very expensive, rightfully so, and almost NHL-like. And so they price out a certain part of the corporate community, which is where we fall in very nicely."

The Crunch also were pioneers in terms of outdoor games, becoming proponents for staging AHL games outside. The original cost to hold an outdoor game was estimated at nearly $1 million, and even after selling sponsorships to the event, the Crunch were still on the hook for at least $500,000 to cover the event. That price tag had scared off some AHL teams, but even a setback in funding didn't stop the team's drive to be the first host of an outdoor game in the AHL.

An original proposal had the game played at NBT Stadium — the home of the Syracuse Chiefs, the city's AAA baseball team — with Onondaga County to put in $350,000 toward the event out of hotel taxes meant to fund local tourism. The Crunch would toss in an estimated $250,000 for the rink and up to $400,000 in other costs. But that deal was nixed by the county's legislature by a 16–2 vote, meaning the Crunch would be on the hook for the entire event if they chose to pursue it, and would have to set it up in a non-traditional venue.

With encouragement from local and state leaders, the Crunch announced less than three months before the event that it would indeed hold an outdoor game and assume the bulk of the risk.

"Our attitude is: why can't we do it? If they can do it at Fenway Park or Wrigley Field, why can't we do it in Syracuse? What was important for us, and it's always important for us, we like to be first at anything we do. If another American League team had done this before, I'm not sure we would have done it as the second one," said Dolgon. "We're always the first. And we were different, because we weren't walking into the infrastructure of a stadium of any sort. We were on a dirt race-track with an old grandstand and no locker rooms, and of all the games in the NHL and American League level now, I still think it stands as the most unique because of the setting."

It was a chance to do something first. "We saw what they had done at the NHL level, and we saw how the league had captured New Year's Day as their day. You look historically: Christmas Day is the NBA's, Thanksgiving Day is the NFL's, and the NHL did a real good job . . . creating this as a day you had to watch hockey," said Dolgon. "Even though we were a minor-league organization in a smaller market, we owed it to our fans to treat them as if they were in New York, Los Angeles, Philly or Chicago, or any other major market."

For an NHL team, $1 million would be a fraction of a club's national and local television deals — not to mention around the sum a Stanley Cup playoff home game would bring in. But AHL teams are heavily dependent on ticket sales for revenue and carry budgets that are a small fraction of their parent clubs'. This event posed a great financial risk for the club. As Sarosy said, "I don't know how many owners would have the courage . . . to do the tremendous risk of holding an outdoor game on a dirt track at the Fairgrounds. One bad snowstorm, that sets you back four or five years."

According to Lindsay Kramer of the *Syracuse Post-Standard*, it was a huge financial risk. "You have to remember, at the time, there was no NHL game tied to it, it had never been done in the AHL before and never even really considered before. From what I understand from

Howard . . . all he got was, 'It's never going to work.' And who would think it would work?

"The phenomenal thing is there was no arena there. The rink was built on a dirt racetrack built for horse racing — average stands, which were long, with no corner seats and some portable seats. You have to make, build and maintain the rink. It's one thing to do it at a baseball stadium where you've got an infrastructure and support. But there's nothing there. There's no merchandise areas, no ticket-taking areas.

"But as far as I've concerned, even though there were some hitches, the feedback is it was a huge smash."

Sarosy concurred. "Industry-wide, this was the first team in history to put on a game. Up until that point, the NHL comes in, buys the game, and puts it on. The NCAA games that have done it, they have the resources of a university. This was the employees and Howard trying to put on a massive game — and the result and the photos were unbelievable," said Sarosy. "I get chills just thinking about it . . . but it was so rewarding. It wasn't just a Crunch thing, it was a county thing and we want our fan base to be proud."

Despite the game being played in an aging grandstand overlooking a snow-covered landscape on a cold February day, 21,508 fans jammed Interstate 690 to get to into the stands and set the attendance record for the AHL at the time. With the NHL in Vancouver on Olympic break, the game got national attention and a national television slot on NHL Network.

Syracuse's 2–1 win over Binghamton was the forerunner of more outdoor AHL games, but without that first leap of faith, there may not have been another team willing to make that gamble. But with the picturesque setting, the Crunch established that it could work, both visually and financially, and the outdoor games became a regular staple of AHL schedules as a result of the Crunch's desire to do something different.

According to Kramer, although there have been other outdoor games, Syracuse's is still unique. "I don't think any of them have quite answered the bell like that one, because they've all been in existing places or linked to NHL games. The locker room area was a combined room the size of between the blue lines, combined, both teams are walking in with a curtain separating them. It's like a mite game.

"There's no reason to expect it would work. But it did."

While the Crunch were making headlines off the ice with promotions, success on the ice was harder to achieve. The franchise only managed to win a single playoff series between 2002 and 2012, and had made just one conference final appearance since arriving in town in 1994.

But the Crunch became the affiliate of Tampa Bay in 2012, and the Lightning has a philosophy of wanting to win.

Syracuse inherited the core of a team — the Norfolk Admirals — that had accomplished something that had never been accomplished in history of the sport. The Norfolk Admirals set a professional hockey record in 2011–12 by winning 28 straight games to end the regular season, and then went 15–3 in the playoffs to capture the Calder Cup title. Norfolk not only broke the AHL record of 17 straight wins set by the Philadelphia Phantoms in 2004–05 — the same number as the NHL mark set by the 1992–93 Pittsburgh Penguins — but also shattered the professional hockey record of 18 set by the International Hockey League's Peoria Rivermen in 1991.

For J.P. Côté, who played that season with the Admirals before joining the Crunch, it was an once-in-a-lifetime experience. "I've never been part of a streak like that. I don't know if anyone in professional hockey will ever be on a streak like that again. . . . It just felt as if we were on top of the world, and you know teams are waiting for you because you're the team to beat. After 10 wins in a row, you have a target, and they put an 'X' on their calendars when they play you," he said. "Then you go to 16 wins . . . nine was the team record and 17 was the AHL record, and 18 was the actual pro hockey record, and we kept winning. The end of the season stopped us at 28, but we actually won 29 because we won the first game of the playoffs. That was definitely something special, and a special group of guys too, there in Norfolk."

The streak also helped the team's players get noticed. "You can see the guys from that team are doing really well, and most of them are still playing hockey, on bigger contracts like the NHL," said Côté. "I think at the AHL level, too, as a veteran, a lot of teams want to associate themselves with winners. To have this on my resume, as this was my second Calder Cup, is big."

With the AHL's rapid turnover, Côté noted just three players remained from that team three seasons later in Syracuse — himself, Eric Neilson and Mike Angelidis. "Most of the guys didn't stay. There's only three of us here, and most of them went on and are having great careers."

For Neilson, who played alongside Côté, the winning just snow-balled and was a thrill. "Amazing," he recalled with a smile. "You're never going to do that again. . . . It was a once-in-a-lifetime opportunity. Winning 28 in a row, I'm going to look back on that and remember the group of guys we won with, how much fun we had when we won. It was almost the more we won, the more we partied as a group, and had fun together off the ice. That actually brought us closer together and that translated to more wins on the ice. We did everything together, we ate together. . . . It was really a family mentality we had there, and that's what I'm going to remember the most."

Norfolk owner Ken Young, who has been involved in minor-league sports for 24 years, recalled the run fondly. "You play three games on a weekend, and the chances of winning all three are not very good, even though we were an excellent team. Each game became bigger than the last one as the streak went on, and it was just so thrilling to constantly see us in these close games, ahead, or in some cases behind with the streak on the line late in the game," he said. "And then we'd score one or two goals and pull it out."

With the affiliation change, the Lightning moved the core of the team to Syracuse in the summer of 2012.

Norfolk was one of the AHL's most popular venues, and moving to Syracuse wasn't popular for some players. As Neilson said, "It was a shocker. I couldn't believe that they were going to do that. Going from Norfolk — and I'll be honest with you, I didn't really like Syracuse to begin with — when I heard where we were moving, I said 'Oh no.' Norfolk, it's beautiful there, it has Virginia Beach. A lot of guys were like, 'I can't believe this is happening.' But when you get [to Syracuse as a visiting player], you only see the hotel and come to the rink, that's all you see.

"Once you get to know the city, and you get out into the community and see the people and meet the people and into the surrounding area, it was awesome. I fell in love with the city. Syracuse is a second home right now, and I'm proud to call it that."

Angelidis spoke highly of the move, and despite leaving one of the AHL's popular spots, they found a new home in Central New York. "Syracuse is a great city, it's got that old vibe, that *Slap Shot* vibe. Good, loyal fans. I like to say Howard is one of those owners who really cares about his players. It's got that old-school feeling, and it's a great place to play. This city took us in right away, they made us feel like we had been there many years.

"It was sad to leave Norfolk, obviously, it's a great hockey city too, and sad the AHL is leaving there, but we're excited to be here, too. The fans have treated us like we've been here for a while."

Côté was happy with the move. "Coming here, they welcomed us. Howard welcomed us with open arms," he said. "They treat us really well, the fans are great and it's a hockey city that has history. You can tell by looking around the old barn, you know, it's what AHL hockey is all about. It's fun to have all these people behind us, and it's even more fun to win for them."

With the combination of the core of a championship team and the crafty marketing of the Crunch, the team reached new heights in the first year of the affiliation. As the Crunch's new coach, Jon Cooper brought an attitude change to the club.

"It was a monumental philosophy change," said Sarosy. "It wasn't overconfidence, it wasn't cockiness and it was a special type of swag — as Jon Cooper describes it. They knew what was expected to win, and more importantly what it took to win. And they were willing to do it."

Erik Erlendsson, who covers the Lightning for the *Tampa Tribune*, explains the team's philosophy of wanting to win at all levels of their system. "They put a huge emphasis on these players who can learn their craft in a winning and positive environment, and winning can accelerate a learning curve. There's a big emphasis on winning at every level they have players involved at."

With Cooper behind the bench for the start of the 2012–13 season, and with Tyler Johnson and Ondrej Palat on the roster, the Crunch were able to reach the Calder Cup Finals for the first time in franchise history. It was the first finals trip for the city since the 1937–38 Stars.

Kramer said the team's run renewed the fans' appreciation. "The year they went to the finals, you could tell people were thirsting for it. It was the first year of Tampa Bay, Norfolk had won the year before and that was the 19th season of Crunch hockey. You just felt so many people had been there for 20 years, because a lot of people stick around here and the fan base had been there since year one, you could see the appreciation seeping from the stands. . . . It was good to see the city get a shot at a winner."

Sarosy said the run was also important for the team to help establish itself — not only to fans, but to free agents. "You have to remember from a Syracuse Crunch point of view, we fortunately had a lot of success off the ice with our promotions, but until that point, we had just one conference final appearance before then. For me, from a hockey point of view, it made us relevant. We always had the accolades for doing the big events that we're very proud of and we can control, but what that affiliation and that run did is made Syracuse a destination for people who wanted to come play hockey, because of what we've done and [how we've] transformed."

In 2014, the Crunch got a chance to break the United States' indoor hockey attendance record with another big event, playing the first-ever hockey game inside the Carrier Dome. Like the 2010 outdoor game, it wasn't an inexpensive endeavor, with the team spending nearly $500,000 to put on the event, although unlike the outdoor contest, it wasn't subject to Syracuse's fickle winter weather.

Dolgon said, as with the 2010 outdoor game, the driving force was doing something that hadn't been done before. "We wanted the novelty of holding a game for the first time at the Dome. . . . It's an old facility but it's still an iconic one here. We've proven that we can be pretty creative toward our outdoor games, and say, 'OK, we're going to break the American League record.' All of a sudden, we're rolling, we're going to do it one better and we're going to set the pro U.S. record [for attendance for an indoor game]," said Dolgon. "We were able to mobilize a community and generate national publicity out of it. So now all of a sudden, it's not just the Syracuse media covering us, it's Yahoo!, *The Hockey News,* and the Associated Press. It's Mike Emrick talking about us."

Assembling the Dome's rink in a matter of days proved to be a major challenge. "They thought at one point it might not get done," Kramer recalled. "It was three-and-a-half days to build the rink when experts said it never had been built that quickly. It probably can't work, but we'll try it. But it did."

Sarosy said a major issue was finding time between SU's football and basketball schedules. "The Dome was so different, it was three-and-a-half years in the making. The hardest part was trying to set the date. How many buildings in America have not only basketball and football together — that's almost unheard of — but also a successful lacrosse program that draws very well? Once we had a date, it was much harder for different reasons. With the Fairgrounds, they gave us the site on January 1 for the February 20 date and basically said 'go,' so we were kind of on our own," he said.

"At the Dome, we got in on a Monday on a very truncated time frame, and [did] what takes two weeks in three-and-a-half days. It was almost a miracle from there. . . . But it was set for us, that was not only the first hockey game in the Dome, but you have that moment of clarity in the moment, to think the largest crowd in the United States to watch a professional game indoors was in your city and watching your minor-league club. It's pretty cool."

For D'Uva, calling the game was a special thrill. "The Carrier Dome was special because it was the first one ever and [I had] called every other sport in that building. To be there just to witness the first hockey event in that building and to broadcast it on NHL Network . . . the event was just a spectacle. And just so much went into making it happen, I'm not sure I could have appreciated it in the moment the way that I should have. But just to look out at the sea of people and to look at a hockey rink . . . you felt transported to another universe.

"Hockey is big here, but it's always been second fiddle to the university, especially the basketball team. But to have been working so hard for a few years to promote the Crunch to get to that next level and as close as we can to number one in this city, to rival Syracuse basketball for the most attention, wow. We've done it.

"We've put Syracuse Crunch hockey — literally — on top of Syracuse basketball. It was figuratively wonderful and literally a special experience. . . . There's something jaw-dropping about, 'Wow, we've done this.' We've done this, we've taken ourselves to a new level that we hadn't really anticipated. It elevated the Crunch and hockey in Central New York to a new level."

The Frozen Dome Classic, like the 2010 outdoor game, was a success, with a crowd of 30,715 seeing the Crunch beat Utica 2–1, breaking the U.S. indoor mark of 28,183 set by the Tampa Bay Lightning in the 1996 playoffs at the Thunderdome. According to Kramer, the hockey had the same buzz around town as one of the school's big basketball games. "You could see the fans going around like a Syracuse-Duke game. And people want to be a part of that. Howard says this is a big-event town, or a unique event town, and it's been proven."

Zettler also recalled the game fondly. "It was great. Those are the experiences that Tampa and Syracuse have been able to give our players. For a lot of these guys, that'll be the biggest crowd they ever play in front of with over 30,000 fans there. To have that kind of support, that kind of energy, not only in the building and around the town."

Off the ice, the Crunch and Lightning have looked for new ways to improve the team chemistry, and after one trip to Bridgeport, management surprised the players and gave the team some days off to tour nearby New York City.

Neilson appreciated getting a special experience during the midst of a long season. "We needed to create our identity and we needed some togetherness off the ice. We realized that, and Tampa realizes that is very important, and Syracuse knows that's an important part of the game. You have to know your teammates off the ice, that's very

Mike Angelidis, an AHL veteran with Albany, Norfolk and Syracuse, was part of the core of the 2012 Calder Cup champion Admirals team that relocated to Central New York that summer. (SYRACUSE CRUNCH)

important on a personal level. We did some stuff in New York that was team-building activities, which was a great hit, and a great success. And you look after that trip, we won five games in a row. I know that had something to do with that trip."

Dolgon said the players showed their appreciation for the jaunt into the Big Apple. "I ran into J.P. Côté. . . . and he said to me, 'First of all, thank you.'

"He said, 'It was the best experience.' He said, 'We always don't know how players are going to react because it's real bonding for them. I can't tell you how great it was.' When you see a veteran like that, he's not a kid, you really realize they get it."

Cooper and his Crunch alumni — including members of those Calder Cup Finals teams — got a chance to play for the Stanley Cup in 2015.

Angelidis even went along for the ride as a "Black Ace," even taking warm-ups before Game 7 in the Eastern Conference Finals.

That was a big reward for the Crunch captain, according to Erlendsson. "Even though he wasn't able to play, it was a big help for him just to be able to skate in warm-ups for that."

Sarosy said Tampa's playoff run was a special time for the Crunch's captain. "Mike is more than thrilled to be there, but he just had his second child. His heart's kind of torn, but he's a human being. How can you not be happy? Mike took warm-ups in Game 7 in New York. Like anyone, they're just trying to get one or two games in, they all understand the importance of that role, and so many guys are sitting out in practice.

"And really, there's not that traditional 'Black Aces' role there, they are filling the gaps at the practices, which is a tremendous role. It all goes back to Jon Cooper. They want to be there for him and for each other, and that's what's cool about it. And you see it from top to bottom."

Young recalled what makes Cooper such an effective coach. "Coop is an excellent coach because he does so, so well with people. And he knows how to motivate, he knows the difference because he gets to know his players well, so he knows what to get out of a guy, whether you do it softly or maybe some other way. I can't say enough good about him."

Erlendsson says Cooper also seems to have a special relationship with his players. "The one thing I noticed when some of those players started to come up into that Lightning lineup, you'd ask them about Cooper, and one of the first things they'd always say is, 'He's our friend.' You don't typically hear players and their coach in that type of relationship, but that's the way he comes across.

"You get the feel he's that kind of guy, can hang out with them and be their friend, but at the same time, it's almost like an uncle relationship; you can horse around with him and crack jokes, but when it's time to be serious, he can get serious too. I think that's why the guys really buy in to what he's trying to preach."

Erlendsson said the role the AHL plays has been a big part of the Lighting's recent success. "Really, since Steve Yzerman took over [in 2010], it's been about development, and you look at guys like Tyler Johnson and Ondrej Palat, they weren't high draft picks, and they let them go down there and they played big minutes and played bigger roles on both sides and they eat a lot of minutes and play the game.

"If you listen to Jon Cooper talk, so much [is] about how much he thinks of the American League and learn[ing] the game away from the spotlight. The philosophy is, let those guys go down there and play, and don't rush them, and make sure they're up when they're ready; and if you [look] at the guys they've brought up, not a lot of the guys have gone back. That's their philosophy, let them play, let them learn, so they're ready when they come up."

Inside one of the AHL's oldest buildings plays a forward-thinking team with a bright future, able to survive and thrive in a market that few thought would support hockey. And its recent success has only put the team in an even better spot.

"The last four or five years, things have come together, said Kramer. "Other cities have failed, there are two- or three-year cities because they're bigger markets, or have more entertainment options, or maybe it's an NHL ownership that isn't quite as connected to the fan base. But I just know it's worked here in Syracuse, and I know it's been key over the years."

Andrews said the team's owner is the driving force behind the franchise — and one of the reasons the team has thrived despite tough competition. "To be really candid, it's all about Howard. Howard Dolgon has made that work. Howard drives that, and we talk about being on the edge in terms creativity and marketing, and no holds barred in terms of marketing and selling his team, and doing whatever he has to do and whatever he can think of to make it exciting for his fans — build interest and to have a better team there."

Sarosy noted how much the Crunch has adapted. "People have to remember when we first came into the American League, we were one of the biggest markets. There were small Maritimes cities, and in a short amount of time, we are one of the smaller markets. It's evolved so much in a short amount of time. . . . It's trying to stay ahead, trying to be as creative as possible, listening to your fan base, listening to your NHL partners, making sure they get what they need out of it, and that harmonious thing, trying to pull it together and moving forward as a collective unit.

"It's not us trying to tell the fans what they like. How silly is that? You have to listen to what they want in their market. In Montreal you could probably open the doors and fill it every time. In Syracuse, we have 2,200 to 2,500 hockey fans that will come if we win every game or lose every game. If we lose, they'll let us hear about it, but that's our market.

"We need to bring Scooby Doo to a game. We need to bring Ric Flair to a game to attract fans. . . . We've done it since day one. We signed Gordie Howe to play way back when.

"Howard owns it for the right reason: his passion. We still run it as a business, but he wants to win hockey games and get some rings and he loves it."

Andrews is full of praise for the work Dolgon puts in: "He works awfully hard with whomever he's affiliated with to make sure Syracuse is a good, competitive team. I think Howard is a bigger force in Syracuse than any other owner in our league. . . . To have 21 years of success in a market as small as Syracuse and with a building as old as Syracuse, and [a] whole host of different affiliates over the years, and probably more bad teams than good, he has sustained it."

CHAPTER THREE

THE BUSINESS

Minor-league sports used to be seen as a small-time venture, but over the last two decades they have evolved into big business for both the owners and the cities involved.

As a result, the American Hockey League business model has changed from a circuit of smaller venues playing in older arenas to a collection of teams in much bigger cities with sparking new facilities and with all the bells and whistles of modern sports, of luxury boxes and naming rights. Most AHL organizations are now trying to sell a higher level of hockey.

What was a 16-team league back in 1994–95 has blossomed into a 30-team league. And of those 16, only five teams have remained intact: Providence, Springfield, Hershey, Rochester and Syracuse. Some of the smaller markets, such as Cape Breton, Cornwall and Fredericton, have been replaced by the large cities of Chicago, Toronto and San Diego.

AHL president Dave Andrews said that when he took the helm in 1994, he was concerned for the league's survival, as it was trying to keep pace with the International Hockey League, which was taking away some of the league's valuable affiliation agreements with the NHL.

"Our original objective was just to survive, to tell you the truth. Twenty-one years ago, there were a lot of markets that weren't sustainable, and we were up against a league with much deeper pockets with its independent owners in those days," said Andrews. "We had history on our side, and we had a commitment to player development and so as in any planning endeavor . . . we had more young players than the other league had. The other league had some delusions of grandeur of trying to challenge the NHL in some ways, and they had big markets and wealthy owners and a plan. But their plan was divergent from what I saw to be our strengths, and I thought, 'If we build on our strengths, we've got a chance here,' because they were going in a different direction.

"So we wanted to pull back that development niche of the business that was shared between the IHL and American League — a lot of NHL teams had gone over [to the IHL] because they could get a better return for their players from the wealthier owners than in a place like Moncton or Charlottetown . . . NHL teams would make a decision to [send their players] to the IHL and if it continued we were done."

Because there were more AHL and IHL teams combined than NHL franchises, there was essentially a bidding war for teams to pay to affiliate with a club, the fee an AHL or IHL team would pay in exchange for having to pay the players themselves. And according to Andrews, that bidding made it a lot more difficult for AHL teams, which had smaller margins.

"There was a period in the mid-1990s where the two leagues were competing for agreements, since there were more teams between us than [there] were NHL teams. Which was great for NHL teams, since they could say, 'If we don't get $1.4 million for our players here in Hartford, we'll take $1.8 million with the Chicago Wolves.' So our guys had to pay $1.8 million to stay in business."

The free-spending ways eventually doomed the IHL, and when the league folded in 2001 the AHL got a major boost. It now had some much-needed stability, allowing the league to effectively corner the market on NHL affiliations — eventually expanding to 30 teams to pair with the 30 NHL clubs.

Six teams from the IHL were welcomed into the fold, which had a huge impact. As the league now covered a far larger area, it affected the expenses of some teams. For instance, some teams that had mostly used economic bus travel now required the more expensive prospect of plane travel and more overnight stays.

"It changed the geographic face of the American Hockey League. A lot of the AHL owners and NHL teams that owned teams in the league [then] really weren't too excited about getting on planes to go play games in Salt Lake City or Winnipeg or Houston," said Andrews.

"We did it in a way that was a win-win. I don't think any of those teams coming in would tell you they were treated unfairly because of the deal, and I don't think anyone on our side would tell you we didn't cut a pretty good deal," Andrews continued. "They came in, they were happy to have a league to come to, they were happy to have a league that had a strong center and good leadership and a whole lot of teams, so you've got some strength and part of something that's going to survive."

The AHL gathered all the IHL teams and spent a day giving them an orientation to the new league, assuring them that they were going to be treated the same as all the other teams.

"We said, 'You're in now. Let's make it work.' . . . If you really created systemically for the National Hockey League a 30-team league to service all 30 NHL teams in a way that it does, it had great value," Andrews said.

The 30-team model also helps teams sustain their franchise values, since there are no further expansion plans or other ways to get an AHL team without purchasing one of the 30 existing ones.

As Syracuse Crunch COO Jim Sarosy said, "The biggest thing that affects our franchise values is the fact that the league is a 30-for-30 league. We used phrases like a 'closed system.' There's no expansion, there's no way to get a franchise outside of having to purchase one from somebody; in a system like that, it's going to help maintain those franchise values."

Just before the 2015–16 season, the American Hockey League also underwent another major shift: 16 AHL teams are now owned by NHL franchises instead of private ownership. Plus there are six new cities in the league, with five of them in California.

It all started when four Western Conference NHL teams that owned their AHL affiliates wanted to have their affiliates in California, within close proximity of each other, for ease of not only calling up players, but also being able to scout their own players regularly.

The San Jose Sharks has owned their affiliate since 2001, with the team first located in Cleveland, then moving to Worcester, Massachusetts. The Los Angeles Kings has owned their affiliate since 2000, when they started play in Manchester, New Hampshire, in 2001. The Edmonton Oilers activated a dormant AHL franchise to play in Oklahoma City, Oklahoma, starting in 2010.

The Calgary Flames has owned their AHL affiliate since 2007. And until 2014, their affiliate, the Heat, was based in Abbotsford, British Columbia, a far outpost that was more than 1,500 miles from the nearest club. "They were flying teams in and covering the cost to play them, and so the Islanders took them up on it and went out there. And that may be the last time they went out west," recalled Phil Giubileo, the Bridgeport Sound Tigers announcer.

Subsidizing visiting teams' travel to get to their home arenas was costly. The city guaranteed C$5.7 million per season, but it terminated that deal after losing C$12 million between 2010 and 2014, according to the CBC. The Heat never averaged more than 3,900 fans per game — particularly with the Heat being the farm team of the Canucks' rival, the Calgary Flames. With the expense of covering hefty travel costs, the team left town, moving their franchise to Glens Falls, New York, for the 2014–15 season.

While there was a push to move these teams closer to their affiliates, there was one holdout: the Anaheim Ducks' affiliate in Norfolk, Virginia, which was still owned by Ken Young instead of the club. Young said he didn't want to sell his team to the Ducks, but faced with having no NHL affiliate to supply players, he had little choice other than to replace his AHL club with an ECHL one — although he wanted to make sure the sport remained in the Tidewater region of Virginia.

"The idea of an AHL West Coast division had been around for a while, but not acted upon. When it finally appeared as though it was going to happen, my choice would have been to buy another team

— but there weren't any for sale. So since they were our affiliate, Anaheim was the logical one to buy Norfolk," said Young.

"I really didn't want to do that, but I wanted to make sure we weren't going dark either. It took some time, that negotiation; it had a bit of conflict to it, but at the same time, I thought both parties would come around. We were fortunate after Anaheim did buy us — and it was strongly rumored at the time they were going to San Diego . . . that we were talking to the Edmonton Oilers [about an ECHL team to potentially replace the AHL Admirals]. Oklahoma City was not going to accept an ECHL club, and we were fortunate to be able to keep hockey in Norfolk. When we bought [the Admirals] 11 years ago, the whole idea was to keep hockey in Norfolk."

Young, who also owns baseball's Norfolk Tides — a AAA affiliate of the Baltimore Orioles — said that his main goal was to keep the sport in town. "The whole area has been good to me in my baseball ownership there, and so when I was approached by some of the city leaders [about] keeping the team there, I said, 'We can do that,'" he said.

"The financial part of it wasn't as concerning to me as having a combination of having a viable product — I at least wanted to break even, of course, but at the same time, fast forwarding a decade later, I didn't want to lose hockey for the area."

Bob Murray, general manager of the Ducks, told reporters that they had wanted to put AHL hockey in California for a while. "The five teams, individually, all decided they wanted to move. We all had different term leases. We didn't own a team, but some owned a team. Everybody had their own relationship, and the ability of getting five teams to agree, in a timing factor, that their leases would end and they could all move at the same time, was a challenge. Otherwise, we might've been able to do this a couple of years ago. We had to find a franchise to buy."

According to Murray, it wasn't an economic drive for the Ducks to purchase the team — although the team would save on air travel. The driving factor was the benefit it would mean for the parent club.

As he told me, "If a goalie gets hurt in the morning, you can't get somebody there. We've seen that happen. There are just so many things that can happen, and we eliminate that this way. Yeah, we should save some money in flights because we've had so many with all the injuries we've had. Think about the guys flying back and forth. But we've had guys lose skates, lose equipment, fly all night to get there and not have equipment. We needed to make this happen."

In fact, the push to move west started more than two decades before it actually happened. "I can tell you the first discussion about putting teams in California came in my first year on the job in 1994, and Tony Tavares from Anaheim was championing the idea," AHL president Dave Andrews said. "It was a laughable idea then and remained a laughable idea for a long time."

But the investment by NHL teams has led to an increased drive to put teams closer to their parent clubs — and not just the California teams, he said.

The salary cap has also influenced that trend. For instance, how much you pay coaches or how many coaches you have won't have an impact on a team's salary cap. As Andrews explained, "Let's use the Kings as an example. They had a team in Manchester and they're spending a lot of money there and they don't see them enough. For that investment, they want to see their value, every day, every game of their players. . . . It's not just California, if you look at the moves we've made in the last few years, not all of them, but maybe 95 percent of them have, one way or another, have brought an NHL team closer to home.

"It took us three years to arrive at a workable agreement between the western-based NHL teams and ourselves to have that happen. It's pretty complicated to move five teams at the same time, and they didn't all own teams and we had to find teams for them to buy — and we didn't have anyone willing to sell. You can imagine how difficult that was to get to a point to make that all happen. Now that it's done, I think the way we've structured our divisions and conference, everyone is pleased except for the schedule differentiation, which, in time, we'll get that fixed."

Ken Cail, who called Manchester's games before the team moved to Ontario, California, said it was sad the champs would move west, but was happy that an ECHL team was moving to New Hampshire.

"Not being able to defend the Calder Cup is disappointing, but I don't think the shift of the franchise is any great shock to anyone who follows the team on a regular basis. There had been rumors that had been around for a number of years now," he said. "When the announcement was finally made, it started to sink in a little bit more, but beyond that, I think we have a great base of hockey fans."

The moves create a different dynamic for the league, as while exposure in California is a boost, it comes at the expense of former AHL cities.

Broadcaster Eric Lindquist wrapped Worcester's final games in Massachusetts, then drove west for the Barracuda's first season in California. "I had a great time in Worcester. . . . I had one of the best setups in the American Hockey League to call a game, and the Sharks are a great organization to work for. It was tough packing up the car and heading out. I made some great friends over the past eight years, and I was a little teary-eyed. I was sad to go."

Lindquist said on the flip side, he was excited by the new locale. "I'm excited about the next chapter, I'm excited about playing games in an NHL arena, and San Jose is one the of the biggest cities in California. It's a huge market. We're talking working on radio and TV and getting everything ready for the season. It's a new start; there's a lot of learning along the way, because it's a new situation with an AHL team playing in an NHL arena. . . . I'm excited to start the season and see what's going to follow this year."

Sarosy said the move of some of the team's rivals out west carried mixed feelings, with excitement for the foray to California along with sadness over the loss of several AHL markets.

"California hockey is unbelievable right now, and you look at the five markets the league has added, the only reason you aren't jumping over the moon is your heart goes to some of the cities that might not have a team. That's where you're tempered a bit," said Sarosy. "But take that away, from an American Hockey League point of view, obviously it's the next logical step."

According to Lindquist, there was strong interest in the Sharks' affiliate from the Bay Area. "A lot of our online listeners for Worcester games were in California. Any time we did the jersey auctions online, I'd say 75 percent of the jerseys were bought by fans in the San Jose area. San Jose fans are usually rated some of the top in the National Hockey League, and they kept a close tab on what was going on in Worcester, and a lot of people that I don't know would reach out to me and say, 'Welcome to San Jose, we're looking forward to Barracuda hockey this year.'"

Lindquist said the move is a big plus just for the fact that a call-up wouldn't involve a cross-country trip. "I've seen guys over the last eight years, I think Jamie McGinn made the trip 12 times, and I know I flew out for training camp every year in San Jose, and I was tired for a few days after the trip. Forget that day, to have guys called up in the morning and play in San Jose that evening, it had to be tough," he said. "But now to walk down the hall and put on a different sweater and play in the same arena, I think it will be a huge advantage. . . . The American Hockey League is more and more of a development league, and it's helpful to have these guys in your backyard and being able to get a good pulse of them on an everyday basis and not 3,000 miles away."

Norfolk's Chris Wagner said he was happy to move closer to Anaheim. "The six-hour flight back and forth from Anaheim takes a lot out of you. I've heard San Diego is great. We have a great fan base in Norfolk, for sure, but it's good for a change."

Wagner also added Norfolk's tough travel made the move palatable as well. "It's brutal. We usually leave two nights before, around midnight, drive through the night, get off the bus at nine or ten and then get off the bus and then practice. Even when we play a game, we get back around four a.m., so it's not like we have a day off. You're just sleeping the whole day.

"It's good to win two of three on the road; then there's some perks to being on the bus, but usually you're just trapped like sardines in there."

Andrew Miller, who played for Oklahoma City, said he did feel bad for the fans the team was leaving behind. "It's sad for the fans in Oklahoma City," he said. "I really wish we'd be staying; you kind of live in the moment right now and not worry about the future."

California native Shane Harper was happy to see teams move out west. "It's really cool; I think it's really cool for California hockey as well.

I mean, it'll be an easier game for some kids to go to, not as pricey. There's more teams now to check out pro hockey. I'm really excited."

Growing up playing hockey outside Los Angeles, Harper said he had none other than Wayne Gretzky attend his seventh birthday party at the Kings' practice rink in 1996. "That was pretty incredible — most people don't believe me — especially being from California, how the heck does that happen?" he said with a smile. "It was pretty neat. Wayne Gretzky was a great guy, gave me a bunch of gifts, and it was a cool experience. I still have some pictures to look back on that."

Harper also said hockey in California has developed a lot in recent years, not only due to the "Great One," but also to the Kings' success. "It's grown a lot. Our era was the start of it. There were a couple of guys before us, but that Gretzky era, kids started to play, and now the Kings have been winning, won a couple Cups, and it's become a lot more popular now. There's a big population, a lot of people playing football, baseball and basketball, but there's a ton of people playing hockey. It's definitely spreading and getting more popular."

Terry Murray — who played and coached for California NHL teams — thought it would be good for the AHL. "When I went to Los Angeles, California was the number three state in the union for players going to major junior hockey. Hockey's been in California for a long time. Heck, go back to the old Western League days with San Diego and San Francisco.

"I think it's wonderful; I think we're exposing a lot of people to the game, and showing that hockey players [are] coming from the Sun Belt — and good hockey players coming from there. It's great for the league."

Elliott Teaford, the NHL columnist for the Los Angeles News Group, says the AHL's growth to the state was long overdue. "I think it's going to be another step forward for hockey in California in the sense that you've seen the NHL growth that's undeniable, and there's been great growth since Gretzky came in the trade from Edmonton.

"There's a great migration to the game for people who have lived here. It's generational now. You have your Beau Bennetts and Emerson Etems and Matt Nietos and Jonathon Blums, but what was missing is that sort of middle ground where you're looking at guys that had to go away to school, like Etem went to Shattuck-St. Mary's, and I think that's sort of filling in the gap now. There's a great high school league the Ducks started in Orange County, and it's not just there, it's in San Diego County and the Inland Empire of Riverside or San Bernardino County.

"Arizona State is starting a Division I program, which will be the first west of the Rockies other than the Alaska schools, and then you'll have others and jump in and start a conference. . . . And then, on top of all that, you'll have the AHL here. I'm not saying it's like the northeast, but it's getting there.

"You're seeing kids getting to the NHL, and you've got to have the influence of college hockey here and already have some pretty good club teams. Now you're going to have serious minor league hockey for the first time since the IHL flirted with California with the Gulls and Ice Dogs, but the IHL was more a money-making league than a developmental league like the AHL is."

Teaford also saw a lot of potential for growth in San Diego, where he felt the Ducks could improve their foothold. "They've talked about growing the game, and southern Orange County has grown so much in 20 years that you now see a crossover. Mission Viejo south, people in that area are big Chargers fans because there's no NFL team and [they] either split on the Angels or Padres," he said.

"The Ducks games are on the Fox Sports network in San Diego, but you can't find the Kings because there's not that much interest in them. It's more interest in the Ducks, so it makes perfect sense to go down there and grow their fan base in San Diego."

Teaford also said adding more professional teams to the mix was the next big step for California hockey. "There's such a natural progression we've had since we've started. . . . You can't deny this has become a kind of a hockey hotbed and this is the next step for it."

The increased ownership of affiliates by NHL teams has afforded them greater flexibility. At the beginning of the 2015–16 season, 16 AHL teams were owned and operated by NHL clubs, while 14 were under other corporate or individual ownerships.

The goals of the two groups aren't always in alignment. Individual owners are looking for a profitable product — or at least one that doesn't lose money — and their teams are usually the ones that put a bit more effort into trying to win Calder Cups. While the payrolls for individually owned teams are usually higher, the NHL teams are compensated with affiliate agreements to help cover costs.

Wendell Young, the general manager of the independently owned Chicago Wolves, told *Crain's Chicago Business* in 2013 that the team splits the cost of between 13 and 17 players on the Wolves' roster with the St. Louis Blues. The actual price paid is based on how many days they spend in the AHL. This gives him a lot of autonomy for an AHL club. Other teams, according to Young, pay lump sums for the rights to a group of players.

Young told the publication that between salaries, front-office staff, an approximate $120,000 payment to the league and the six-figure cost to equip the players, the Wolves spend several million dollars per year that the Blues would have spent had they owned their own franchise.

The Syracuse Crunch's agreement with Tampa Bay requires them to pay a fee — one of their biggest yearly expenses — to their parent, Tampa Bay Lightning, but the NHL team covers the cost of the players' salaries. The agreement is a complex, negotiated contract that goes all the way down to who covers the jerseys.

"In our affiliation agreement, it gets down right to who's responsible for the socks. It covers every single item. Every [affiliation agreement] is a unique document," said Sarosy. "And we have been in that position before; back in 1999, when we were with Vancouver, they gave us five roster spots and we were responsible to fill those spots, which we did, and got guys like Ryan Bonni, Reggie Savage, Trevor Doyle and Martin Gendron. We have done it that way, but we currently are with Tampa Bay and we're more in the norm for the league, as our affiliation fees are paid, and in terms of decisions and expenses, it's all under Tampa in terms of salary coverage.

"What we'll negotiate is, for example, they'll buy the gloves and the helmets, and we'll buy the jerseys and the socks kind of thing. I don't want to say it's typical, because they're not typical documents, but that's what it's like right now. For our agreement, Tampa Bay is responsible for the sticks, we pay for the jerseys. We negotiate right down to how much of the year's supply we're responsible for."

Team-owned AHL franchises don't have to pay for affiliation agreements, and with the salaries already covered by the parent club under the umbrella ownership, they typically regard the cost of running another team as a product of their main operation. These teams don't always splurge on veteran players, other than ones that fill the NHL team's needs. They tend to emphasize player development over winning, outlaying less expenses than an independently-owned team would in most cases.

The growth of NHL-owned AHL teams certainly has been a shift in the league, and with two NHL clubs — Winnipeg and San Jose — hosting their AHL teams in their own arenas, it will be worth watching if more NHL teams down the road opt to bring the business completely in-house.

A lot has changed since Sarosy joined the Crunch two decades ago, and the biggest change for him is the markets the league now plays in. "The biggest difference from day one to today is that the strength of the relationship with the National Hockey League is second to none. That goes back to Dave Andrews and what he's been able to accomplish. The business model has changed a bit, our travel budget has grown, our equipment budget is insane now, and the growth areas have been there. We were one of the bigger cities in the American Hockey League [back in 1994], and we were playing the Halifaxes and Cornwalls. Fast-forward 20 years, we're one of the smaller markets, especially in building size.

"You see these legit NBA and NHL arenas that teams are playing in — but bigger is not always better. We're relevant in our own market and proud of what we've been able to accomplish, and unlike the Rochesters and the Hersheys, there's no major university in their cities. We've found a nice spot in the sports landscape in Central New York and we try to maximize that and continue to grow."

Opening the AHL to new markets notwithstanding, the business and marketing of the league has changed as well, with technology playing a major part. News organizations have been cutting budgets across the board, in some cases reducing coverage of local sports, and in larger markets moving the AHL franchise further down the priority list. But now teams are able to bypass traditional television and print media and reach their fans directly.

Howard Dolgon, owner of the Crunch, says social media has allowed teams to reach more fans directly. "One of the ways it's changed dramatically is the way we communicate with our fans. Because the days of being a dominant player in print or TV, those are over," he said. "People are getting their TV sports more from ESPN and less of the local stations, and in this market in Syracuse, as opposed to New York, there's a lot of locality. People are getting away from reading, and that front page article in sports — once the paper is printed, it's only four days a week [in Syracuse] — it's a smaller [impact]. People are getting their news from Twitter or Facebook, and more electronically, so we've had to adapt how we communicate. It's been a big change in how we do business and we're still learning to do that and get better at it."

Sarosy credits Dolgon for spearheading one of the team's successful social media ideas, a 2015 YouTube video in which Vance Lederman, the team's senior vice president of business operations, offered to let Republican presidential candidate Donald Trump coach the team. In the video, Lederman says "So, Donald, I've got an offer for you; you're a big man, you want to be for all the people. I invite you to come Syracuse to be a professional hockey coach." Dolgon followed up with some Tweets aimed at the Republican candidate, including one that read "Who wants @VanceLederman to challenge @RealDonaldTrump to a dance off sans shirts. Live on CNN. Better than debate."

The post was a hit not only locally, but the story got picked up across North America by CBS, the Score and the *Hockey News*.

"The birth of that came out of our brainstorming sessions, and Howard Dolgon, it was another of his countless ideas that he's come up with. If you look at our history, that's something we've done all throughout, [from signing] Gordie Howe for a fifth decade to inviting Britney Spears here or Kris Humphries," said Sarosy. "For us, that helps us grab national attention. . . . Dan D'Uva shoots the video, we put the script together and within an hour, it's on the cover of NHL. com, CBS Sports and Yahoo! Sports."

While the video won't sell any more tickets per se, it does help the team's branding not just locally, but also across North America, Sarosy said.

"People here say, it's not going to sell you any tickets, and it's not. But it reinforces our national brand and makes our sponsors feel good. How many American Hockey League teams — for a non-hockey thing — are on CBS, Yahoo! or NHL.com? It's not something that happens daily."

The emergence of the internet and audio and video streaming allows AHL teams to reach fans far outside their home markets, on individual radio streams as well as the league's out-of-market product, AHL Live.

Lehigh Valley announcer Bob Rotruck says his reach now extends far beyond what his radio signal could ever deliver. "I grew up with an AM transistor radio and a headpiece in my ear, listening to whatever games. A lot of people don't know this now, but at nighttime you could pick up AM radio from out of town before internet radio, so when I was a child of the '80s, I would grow up not only listening to Cincinnati Reds games, but Chicago Cubs, Milwaukee Brewers and the Philadelphia Phillies.

"You could say I know WOR in New York and on and on, and then the hockey games in the winter as well. I'd be able to pick up the Dallas Stars games all the time, and before that the North Stars on WCCO. . . . I listened to a lot of Blackhawks games with Pat Foley, and Detroit and St. Louis had Ken Wilson for a long stretch. And those were the announcers I loved listening to.

"I'm doing the same thing. And it is an older-school thing, but the fans are able to watch on AHL Live video, which makes it not quite as old school. But there are a lot of fans who are hanging with me on the internet radio.

"I feel like there is a romance with the AM radio, but now these fans can actually reach out to you. That's the advantage of the modern technology and the social media. I'm really active on Twitter, and fans even find me on Facebook.

"I just had recently a couple of tweets, this guy who's a loyal Phantoms fan from Brazil, who listens to the internet broadcast all the time. Maybe he's originally from Philadelphia; that, I don't know, but

I thanked him, thought that was awesome, retweeted that, and that sparked someone saying he was listening from Australia."

The increase in video and audio options certainly has a drawback for AHL teams though, as a hockey fan looking to catch a game now not only has the option to go to their AHL arena, but could also catch any NHL game they wanted via a broadcast package.

Rochester broadcaster Don Stevens has noticed the difference in recent years. "The thing that now is the biggest difference as far as hockey in this community — or any community — [is] there are so many things going on now. There are so many things available to choose from for your entertainment dollar. Anybody can watch any NHL hockey game on TV any night of the week, or any other sport or event," he said. "It's all on TV — you don't have to leave your home or anything. So it has had an effect on the fan base of people coming out to watch games. Rather than just providing a product of the sport, now you're also having to provide the different entertainment things to get people to come out to your building. That's changed a lot."

Barry Trotz, who coached in Portland from 1993 to 1997, remembered how the Pirates were one of the first AHL teams to emphasize that element. "Our owner, Tom Ebright, was way ahead of his time. His daughter was going to school at Vanderbilt in Nashville and he would go watch the minor leagues — the East Coast League's Nashville Knights — and they were owned by a wrestler, an accountant and a promoter.

"They had these fireworks and stuff going on, and that wasn't done at the American League level or the NHL level. He brought that mentality to Portland, Maine, and turned that place into an event. It was a little bit chaotic . . . the Maine Mariners were probably drawing about 1,800 fans a game before we arrived, but we were drawing 7,400 in a 6,700-seat building.

"I was walking across the ice early [in] the year — and we had a good team — and [Worcester coach] Jimmy [Roberts] was walking across the ice and he goes, 'Hey, kid — what is all this crap going on? It's like a circus.' I said, 'I know, Jimmy. I'm not used to it, but this place is packed. It's entertainment. You've been here before, there was no one here, now this place is going nuts.'

"I think Portland in the minor leagues set up what you see now in game presentation, giving the fans more than just a hockey game. That's what the minor leagues do, they prepare the next level, the next rules. I think Portland was groundbreaking that way."

Dolgon added there's also a lot of competition for fans' entertainment dollar, not only from other sports products but other types of entertainment such as movies, concerts and dining that fans can spend their disposable income on, other than just hockey games. "Like anything else, there's more for people to do. Things come and they go. When they're here, they're our competition."

In recent years the AHL has also looked to grow the league by playing games in different venues, indoor or outdoor, which provides exposure in larger markets where they may take an interest in the farm teams, but also gives the players a taste of performing under the bright lights of a big stage.

In 2012, Norfolk played Hershey at Washington's Verizon Center, which Ken Young thought was a special opportunity for his club. "It's good for the players, especially for the younger players, and it was one of those situations [where] it was exciting for everybody to go into a major arena, with a very good crowd, and play on NHL ice. It was a good experience. It's one that, [if] we were faced with that opportunity again, we would do that."

In the past five seasons, Syracuse has played an outdoor game at the New York State Fairgrounds, and inside at the Carrier Dome, as well as Montreal's Bell Centre and the Verizon Center.

As Crunch broadcaster Dan D'Uva recalled, "The Bell Centre was neat because the place was packed, starving for hockey; Montreal fans had not seen hockey [due to the lockout], and the place was packed. It was one of the most one-sided games the Crunch have played, it was 4–1, but it was a dominating performance. They controlled the game in every shape and form. To be in that booth and the press meal was out of this world. And that was, 'Wow. This is up a notch.'

"And I've covered the Devils, been at Prudential Center, Madison Square Garden and a couple of NHL rinks, calling the game; they have engineers looking after you and you think, 'Wow, we don't have this in the American League.' Just the number of the people [18,582], the intensity of the place."

For those who get to participate, it can be a career highlight. For instance, Brandon Manning still recalls a great game he played for the Phantoms, where they won 4–3 in overtime. In was on the heels of the 2012 Winter Classic, and the then-Adirondack Phantoms played the Bears in a game at Philadelphia's Citizens Bank Park in front of 45,653 fans.

"That was a huge day for us as an organization. To play in front of that many people in that kind of atmosphere was real exciting. Just going into the Phillies clubhouse and seeing what that was all about from the start, and to go out on the field and you're in a hockey rink on a baseball field," said Manning. "I'm a big sports fan myself and so I've been at a few ballparks, so that was an awesome experience."

Rotruck said the experience was a thrill. "This was our championship of the season. Ben Holmstrom scored with 21 seconds left to tie the game, and Shane Harper, who's such a great kid, won it in overtime and did a TV interview after and couldn't speak. I was trying to find the right words as well."

Before the game, Rotruck wasn't sure how it was going to go. "I thought, 'I'm going to do an outdoor game in January and I'm going to freeze my butt off.' . . . But it was 50 degrees that morning, and they had the morning skate and it's a picture-perfect sunshiny day, and guys were staying on the ice a lot longer than they usually would for a game-day morning skate because it was such a beautiful day. And the game itself, it was like baseball weather, I'm smelling burgers because I'm in the Phillies broadcasting booth. And I'm a baseball guy too — the first game in a baseball stadium and I'm calling a hockey game."

The game was a career highlight for the veteran broadcaster. "We go to Hershey the next day, and Hershey's building is pretty big, and then you say, 'It feels teeny.' It feels miniature compared to this 45,000 thing, and that was the peak of my broadcasting career. It was an incredible evening; no matter what happened, it was incredible, and then for them to come back like they did. I couldn't sit down, I was dazed and somewhat spaced out after the game. I felt like I played the game. I was exhausted. I forgot my coat in the booth. I left a present for the Phillies announcer for Opening Day. I was so out of it, I forgot to take my coat when I left."

The next season, the Bears played a game against Wilkes-Barre/Scranton at Hersheypark Stadium — right next to the team's historic Hersheypark Arena.

Mark French, the Bears' coach at the time, said even though the team lost 2–1 to the Penguins, the game still was one of the favorites of his career. "Once you get through the feeling of disappointment, I think each guy that participates, they will feel it is a very special event, and probably in their hockey career, ranks pretty high for them."

Dany Sabourin, who backed up Marc-Andre Fleury in the 2008 Winter Classic and Braden Holtby in the 2012 game in Philadelphia, said getting a chance to actually play outside was fun. "It's a totally different experience," he said with a smile. "It was nice to play. You remember when you play outside as a kid and having fun. Even though it's for two points, it's so different, you have no choice but to think about when you were a kid and playing outside."

According to Bears' broadcaster Scott Stuccio, the event took a lot of planning. "The whole weekend was planned before [that] season," he said. "It's like Christmas morning. It all comes together and bang, it's all finished. Comparing it to Philadelphia, 45,643 people dropping down to 17,133, it's a family-oriented atmosphere; to have this stadium host hockey for the first time ever, you couldn't have it any better."

AHL president Dave Andrews said the outdoor events are special for the league. "Those are great events. I've enjoyed attending them. The one in Hamilton was great, the one in Hershey was great. We had only one that wasn't great, and that was the one in Hartford. The one in Rochester was really good and the one in Philadelphia was fantastic."

Ticket sales are the lifeblood of a team's finances, because most teams don't have more than a cursory television contract with a local provider. The scale of an AHL team's finances are much more restricted than an NHL club's, in big part in absence of the league's national and local television dollars that can help reduce the risk if a team can't sell tickets.

To give an idea of the scale of an AHL team's finances compared to an NHL team's, consider that Terry Pegula bought the Buffalo Sabres and its holdings in 2011 for $189 million, and the franchise was valued at $300 million by a November 2015 *Forbes* estimate. Pegula bought the AHL's Rochester Americans later that same year for around $5 million — the average annual value of the five-year contract Matt Moulson signed with the Sabres in free agency in 2014.

An AHL team operates on a much smaller scale than the NHL in every aspect, from expenditures to staff sizes. "Not having access or being privy to the numbers on all the teams on both sides, I believe our organizations cost substantially less to operate than a National Hockey League franchise on so many things. Rent and payroll are two huge ones off the cuff," said Sarosy.

While some teams have up to 50 employees working for the club, Sarosy noted his staff was just 14. "Like anything, the market ranges from the Binghamtons, Syracuses and Uticas to the San Antonios, Chicagos. I'm sure they're all over the map," he said. "You're usually in that $4 to $5 million range to operate a franchise, and a big part of that is the affiliation fees for the independents. The teams that aren't independent have a drastically different model than us, but teams can be all over the board. What I can speak of, from a financial point of view, is for an independent team like the Crunch and the teams we're surrounded by, your bigger expenses are your affiliation fees, your lease, and then your salaries. And then you get into your travel and your equipment — and your equipment is not a boilerplate for every team."

In a way, the AHL is very much a throwback to hockey's earlier era, heavily dependent on ticket sales and without the large influence of national television dollars that give NFL, NBA, MLB and NHL owners a bit more financial security. For the Syracuse Crunch, for instance, ticket sales and corporate sponsorships are far and away the main source of income, Sarosy said.

"Every team will have a different model there, but for sure, the two largest areas are ticket sales in all its forms — season-ticket holders, groups, single-game sales — and then your corporate sponsorship. Concessions and merchandise, while it's extremely important, it pales in comparison in terms of amounts to those other two categories," he said.

For the 2015–16 season, attendance for the AHL regular season was an all-time high of 6,693,526 — an average of 5,982 per game. The five teams that had the highest average attendance figures were Hershey, San Diego, Lake Erie, Ontario and Grand Rapids, with two of those being teams that relocated to California that season.

Ticket philosophies also vary from team to team, largely depending on what kind of lease they have. Some teams — like the Crunch — are loath to give away or sell heavily discounted tickets, while others with lower ticket bases may look to attract more people in the building cheaply to try to make money that way.

"I've spent countless hours talking and thinking on this topic alone, and we do not discount our tickets greatly," Sarosy said. "You have to create a value for your product. In this market, in this situation, it's a tremendous disservice to your corporate partners and your fan base if you walk into a local supermarket chain and see a stack of your tickets there, and the next time we're asking them to pay $17.50 per seat per night. It can almost be looked at as a slap in the face.

"My understanding is, why some teams do it is they may have a phenomenal parking deal, that we don't have in Syracuse, or their concession deal may be off the charts, so it's OK to have a lower ticket price, they may have a smaller ticket base and want to get people in the building in terms of revenue. Ultimately, I think it's a flawed process because it collapses in on itself on some point. You have to have value for your brand, and by papering the house, it's disrespectful [of] what you're doing. You're not growing your base that way at all. It's more of a short-term solution and an immediate fix rather than a long-term solution, in my opinion."

A good schedule is one of the key factors of drawing crowds. With a 76-game schedule (68 for California clubs), up to 38 games at each venue, and most teams looking to book weekend dates to maximize sales, it's a complex process to put together a schedule that works for all the teams. Once they check their building availability during the season (dependent on the schedules of each of the building's tenants, as well as scheduled concert dates and other events such as ice shows and the circus), each team submits available dates and requests for certain opponents to the league. With three teams — Lake Erie, Milwaukee and San Antonio — sharing buildings with NBA teams, the AHL waits until that league releases its schedule to finalize its own.

"It's a very involved process and a thankless process for the league. Inevitably, you're never going to make everyone happy. We're required to send in dates — we rank them — primaries and secondaries, and we rank them one through whatever and submit more than you actually are going to get. And that process is simple," said Sarosy. "We talk with the local building and find what they have booked already and gobble up everything that we can and send it over to the league. Then you get your guaranteed home dates, which are great from a marketing point of view; we can start selling some group and theme nights, and it's very important to know opening night.

"It's a challenge, because minor-league baseball teams might know their schedule almost two years in advance. But they aren't sharing the building with NBA teams, and Garth Brooks isn't coming in, and that sort of stuff. But every year it becomes a little bit cleaner and a little bit better, and it's quite an extensive process.

"The league will take every request, but they have the final say, but what you say is common. You say, 'We want to play the Texas teams,' or, 'We prefer not to go there,' for whatever reason. Howard is our point person on the schedule. I'm sure we've gotten some of the requests and very sure we haven't gotten all of them."

It also gets tricky for a team like Toronto that is shifting conferences, as the change means the Marlies are facing a new group of opponents. Brad Lynn, the Marlies' director of hockey operations, who is in charge of the budgeting and travel for the team, had a fair bit of catching up to do.

"It's a challenge for me not knowing one side of the league. I've been working for this team for five-and-a-half years, and I've never been to Providence, Bridgeport, Portland, you can go down the list. Learning those new cities and what works, what doesn't, that's a bit of a challenge," he said. "It's a great league in the sense that people will help you out a lot if you need it."

It also can be more of a challenge come playoff time, when arenas already have dates booked and teams have to get creative with scheduling — or even move games to another arena.

For instance, during the 2015 Calder Cup playoffs, Hartford's XL Center was booked for an event during the second-round series between the Wolf Pack and Bears, so two of Hartford's "home" games were played in Worcester — the home of the team the Bears had just eliminated.

With the push out west and the first five teams moving to California, it seems likely that there may be other teams looking to shift their AHL teams out to that circuit for the ease of travel.

Former Wolves coach John Anderson said in 2015 he would be surprised if that was the last of the movement. "Obviously, I was shocked when Abbotsford came in, and St. John's. You have to take a dogsled to get there. But, I guess that's the markets that are available. When I coached in Phoenix, there was talk of them bringing their club to Prescott Valley, which is an hour and a half away, and that would fit in with the five teams that are [in California] now. I wouldn't be surprised if that doesn't happen in a year or two.

"It was inevitable, it makes sense. Phoenix, we would call guys up and it would take them a day to get there, and they'd be exhausted coming from Portland. It's too far." Anderson turned out to be right. In 2016, the Coyotes bought their AHL affiliate in Springfield and moved them to Tucson, Arizona, 128 miles down Interstate 10 from the team's arena in Glendale.

Ken Young, who sold his team in 2015, felt the league did a good job balancing the demands of the National Hockey League, which owns over half the league's franchises and the independently-owned clubs — not an easy feat. "I would say for us, the AHL is really a good league. Dave Andrews is one of the best sports league presidents around. He had such a good handle of it. I ended up on the executive committee for a few years, and you get a good flavor of what's going on and what's important in working very closely with the NHL, trying to please them without hurting the financial structure of your league.

"Over the last four or five years — and Dave was the catalyst here — of making sure the NHL — who owns close to half of the AHL teams — and we could work together in a positive way, part of that was reducing the schedule a little bit and some other things, and that's where I saw the changes in the last few years.

"I think Dave guided it very, very well so it worked out for both the NHL and the AHL owners."

CHAPTER FOUR

THE HERSHEY BEARS

Rolling southbound on Interstate 81 through Pennsylvania, the National Hockey League feels very far away. Once you exit off of Interstate 78, you're in the heart of central Pennsylvania's dairy farm country — the abundance of milk was one of the reasons chocolate magnate Milton S. Hershey placed his corporation's headquarters in the town eventually named after him in 1905.

Heading on back roads toward Giant Center, there are silver metal silos and few stop lights. Once you cross U.S. Route 22, a couple of billboards start popping up, advertising Hershey's attractions, and you soon see a "Welcome to Hershey" sign with a dancing Hershey's Kiss that proclaims the burg the "sweetest Place on Earth." Past the hotels, the outlet mall and restaurants and Hersheypark's roller coasters, Giant Center's electronic marquee comes into view.

In a league that's known for rapidly changing rosters — and even teams — the Bears are a throwback to the early days of the league when the hopes of this company town took on the larger cities of Baltimore, Buffalo and Pittsburgh, and had a lot of success doing so. Originally founded in 1932 to help entertain the company's employees, the Hershey Bears joined the American Hockey League in 1938 — the league's third season — after spending six years in the Tri-State Hockey League (renamed the Eastern Amateur Hockey League).

Simply put, the Hershey Bears are the crown jewel of the American Hockey League, the league's version of the Montreal Canadiens or New York Yankees. The Bears are the oldest continuously operating team in the league, having played in every AHL season since joining in 1938. The club has also been the league's most successful in terms of Calder Cups, capturing a league-record 11, including three since 2006.

Even now, the Bears represent a town of just 14,257 playing against teams from the cities of Chicago and Toronto — which could hold the entire population of Hershey 180 times over. And Hershey has won the same number of Calder Cups since 2005–06 as any other AHL club has in the last 30 years.

The Giant Center's rafters reflect the team's success, with 11 banners honoring each Calder Cup win. Banners honoring retired numbers and Frank Mathers's place in the Hockey Hall of Fame hang across the ice, but none commemorate any other team accomplishment of conference or divisional championships. A Reese's Peanut Butter Cup advertisement placed in the upper deck proclaims, "It's all about the Cup." It rings true — nothing else really matters here.

Giant Center, opened in 2002, is a smaller version of a modern NHL building — a circular arena sitting in a large parking lot. It seats 10,500 for hockey, and many of those chocolate-colored seats are filled on game nights. This is a team that regularly finishes atop the league's attendance figures.

Unlike a lot of the older AHL buildings, the Giant Center features tiered seating levels, not to mention luxury boxes, club seating and a specialty restaurant. Walk through the concourse into the seating bowl itself, and you see the modern configuration that is similar to the shape of the roof of the historic Hersheypark Arena, which served as the team's home from 1938 to 2002, and is now used as the team's practice facility.

That history also seeps all the way down to today's Bears.

"The fact they play in Giant Center and look up at those banners every day, they practice in [Hersheypark Arena] where the banners are back again, to know this team is the oldest in the league, has a chance to win the most number of Calder Cups in the league and be in the finals the most number of times, with a chance to play for it, it means the world to them. Doug says this a lot too . . . for him, it's about winning, being the best," said Scott Stuccio, broadcaster for the Bears. "It may not be so much about raising the banner as raising the Cup and getting the ring at the end of the season."

Eric Fehr, who came up with the Bears before starting his NHL career, has high praise for Hershey: "Hershey's a great city to play. Some of the best fans in the league, a good building that's full most nights. It's almost an NHL-type feel in an AHL arena."

Fehr's teammate the year they won the 2005–06 banner, Brooks Laich, echoed those sentiments. "It is such a hockey-mad environment, it's the place you want to be in the American Hockey League to play hockey. You know you're going to have a good team, you're going to be well coached, you're part of a great organization, you're going to be developed as a player and you're going to be treated like royalty in town," he said. "I can't say enough good things about Hershey — it's the best place to play in the American League."

Graham Mink concurred. "I loved playing in Hershey," he said. "I played three years there, and they were the three best years of my career, really. I loved it there. If you're not going to play in the NHL, there's no better place than Hershey to play, in my opinion. It's fun. It's a big-time feel, there's a nice new rink, the place is sold out every night, people are very passionate about their hockey team and their hockey players."

And part of what makes it a great place to play is the community. As AHL veteran Andrew Gordon, who spent his first four years in the league in Hershey, said, "The town really embraced you. You couldn't go to the grocery store without people asking for your autograph or patting you on the back, or go to [a] restaurant without people giving you 50 percent off or even picking up your tab."

That community feel really contributes to a unique AHL environment. As Bears coach Troy Mann said, "I think it's just the people. It's people within the family itself of the Bears organization, and then you've got the small community outside Hershey. . . . It's a small-town atmosphere, where the players and coaches can pretty much go any-where and be recognized by someone. Even if it's just being recog-nized at Hersheypark in the summer, or if a security guard recognizes you, that makes it special just being part of the community.

"Let's face it, we've led the league in attendance nine straight years, there's an expectation to win, and any time you come to coach here or play here, you know the expectation is to win, but that same time, you've got that great support. It's second to none, really."

Hershey is a special place, said Bridgeport broadcaster Phil Giubileo. "I love calling games at Giant Center. It's a great atmo-sphere, it really is. It's such a great building, and it's a great fan base. When you go there and it's 10,000 fans and a loud atmosphere and feels like an NHL building — I've been lucky games to call NHL games at Nassau Coliseum and other buildings — so to be able to go to Hershey and feel that, that's amazing."

Wendell Young, Chicago Wolves' general manager, said Hershey was one of his favorite places in hockey to play. "We had the advantage with the fans, and . . . one of my favorite experiences as a hockey player is being in Hershey. The town, it's not a big town, but you don't know where all these people come from — you go to a game, and I've been to games in the new building, and I don't know if there are 10,000 people [living] around here, [or if] they just import them.

"Everyone's into the game, it's a fun place, great people — it's just a fun place to play. I loved playing in Hershey. It wasn't just the fact we had a winning team. The organization is run so well and people are treated properly, and the fans appreciate good hard hockey."

Along with that support and attention, however, comes added pres-sure, said Tim Leone, who covered the Bears for the *Patriot-News*. "Obviously, it's the most historic and tradition-rich city in the league, and with that comes more of an onus to win than any other city. I think it's a little more pressurized than those situations, say to compare this to a Bridgeport, where the Islanders can approach it as a purely develop-mental situation, where here winning needs to be part of a component for the fans," he said.

Sometimes those higher expectations can be too much for some players. "There is a lot of pressure, so it's not for everybody. Some people go there and don't like playing there because they don't do well. People expect you to win, so if you don't, it's not the best place in the world to play," said Mink.

"I was fortunate enough to be there for two of my years and win championships both times," he said, having won a Calder Cup in 2005–06 and again in 2008–09. "It was a great experience for me, and fun. I love Hershey. It's a well-run organization as well, very family-like feel, very comfortable there. I wish I could have played more years in Hershey."

Brian Willsie spent two different stints in Hershey, once as a young player and then as a veteran player, and he noticed a big change in the team's focus, given the change in the parent club.

"It was [a] different mindset; I don't know if it was the parent club or not, but with Colorado's stint, we were really just all prospects. They sprinkled in the odd veteran, but my first three years from 1998 to 2000, we were probably averaging 23 years old. We had two ex-players as coaches — Mike Foligno and Jay Wells — who just really pushed us hard. We learned to be pros, and you learned to sink or swim," he said. "You got with it and got with the program, or you were shipped out or sent to East Coast League team. It hardened a lot of us, and most of us ended up going up to the NHL within five years of our entry-level deals."

Willsie returned years later to help the Bears capture a third straight Calder Cup in 2010–11. The new arena wasn't the only change. The team had won three Calder Cups after affiliating with the Capitals in 2005, and the expectations were high.

"They pushed a few more veterans to help out the prospects and it really produced that winning team year after year. We talked about it during the season and after. We had just as good a team as the ones that had won the two years before. Mathieu Perreault was there, [Braden] Holtby was our goalie and we had Sheldon Souray. We had a team that could win. But those long seasons they had been through, playing into mid-June, and even the year before that one, they had played into the semifinals. Year after year after year, when you're a 20s kid, maybe it wears mentally and then you get to that point."

That year the Bears failed to make it out of the first round.

"I think if we had gotten out of the first round we could have had a big run, but it was one of those, 'Oh we lost, but now I'm going to have a bit of a summer.' You hate to say it, I'm not sure if it was like that, but there was a lot of pressure to really perform. Three-peats and dynasties are really, really rare, and I can see why. There was a lot of pressure to do that again. It was really hard for the players to get their mind around it again," Willsie said.

The team's architect, Doug Yingst, has been with the Bears for an impressive length of time. In fact, he's been with the team longer than 28 other current AHL franchises have been in existence. From when he arrived in 1982 to when he retired in 2016, Hershey won five Calder Cups, just one off the franchise total of the Rochester Americans, who have been playing since 1956.

As we talked, his team practiced below at the historic Hersheypark Arena, an arena built in 1936 that remains a slice of the AHL's past. At one end of the ice is an older grey scoreboard simply reading "HOME" and "VISITOR" in the classic typography you'd see in an old movie marquee. The scoreboard, which would be similar to one you'd see at a town rink with light-up bulbs and extra rows for penalty times, is surrounded at each end by an American and Canadian flag.

Underneath hang the eight Calder Cup banners that the team won when playing in the venue — and unlike the minimalist ones across the parking lot in the new arena, these feature the team name, the old "skating bear" logo, the year and "Calder Cup Champions." Between the 1968–69 and 1973–74 banners is a white board with "AMERICAN H.L." at its top, where information was posted in that same movie-theater lettering. The seating bowl rises steeply from the ice up to the yellow beams and white roof, and there are five groups of seats varying in color from brown, red, blue and yellow.

"If you look at the history of the building that we're actually sitting in, and how it was built, why it was built — for the community and for the employees," he told me. "That history and tradition continued throughout the years, and has only grown, and our fan base has obviously grown since we moved over to Giant Center. This is 'AHL Hockeytown.'"

Back in the day, this old barn did give the team a big home advantage. As Willsie said, "You don't realize it at the time because you're a 20-year-old kid, but I mean, what an arena, fan support, all that, it was pretty awesome. We were a young team, didn't have a lot of older veterans — Colorado didn't do that at the time — and we just relied on each other and got really close. We just really enjoyed the town. It's a hockey town — it's a small town — and many of us all came from small towns in Canada. We weren't big-city kids and could really relate to that. Then from there, we moved to the new arena; it was state of the art, and just like some [of] the NHL arenas you'd hoped to play in or got a few games in.

"Then, you'd go back to Hersheypark Arena to practice and you'd be like, 'Oh man, do I ever miss this place.' The atmosphere and the small confines, I almost didn't really realize it at the time, but it's to the advantage of the home team. We had Scott Parker some of those years, and always had tough guys and the fans are right on top of you — I think it's illegal to build arenas that steep anymore — and the glass had a big give to it. It was a special place to play, and it could be one of those things you didn't realize how good it was until you weren't doing it anymore."

John Walton, former AHL broadcaster, isn't shy about his affection for the old barn either. "It is the greatest hockey arena still standing in North America, and with the new roof on the place hopefully it'll be there 100 more years. Going there as a visitor, you were always welcomed by the people . . . sitting around you — you sat in the stands. The stats were passed to you by fans like you were passing change to someone at a ballgame who just bought a beer; it was kind of the same way to get your game notes there. It was a beautiful place for hockey," he said. "For anyone who ever got to call a game there, and I can say that I was lucky enough that I did, it was a piece of hockey history I'll never forget."

Yingst makes it clear that winning isn't secondary for the Bears. "There's no question. Winning is the challenge; it's the challenge every year to put the team together, it's a challenge on the business side because you have these high standards and every year it's to meet the standards and do better than the year before. Every year it becomes

Defenseman Connor Carrick spent parts of three seasons in Hershey before being traded to Toronto in 2016. (SYRACUSE CRUNCH)

a challenge to put a winning team on the ice with the assistance of our NHL partner, and we believe in winning and developing — not developing and winning.

"And it goes back to not only with Washington, but with Philadelphia, we were with them . . . 12 years and they really felt winning was the key to developing their younger players and so that's what we do. It's about our fans. As much as they love the prospects and love seeing the prospects, they want to see them winning."

Marshall noted the different vibe in Hershey. "It was cool. It was different, the relationship between the Bears and the Capitals, it was like there were two different teams. Hershey is run in a certain way, they want to win, and they have their reputation. It's different from other teams where it's completely attached. The management has more stuff to say when you're really attached, and sometimes in Hershey, management will say, 'We want to see this guy play, he needs to develop,' but at the same time, on their behalf, we want to play, we want guys with experience. You want to win. We have our reputation."

At Giant Center, games are usually loud. The Bears have led the league in attendance each year since 2006–07, with a 2015–16 average of 9,790 — 1,100 fans more than the AHL's second-best club, San Diego. On a game night, the crowd is decked out largely in the chocolate-and-white jerseys bearing the names of the players who have come through town in recent years, part of the Washington youth movement that started with the Capitals' rebuild when the team re-affiliated with Hershey in 2005.

The crowds are usually loud — chanting the signature "B-E-A-R-S, Bears Bears Bears" chant capped with a "Woo" — and make it a dynamic atmosphere to play in.

Tim Kennedy, who spent 2014–15 in Hershey, said he liked the energy the Hershey crowds brought. "It's a nice place to play, it's a nice family town. It's a great area, great fans, obviously; we get at least between 8,500 and 10,000 fans a game so it's something you can't beat when you're playing in the minors, so it's a nice change. Some places you play, they say there's 3,000 but there's maybe 800 people there. It's nice to play in front of a crowd."

Philipp Grubauer, who spent three seasons in Hershey, spoke highly of his AHL stop. "I think Hershey is one of the best places you can possibly play in the AHL. I'm really proud of the attendance there. We really draw 10,000 fans every night, and it's really nice to play in front of those crowds every night."

Connor Carrick, once one of Washington's prospects, also says he enjoys the experience. "It's a small town, so we get very good fans. All over town, you go out to eat, you're going to see a lot of Bears jerseys and a lot of Bears shirts, so the support of the town's great. I'm very lucky to play there."

The tradition also means the Bears ink some of the AHL's top free agents and are a destination spot for veterans as the team looks to capture its 12th Calder Cup.

Chris Bourque, who won three Calder Cups in a previous stop in

Hershey, inked a two-year deal with Washington in summer of 2015 that was worth $375,000 at the AHL level — one of the league's highest two-way salaries. Aaron Ness, the captain of the Sound Tigers, signed a one-year deal for $300,000 in Hershey, and goaltender Justin Peters, third on Washington's goaltending depth chart, earned $950,000 on a one-way deal even in the AHL.

Bourque — the son of NHL great Ray and brother to Bears team-mate Ryan — who had NHL stints with Washington, Pittsburgh and Boston, has become a key veteran in the AHL, becoming a four-time All-Star and winning the league's Les Cunningham award for most valuable player in the 2015–16 season, as well as the Jack A. Butterfield Trophy for most valuable player in the Calder Cup playoffs in 2010.

With some of his best AHL moments in Hershey, Bourque said he was thrilled to be back in Hershey after helping knock the Bears out of the playoffs with both Providence in 2013 and Hartford in 2015. "I was thrilled to come back when I had the opportunity to sign here. It was easy for me to do. I'm happy to be back," he said.

Even visiting teams like to play here. Former Bear Patrick McNeill recounted what it was like to take the ice as a visitor. "It's pretty cool to see familiar faces and everything, but once you get in warm-ups, you're getting close to game time and push out all the memories, because you're trying to get down to business. But after the game, you look around and see the banners and remember the good times that you had here. So it's always special to be here."

Sean Collins said a road game in Hershey was always one he'd look forward to. "Hershey's got a great reputation. It's a game you'd circle on the calendar, and it felt like an NHL atmosphere in the AHL. Playing in Springfield you'd maybe play in front of 2,500 or 3,000 fans, and you'd go to Hershey and play in front of 10,000. It's an electric atmosphere."

Up above in the press box, the Bears have provided a broadcast pipeline to the National Hockey League, as former Atlanta Thrashers voice Dan Kamal, Tampa Bay Lightning radio voice David Mishkin and John Walton all joined the NHL after time in Hershey.

Walton, the latest call-up, spoke highly of his time there. "I was fortunate, and much more fortunate than most. . . . I was in a place in

Hershey where if there were 30 NHL jobs, I had the 31st best job in the world. To have the fan base we did, we were Hershey's NHL team," he said.

Current Bears broadcaster Scott Stuccio, who came down Interstate 81 from Wilkes-Barre/Scranton to take Walton's spot, says being in Hershey is a thrill.

"To call games in Hershey, you know it's expected to win, the teams are expected to go far, and you're expected to have some award-winning players amongst the league on your team and your community, and it's been a whirlwind. Since coming to Hershey, it's been a life-changing event for me in many ways. I met my future wife here, I'm establishing my life here and I'm working for the greatest organization in the league, hands-down."

AHL president Dave Andrews called Hershey a special place for hockey. "I think in terms of standing the test of time as an outstanding franchise in terms of their fan base and their competitive level and their leadership, there's no one at that level in our league. We have some other historic franchises in our league — the Rochester Americans come to mind, and others. But, I mean, Hershey has been the gold standard for a long time. And they do everything right. They're a very proud organization and have a high performance standard for their staff and for their team, and the expectations for their fans are very high.

"It's a terrific place to go and watch a game. It's a team you can count on in almost every way. Who are the best in the American League and who has been the best in the American League? The Hershey Bears. There's no question."

CHAPTER FIVE

THE LIFERS

If there's one constant in the American Hockey League, it's change.

While National Hockey League rosters turn over at a gradual pace through the course of a season, AHL rosters undergo a much more rapid churn. The numbers of call-ups to the NHL, demotions to the ECHL due to injuries, trades and other reasons mean most AHL teams will often dress several dozen different players in a campaign, rather than sticking with the roster they have at the beginning of the season.

Amid the change, the continuity in a team usually comes from the veterans, the guys there to help the prospects along and give the parent club a bit of insurance in case some of the players on their NHL roster get injured and they need a player to fill that role. These veterans may not be in an NHL franchise's long-term plans, but they play an unsung role in their teammates' development. Their value isn't just what they do on the ice, but also what they do off the ice, passing on their knowledge to the next generation of prospects and playing a vital role in the community.

A classic example of this is Eric Neilson. During his three seasons with the Syracuse Crunch, Neilson wasn't an everyday skater — he dressed in only half of the team's games. His role was to provide muscle when it was needed, an art whose place is being diminished. While he wasn't a player that would capture a scoring title or an MVP award, Neilson did win the 2013–14 Yanick Dupre Memorial Award for his contributions off the ice, given to the AHL's man of the year for his service to the local community.

Indeed, veterans play another important role. They often become the face of the franchise, whether it's being on advertising or video promotions, or going out into the community. While most teams have to advertise their brand with a logo, veterans allow them to put a human face to the club. For instance, despite the lack of playing time, Neilson was easily the most recognizable member of the roster, thanks to his work promoting his club.

During breaks in play, fans at Syracuse's War Memorial Arena were greeted with a video of Neilson's Ric Flair-like "Woo!" on the scoreboard. He was the only Crunch player pictured on the team's 2014–15 press credentials, and was a big part of the team's marketing plans — he was one of the few players the team was confident would be around the entire season.

Neilson's likeness has a special spot with Crunch COO Jim Sarosy, as his bobblehead — in this case a bobblefist — sits on Sarosy's desk.

"I hope everyone has a chance to have an Eric Neilson in their life. I spent three years with him, and legitimately, he's never had a bad day. What our fan base sees, that upbeat personality, that's how he is. It's almost exhausting at times. He's wonderful," said Sarosy. "I have one bobblehead at my desk, and it's poor Eric Neilson. He gets it, and understands his role — that's not something you can say about everybody. His role is not only to contribute on the ice but to be a positive influence off the ice, too, and he does more of that lifting people's spirits more than almost anyone I've ever met in my life."

Neilson also has become a staple on the team's radio broadcasts. "He should go into TV. He's terrific, so when he and I are on the air together, we're just hanging out," said D'Uva. "We're calling a game and he's got a great story here or there, his view on something. . . . He once started singing Johnny Cash in the second intermission."

Following a game at Bridgeport's Webster Bank Arena, Neilson, dressed in a suit, walked out of the locker room in the basement beneath the stands to meet with me. While he didn't play in the game, he was there to be part of the team — before our interview he made sure to help load equipment on the bus waiting to take the team on a five-hour bus ride home.

The Crunch were in a good mood on this Sunday evening, having won three games in the previous 48 hours. Syracuse managed a 2–0 shutout win that wasn't pretty (but it counts the same in the standings).

"It's rewarding, all the hard work you put into the game and get the two points out there," he said. "It's not like the NHL where you're hopping on a plane and eating sea bass and filet mignon after a game. We ate pizza and chicken fingers last night for supper. To come out on the road and be successful, it's hard, it's tough. When you do it, you get rewarded; you have to enjoy it and have fun with it."

Neilson went into pro hockey looking to make it to the NHL. A fifth-round pick of Los Angeles in the 2004 NHL Draft, he spent the early part of his career in the ECHL. He was a tough guy in a time when that role was being phased out of the game, and so he went to the AHL, to Peoria, to Hamilton, to San Antonio, to Norfolk and to Syracuse. He hasn't been able to make it to the top level, but along the way his goal has shifted. It's now to help his younger teammates prepare for their chance to live out their dreams.

"It's nice when I get to see a young guy come in and get to see his maturity level, not just on the ice but off the ice, and then see him mature into a professional hockey player. They finally get called up and play in the NHL, and I'm watching him on TV and I remember when he first came into the American League and he didn't know how to be a pro, and now all of the sudden he's in the NHL," he said. "That's really gratifying for me, I'm almost like a proud uncle or some-thing. . . . That's the best feeling when you can see those young guys reach their goal and reach their dream. That's why we're here. The

Eric Neilson, shown here diving to block a shot, played for Peoria, Hamilton, San Antonio, Norfolk, Syracuse and St. John's, but never got to play a game in the NHL — but he helped countless other teammates live their own dreams by being a mentor for them.
(SYRACUSE CRUNCH)

American Hockey League is here to develop players. While we're all believing, wanting and striving to make the NHL, some of us won't do it for whatever reason. But the guys you play with that really work hard and deserve it, they get you thankful and happy for them."

Graham Mink, another AHL veteran, said there is a thin margin between making the NHL and not making it, and that's not something a player can always control.

"There's such a fine line between the American League and the National League, and the hockey in the AHL is very, very good," he said. "You've got the top 20 percent of NHL players, and they're dipped in special talent. The rest are great players, but they worked their way in there. They've been fortunate and they've had good opportunities.

But there's a lot of good players in the American League — the majority of the American League — that could be in those positions if they have been given those opportunities."

Drew Bagnall, who retired from pro hockey following the 2014–15 AHL season, said sometimes the stars don't align. "I think, just from a player's perspective, so much is outside of your control. It's tough to do your job as well as you can, but if the stars don't align, if no one gets hurt up top, you don't get to play in the NHL. Some guys think if you're the best player down here, you get that NHL job. But every year, there's a crop of first-round picks they have to see, and I don't think people really realize how cutthroat and how small your window is to make it to the NHL."

With new talent replenished every June at draft, it's difficult for a player who stays in the AHL for any length of time to get a chance to move up. Some players go through their entry-level contracts without a regular NHL role, and once that expires, the pathways for a player start to dwindle.

The American Hockey League employs the development rule, stating that of the 18 skaters to dress in a game — not including the two goaltenders — 13 of them have to be qualified as "development players." Of those, 12 have to have played fewer than 260 AHL, NHL and European Elite League games combined — or just over three seasons' worth of games based on the AHL's standard 76-game schedule used prior to the 2015–16 season — and one skater can have up to 320 games, adding another season.

That restriction puts a premium on young talent and it limits what an older player can do after spending a few seasons in the league.

Unlike NHL unrestricted free agents, players who are 25 or older and haven't played 80 total games in the NHL, and have played at least 10 games in three different seasons of the NHL, AHL, ECHL or European Elite Leagues, become unrestricted. NHL unrestricted free agents can earn big dollars signing with another club. In the AHL, however, unrestricted free agents have to start thinking about survival.

With the reduced roles veterans play in today's AHL, roster spots are getting tougher to find. Sometimes a player might think he has a better chance to reach the NHL with another team and sign a two-way contract that could earn him a substantial raise if he can crack the 23-man roster.

For instance, Sean Collins signed with Washington in the summer of 2015 on a one-year, two-way contract, paying him $575,000 if he played with the Capitals and $200,000 if he played with Hershey. He hoped the team's salary cap situation would give him a better shot at reaching the NHL. "They spoke with my agent during the free agency window and they're a cap team. I'd be making minimum if they need a depth guy in their bottom six or [a] 13th forward call-up guy," he said.

A player might continue with the same organization if the staff wants to bring him back and he feels he still has a future there. Sometimes a team looks for a veteran on a successful team to help the team's Calder Cup chances — it's usually the added value that is the important factor on who plays on in the AHL.

Colton Gillies knows how quickly the door to the NHL can close, and how tough it can be to keep an AHL job. A former first-round pick — sixteenth overall — he played in 154 games in the NHL. Gillies's career didn't pan out as he had hoped, and he spent two years in Rochester and Bridgeport trying to earn his ticket back to the NHL. Along the way, he tried to pass on some of his knowledge to his teammates.

I met with him after a game, and despite being tired, Gillies took the time to chat about his role in the AHL. "In the minors it's about development, and being an older guy and experiencing being up and down, knowing what it takes to be there, you try to relay the young players the message as much as possible," he said. "You only have so much time — I'm 26 — before you're not a prospect anymore, and you're not in their plans. There's a lot of good players in this league who don't get the opportunity to play in the NHL, and it's maybe because the team thinks their time has passed and they're not in their plans."

Gillies draws on the experiences he had when he first came into professional hockey from the Western Hockey League, and what he learned about how to deal with the dream of the NHL being that close, yet seemingly so far away.

"I know when I was in Houston and Minnesota, your goal is to get to the NHL. Your dream's not to play in the minors, your dreams are to play in the NHL. Back then, it was, 'I think I played well, hopefully I get called up,' and you're watching to see if guys got injured up top and see if there's a call-up. But at the same time, you want to commit yourself to this team down here."

As the roles change, so do the perspectives. Bagnall noted that with a constant stream of prospects coming in every year, some draft picks worry a bit too much about getting promoted rather than doing what they need to do to earn it. "I think you especially see it with the young guys, maybe they have the mentality that they belong in the NHL, and they get so concerned with what's going on up top, they don't necessarily take care of what they have to do down here. If you take care of where you are, you'll get to where you want to be. Someone told me that long ago, but it's so true. You look through the years, eight years in the league, I still think that and say it to the young guys all the time."

Many players learn to accept that there is an element of their fate that is beyond their control.

"That's when being a professional comes into play. You can be equipped with experience and get frustrated when another guy gets called up. Earlier in my career, I had more of a roller-coaster career, and as you get older and more experience[d] you try to get your game to be more consistent," said J.P. Côté. "You want to keep improving, but there's so many things you don't control. The guys who are not focused and team-oriented enough, the leaders of the team have to bring them back with the group, and keep pushing the same direction."

And as Kevin Marshall told me, it can be a big challenge for younger players to buy into the team concept of putting the goals of the team ahead of their own — especially if it means putting up less individual stats.

"That's the biggest issue in the minors within teams is to try to bring everybody together and win together and understand that by working together, by winning together, we're going to have success as individuals. It's so hard, because you're right there, and it's tempting to look at the team and say, 'I have to play well tonight,'" he said. "'We lost 4–3, but I got three points.' So am I happy? Am I mad? I'll be happy because

Veteran defenseman Kevin Marshall, pictured here playing for Toronto, knows that part of being a player in the AHL and hoping to earn a promotion is putting the team's success above your individual stats. (SYRACUSE CRUNCH)

I'm getting points, but at the end of the day, I don't think within a team that's how it should work. It should be us. We're going to win together and have success together and think right now about the Marlies or whatever AHL team you're on, instead of thinking about the big club.

"But it's hard, because they're young kids; you're a step away from making the big bucks and a step away from living the dream. Or you're a day away from being on a five-hour bus ride. And it's huge to not think about it."

While some of the first-rounders may get a bit more of a look, of course it doesn't mean that they'll become NHL players.

"There are some blue-chips prospects in the AHL, but the line is pretty thin. I've seen a lot of blue-chip prospects really languish, and

I've seen guys play in the [ECHL] the year before — really unsung players and unheralded guys — and they go right through the American League and spend long careers in the NHL," said Mink. "It's not an exact science by any means. It's kind of a crapshoot. When you're in the middle of it, the expectations that everyone has and the draft picks they have pinned on them don't mean anything when you drop the puck. It's kind of like, what do you do when you're on the ice, what ice time do you earn, how do you fit in with the team?

"There's definitely an advantage to being a high draft pick, and there's a little bit of a self-fulfilling prophecy that comes in there. There's a little bit of interest at the top level to have your top picks do well and become established NHL players. For the bottom-two-line players, they're looking for who can get the job done, and who can't," Mink continued. "But that doesn't mean teams [are] afraid to admit they made a mistake and just move on from a guy just because they spent a first-round pick on him."

Even players who get their chance in the NHL sometimes have to deal with coming back down to the American League. And as Brendan Mikkelson, who played in 131 games in the NHL before being sent down again, told me, it can be hard to accept.

"My first time coming back down was tougher after being in the NHL. For some reason, [you] think because you played games in the NHL, whether it's for one game or ten or twenty before coming down, you somehow feel you're a way better player," he said. "For some reason your expectations go up and so you think you should come down and think you should just dominate. That was always the toughest part, coming down after a recall. Going up, you're so focused and want to do well, so your mind is in a pretty good place as far as doing your job and really being simple in your game, but you come down and you all of a sudden . . . think you should be a different player, but you're not. You hope to get better all the time, but the shape of your game won't change in that small amount of time."

For those who know their time in the NHL is over, they have a choice. And many decide to keep playing a game they love and help nurture younger players along the way. When Derek King, who played

831 NHL games, got sent down for good to the IHL in 1999–2000, he got a chance to rediscover his love of the game.

"I got sent down from St. Louis and I knew my career was pretty much over. I went down to Grand Rapids in the IHL and that's when it kind of hit me that these guys love the game. The paychecks weren't that great and their goal was to get to the NHL and they were going to do whatever it takes," he said.

It wasn't easy at first, he confessed. "You're not making a lot of money here, you're banged up, you're playing three games in four nights and riding the bus, but it brings you back and you appreciate the game. Maybe you lose that when you're up with the big clubs. These guys are passionate and I think it's great."

After two seasons in Grand Rapids and one in Germany, King returned to the AHL incarnation of the Griffins as a player-coach, which eventually led to being an AHL assistant coach.

"When the IHL folded, and player-coach came about in the American League, I jumped at it. I felt I could add some type of education to the players [from] all the stuff I went through as a player, and hopefully they can get something off of me," he said. "I enjoyed seeing guys I played with ending up being in the NHL years later."

Veterans in the AHL can still make decent money. If they're not signed to a one-way deal and sent down, which would require them to be paid at least $575,000 in 2015–16 money, they can earn up to roughly $400,000 for a season's work — although unlike the NHL, those contracts are usually handed out year-by-year and don't usually last for more than a few seasons.

American Hockey League president Dave Andrews said the veterans embrace the role they have and know the importance it has on prospects. "Most of our players still have the dream. Those who are beyond that, the veteran players in our league, are well compensated and they understand that's what they do. They're franchise players, they're leaders, they're there to bring these young players along. There's a place in our league for them," he said.

"I think back when I first started, a lot of the veteran players were just guys on their way down and hanging on. There was no great purpose for them, and the goal wasn't understood or clearly laid out for them by their organizations. Now, you see very few older players in our league who don't take great pride in [it]. They have a job in the American League for a reason."

Andrews also said a veteran can even play a bigger role in a player's development than the team's coach. "The impact of a good veteran player on a team is greater than the impact of a coach. It'd be interesting to talk to players who have moved on to the NHL and ask them who influenced them in the American League — they'd probably tell you it was someone they played with."

Dave Starman, a hockey analyst who scouts for the Montreal Canadiens, said getting the right veteran in the room can be a big boost. "There's a guy who wants to keep playing, and enjoying playing, and a coach on the ice and in the dressing room who's still wearing skates, and potentially starting to work on a coaching or scouting career," he said. "There's definitely a happy medium, you don't want to overstock on vets because you're wasting space, but you want to develop these kids. You put somebody in the room who's gone through it and can explain to them what the process is, I think it's huge."

A good example of this is Joel Quenneville, who went on to become a Stanley Cup–winning coach with the Chicago Blackhawks. Starman recalled how much Quenneville helped Baltimore players when he was sent down from Washington at the end of his NHL career in 1991.

"Joel Quenneville, he helped more guys on that defense corps in a big way, because he was like their coach even though he was playing with [them]. He was one of those guys who could help see the forest through the trees, he could get in the guys' ears and he was a stabilizing factor," said Starman. "You get a Joel Quenneville to finish his last year with your American League kids, you're living right. That's what I think a lot of GMs are looking for when they [try] to get a vet signed."

Crunch owner Howard Dolgon also speaks highly of older players. "You look at our veterans, the Côtés and Angelidises, they're not going to blow you away on the scoreboard, but they're going to blow you away in the locker room. They're going to take that 20-year-old kid who may be used to scoring two goals a game in junior hockey, and now all of a sudden hasn't scored in five games, and keep him on an even keel. That's the value of having them on the roster, and they understand that having character in the room is going to help."

While AHL teams usually don't have final say in their own rosters — the NHL team almost always calls the shots — they can lobby and push to keep certain players to try and help the team.

Some teams in the league put a premium on winning at the AHL level, feeling that longer runs in the Calder Cup playoffs will help prepare young players better for the NHL by getting them used to playoff battles. Others teams opt to let their younger players get more ice time and not use as many veterans, a sink-or-swim attitude that may not lead to more wins, but helps players gain experience and opportunity to play. There also is a blend of the two, where AHL success is important, but not an overriding factor in decision-making.

Sarosy explained that Syracuse's parent club, Tampa Bay, wants to see the affiliate have success, as it promotes the idea that young players can learn from the triumphs and failures in the Calder Cup playoffs. "Tampa does not believe winning is an innate trait. You have to learn to win, and they surround their assets with the players that are needed. As does Syracuse," he said. "Tampa wants their kids playing four rounds of playoffs each year, they want them playing special games in the Bell Centre, they want them to go to training camp in France because that's going to accelerate the development process. You don't want to be on a staff where's everyone's miserable because they're losing and be out of it."

In Hershey, a premium is put on winning in order to help develop players.

"I know the Capitals' and Hershey's philosophy since they came together [in 2005] is 'you can win by developing and develop by winning,' so it's been the model. I know when I came in as an assistant that's what I was told, and when you have 10,000 fans every night and the most Calder Cups league history, that's what you come to expect."

These are the teams — the ones that place winning and leadership at a premium — that are good potential landing spots for veterans. Many players want to be on teams where being a role model is valued.

As former Syracuse coach Rob Zettler, who spent time at the end of his own career helping mentor younger players in Portland, said, "I think part of development is bringing in a couple of older guys to help the younger guys develop. Frankly, that's why we have a number of high-quality veterans on our team like the Angelidises, Côtés and Neilsons — guys who are helping our younger guys become better players, better people, and helping us winning hockey games."

But it does take a special kind of player to mentor the younger prospects, said Bridgeport coach Brent Thompson, who played 121 NHL games but spent most of his career in the AHL. "You look at the vets around the league that have played seven to 10-plus years and they're still banging around the American Hockey League. I think it takes a special person, a special character, and a true love for the game of hockey. They're doing it because they love it, they're making a living, and those guys have a big impact on the young guys coming through. You have to find the right person or the right veteran that's been hanging around . . . I played 15 years, hanging around the minors and grinding through on the American League on the bus every single weekend.

"You definitely have to have a special appreciation for what you're doing with your life."

Gillies, who played in the 2011 Calder Cup Finals with Houston, feels that being part of a successful AHL club can help a player stay in the league.

"Every team wants winners, and for myself, this is a one-year contract. We haven't been as successful [in Bridgeport] as we have been in the past, but teams look for players who win games, and being successful leads to good opportunities. Hopefully, for myself, going forward, people see my hard work and leadership and getting on with the younger guys and hopefully that's viable to them."

For other teams, winning at the AHL isn't necessarily a priority for the NHL club, and that becomes a delicate balance for some, says Mink. "That's the hardest part of the American League, you want to have success and do well at the American League level, but then you're also a feeder system for the NHL — especially those teams that are owned by [NHL clubs] — the NHL success comes first. Sometimes you have great teams in the American League that don't stay together, simply because of that. I don't want to say they don't care about winning, but ultimately, winning in the American League is secondary to any type of benefit the NHL team might have."

In the salary cap era, developing and keeping tabs on young players in the AHL is increasingly important for NHL teams. To put it bluntly, clubs need economical ways to fill out rosters. Brian Willsie spent 381 games in the NHL, as well as significant time in the AHL before becoming a member of the Colorado Avalanche's player development department. And he has noticed that there has been a much greater emphasis on development in the last two to five years.

"We used to call the AHL the 'Mushroom League' — they throw water on you, throw shit on you, keep you in the dark and wait for you to grow," he said with a laugh. "That's the way it was, you put your nose down and worked and you waited for a call. Now, there's NHL general managers, assistant general managers, development coaches, all these people at American League games all the time, and really working with the prospects."

"NHL teams are putting so much more into development now. They have staff at all the AHL games, work with their prospects on a weekly — or even daily basis — because it is so crucial to have those young guys with entry-level contracts to play in the NHL with the salary cap," he said.

According to Andrews, one of the biggest changes in his league has been the amount of money and attention the NHL teams invest in their affiliates.

"What has changed in the landscape since the last two NHL Collective Bargaining Agreements is the value to every NHL owner and general manager of player development in your system. It's crucial. You can't be successful in the NHL without a strong development program," he said, noting that the AHL is one place you can spend money that doesn't count against the cap.

Andrews recalled that when he was with the [Cape Breton] Oilers, the team had a full-time head coach, a volunteer assistant coach, one medical guy and one equipment guy. And that is a sharp difference to any team in the league nowadays where you have a head coach; two full-time assistant coaches who are well salaried; full-time video coach; probably two or three medical guys — and that doesn't include guys coming from the NHL club — the player development coaches, there's at least a couple of them; the goalie coach that comes in; the strength and conditioning guy; the nutritionist; the sports psychologist," he said. "They're feeding these guys in-arena; they're having their breakfast there and having meals after playing a game at home. The investment in players has become massive compared to what it used to be.

Côté also noticed that teams are paying much closer attention to detail, and that's to help prospects along, not only on the ice, but off.

"A couple of years ago you could see the philosophy change with some of the younger groups from when I was young, and you could deal with more of a dictator kind of coach. That's more of the 'old time hockey' kind of thing, and that's how I was brought into the league and into hockey, really," he said. "Now, you have to carry these younger guys a bit more, stay close to them and hopefully get them a little more support and let them know what is going on."

Some of the veterans become AHL team captains. Leading by example in those roles often means that they have to put the goals and dreams of others before their own. But it's a role they are happy to fill.

As Bagnall, who wore the "C" in Rochester, told me, "Your job as a captain is to develop players in this league. At the end of the day, the best way to do it is play the game as best you can. You're trying to teach things you picked up throughout the years, and you want them to know now what you didn't know at their age.

"You just end up having a huge family across North America and overseas if you play enough years in this league," he added. "It's pretty awesome to be able to stay in touch with those guys and see where they're at."

Matt Ellis called being named captain one of the highlights of his AHL career. "Being named captain at a young age in Grand Rapids was a huge honor for me. I wore the 'C' there for two seasons; I was able to wear the 'C' in Portland and the 'C' in Rochester, and those are memories that hold a real soft spot for me."

Ellis went on to play 356 games in the NHL. He took some time while in the Sabres locker room to talk about the role of an AHL captain, saying that you need to "kind of be a jack of all trades. You have to worry about what you bring day in and day out, but at the same time, part of the role is holding guys' hands and bringing them along for the ride," he said. "For me, it hasn't been that hard. You put your work boots on day in and day out, be a good pro, go to work and lead by example. When guys ask, you share your experiences and share your stories.

"I've seen a lot, had to endure a lot, and you try to bring those experiences and help the young guys grow, and at the same time you help them understand the importance of day-to-day being professionals and coming to work and that mentality [that] you're at the American League level trying to get to the NHL.

"It's team first, playing to win a championship at that level. It's something that you have to achieve, and it's something that's always in the back of your mind — if you're a champion, no one can ever take that from you."

Steve Oleksy, who captained the Bears, stressed the importance of reinforcing the team mentality. "I think it's important to be a kind of a channel between the coach and the players to make sure everyone's working together. I think that's when the team has the most success. I think we have a lot of leaders in the locker room, not just myself, so I think it's important to bring everybody together, and far as my play, try to show up every night and lead by example."

Coach Troy Mann explained why he picked Oleksy to wear the "C." "First of all, you want a guy who's a real person, and a guy that puts the team first," he said. "I think my coaching career is similar to Steve's playing career. He battled through the lower minors, trying to get some recognition and that's what he did. He just kept working, and I think his work ethic got him to an NHL contract and 62 games there."

For Mike Angelidis, Syracuse's captain, it also requires a lot of hard work and leading by example. "You try and teach guys on how to be a pro hockey player, and bring passion to your game. As a captain, you have to lead by example," he told me. "You can't ask a guy to go out and do something if you're not willing to do it yourself. I have to hold myself accountable, and have the guys hold themselves accountable."

Angelidis was rewarded for his efforts by the Lightning with a three-game call-up in March.

"That's one of the reasons Angelidis has come back, because how much he loves this organization and the opportunity they have given him," said Erik Erlendsson, lifetime Lightning beat writer. "He made that late-season call-up there, and they spoke so highly of how he worked with the younger players and understands that role down there. He's trying to get to the NHL — that's his number one goal — but he understands what they're asking of him and he's more than happy to do it.

"In a game against Boston, they got into a couple of fights, and the admiration from his teammates and coaches after that just was a wonderful example of a guy like that given an opportunity to come up and make an impact."

The Lightning also valued his contribution, signing him to a one-year, two-way contract for the 2015–16 season, paying him $650,000 for the year at the NHL level, and $200,000 at the AHL level, with $300,000 of that guaranteed. And with that provision, he was called up for several stints that season to not only fill in for injured forwards but to also contribute to the development of Crunch teammates.

Maggie Walters, who was the director of communications for the Crunch before taking a job with the Blue Jackets in 2014, said the parent club can help set the tone for players. "With Tampa the expectations for the players [were] super clear. You have guys like Mike [Angelidis] and J.P. [Côté] who are setting the tone, letting the guys know what it's all about to be a professional, and the community work is part of that."

Ken Young, who owned the Norfolk Admirals, with some of those same veterans on his club before the affiliation change, said that group was effective off the ice for being a part of the community. "Neilson and so many players on that team, they were great in the community and they got out into the community. Whether it was hospital visits or just going into the restaurants in the evening or after a game . . . they handled it so, so well. I think that was part of the success — not just the winning, although that had a lot to do with it — but the fans got behind that team."

Public relations work — all those school and hospital visits — can be almost like a full-time job for some players. In Syracuse, players average anywhere from 150 to 200 appearances per season — which is a lot considering players are only there for 192 days in a season. As Sarosy said, "It works. They have that interaction if it's a youth player or in a corporate setting, they go around from cubicle to cubicle and say, 'Hey, how's your day? Can you come see us this weekend?' The connection is so important and build[s] up the fans and continue[s] to do that."

Former Bears general manager Doug Yingst agrees that getting out in the community is essential to building a bond with fans. "I could never understand if you were an NHL-owned-and-operated team — we're almost 50-50 and independently owned teams — and there's no relation to the community," he said. "We need the Steve Oleksys and veteran players going out in the community more and going to schools and readings. Some teams are for development purposes only. They don't have that, and therefore they don't have more of a fan base and they lose more money."

The role of an AHL veteran is important, not only to try to keep their own dreams alive but to also nurture the dreams of their younger teammates and help market their team. For some, even with their role in helping others reach their goals, they get a chance to be called up to the NHL. Those are the nights the players skate for, giving them memories they won't forget.

Mink, who played seven games in the NHL during his career, recalled them all fondly. "I was nervous. The first game especially, it's a whirlwind. It's fun. I enjoyed every minute of it when I was there. I was hopeful it would be for longer, but it wasn't; but I didn't let the significance of the fact I was playing there go wasted at the time.

"There were a couple of turning points in my career where I was really close to making teams out of camp and it just didn't end up working out, and then for whatever reason, there wasn't an opportunity with injuries or whatnot. It would have been nice to get that, but I didn't.

"But I still feel fortunate to look back and have those seven games."

CHAPTER SIX

ON THE ROAD

It's a Sunday night in Hershey, and a sellout crowd of 10,803 files out of the arena following a 5–1 Portland victory over the home team. The teams have finished a whirlwind weekend of hockey, completing three games in three days against three different opponents in three different cities — or in AHL vernacular, the dreaded "3-in-3." The Bears started their weekend in Providence on Friday night, bused to Hartford for Saturday night and returned home for this 5:00 p.m. start at Giant Center — a journey of around 740 miles.

"It's hard with the travel," said Bears captain Steve Oleksy, admitting the mileage had taken its toll. "We've been playing well as of late, too. It's bound to give out at some point, but unfortunately tonight was the night. We played a good game in Providence there, but we didn't get a bounce to go our way tonight."

For their part, the Portland Pirates travelled almost as far to get to tonight's contest, nearly matching the Bears' weekend mileage even before beginning their long trip home. The Pirates started in Syracuse on Friday night, drove down to Allentown for a Saturday game, and then rolled into Hershey, having covered nearly 700 miles since leaving Maine just days before.

Outside the Portland locker room, Pirates goaltender David Leggio talked about what it was like to have a win after such a long weekend. "I thought we played awesome for a game three nights in three cities," he said. For Leggio, who had spent a year in Hershey, the win was special. "It's the best place to play in this league. But it's nice to get a win. To get six points in three nights, the guys were really pumped up to get that."

The goaltender acknowledged how hard these stretches can be on his teammates. "The goalies normally don't play all three, but the skaters are just battling. It's not really natural for humans to play three games in three nights, and guys have to fight a mental battle. You see guys in this league, they fight through it, and they play as hard as they can."

While the Bears just had a short drive to get back home, the Pirates' journey wasn't over yet. Decked out in team-issued black CCM track suits with the team's logo, players put their own gear on the bus before driving back to Maine. The 480-mile trek will take them nearly eight hours; they won't be home until the early hours. And that's not the worst trip they've ever had.

Pirates coach Ray Edwards, chatting in the hallway outside the visiting locker room, had a quick answer when asked what his most memorable bus trip in the AHL was.

"Last time we were here. It took 14 hours to get home. I never slept."

The Pirates' fateful trip came on Valentine's Day 2015, as a blizzard dumped up to two feet of snow in parts of New England, leaving a mess along the interstates from Pennsylvania to Maine — the entire route of their journey. "It was storming the whole way, but our bus driver tried to trudge through and got the hard hat for that trip," he said. "We left here at ten o'clock at night and we didn't get back to Portland until noon."

Perhaps the biggest complaint players in the AHL have is the travel. It isn't for the faint of heart. The NHL's collective bargaining agreement limits teams to playing more than back-to-back games. In the AHL, the 3-in-3 is common, with teams playing three games — almost always in at least two different arenas — in three days, usually with the Sunday game being an afternoon affair.

The NHL requires that teams arrive the night before for a road game, and be put up in a hotel of a certain standard. The AHL frequently uses same-day trips to play in nearby cities, and varying from team to team, travel budgets can vary on overnight stays. Games are mostly held on weekends to maximize ticket sales — the lifeblood of the finances of a club — and with a sport as physical as hockey, playing that kind of schedule doesn't always produce the most entertaining hockey.

The AHL also features its own Continental Divide, as teams on one side rely more on buses and the other on commercial air travel.

In the Eastern Conference, teams based in New England, New York and Pennsylvania almost always ride the bus, with not a ton of time spent overnight in hotels. While there are less extended trips, there are a lot of short trips and more 3-in-3s. Out west, teams are more reliant on commercial air travel and spend more time away from home in hotels, but have a more spread-out schedule.

As a result of the heavy travel to get to 38 road games a season, almost everyone who has played in the AHL has a bus or airplane tale that could make the most hardened traveler wince.

For John Walton, who called games for the Cincinnati Mighty Ducks, one particular road trip from the late 1990s came to mind for all the wrong reasons. The Mighty Ducks had four games in five days, traveling from Fredericton on the Friday to St. John's, and then a 5:00 p.m. start on Easter Sunday in Hartford, which was a 10-hour drive away. "It was god-awful," he said. "On the way to Fredericton, we were sidetracked, because our bus driver knew of a shortcut. But that turned out to be a seasonal road — which I'm sure was a very lovely shortcut to St. John's in July — but not maintained in the winter. Guys were getting motion sick in the back, and we all had to get off to get some air. A couple of guys were throwing up, and I said to assistant coach Eddie Johnstone, 'The only way this trip could get any worse is if a bear comes out and eats one of us.'"

By the time the Mighty Ducks rolled into Connecticut's capital on Easter morning, Walton said the team wasn't exactly at their Sunday best. "We had nothing left in the tank. [Coach] Moe Mantha and I helped with the gear at 7:30 in the morning, and we looked awful, I'm sure. We walked into the Hilton in Hartford with everybody dressed in their Easter Sunday finest and we walked in with our Ducks tracksuits. All we wanted was a meal. We sit down and the two of us eat, and everyone around us is like, 'I'm not really sure they should be here.'"

Jody Gage, a 17-year AHL veteran, said a pair of fateful trips stood out from his playing days, both involving a bus problem. "One time coming back from Hershey, we went down a hill and couldn't [get] up a hill or get back up the other hill, so we spent the night on the highway because of the ice conditions," he said.

The other trip was even worse, he recalled. "We were on the Thruway in 1987 to Adirondack and *our bus caught on fire*. And it was cold. That was tough, we had wait another 45 minutes for another bus to come. That was probably the most dangerous one, as I was at the back of the bus and could see the flames outside the window."

Troy Brouwer, who played in Norfolk, remembers one trip back to Virginia when winds prevented the team from entering the Chesapeake Bay Bridge-Tunnel. "One time, the bridge to get back into the Norfolk area, there was a wind warning, so we had to sit on the bus until the next morning to wait for the wind warning to come down. Luckily, we had a sleeper bus."

Broadcaster Todd Crocker worked for a number of years in Hamilton, where the Bulldogs would take extended bus trips. He doesn't miss those long bus rides, to put it mildly. "People romanticize travel in the American League," he said. "I tell you what, you ride on a bus for six hours somewhere, like Adirondack from [Hamilton], and that will about cure you of that romanticism. I remember with the Bulldogs at the time we took a 17-hour bus trip back from St. John's. It was awful."

Jim Sarosy of the Crunch laughed, recalling a former NHL-star-turned-AHL-coach's reaction on his first AHL bus trip. "Stan Smyl was our coach. Up until that point, had spent his entire life in the NHL. He was a phenomenal player, and he was used to getting on the plane and shrimp cocktails were waiting for him.

"We're driving down Interstate 81, and I kid you not, a deer runs in front of us a little way down the road. A few seconds later, a hunter runs across, chasing the deer. And the look on his face — it's something he never expected."

With a group of 30 players and staff sharing a small space for an extended period of time, the bus isn't usually aromatically pleasing, according to Joe Beninati. "It was . . . not regal. It did not smell of rose petals," he said. "It was not that pleasant, no."

Crocker agreed that it wasn't exactly a sweet-smelling ride. "The one thing about travel with a bunch of young guys, there's other things that happen on the bus that are not exactly pleasant. You might say, gas isn't just in the tank. It's like, 'Holy smokes.' There are some times where you just say, 'Get me a breath of fresh air.'"

With little to do on bus rides, movies became a big part of helping pass the time. Marty Biron's primary job when he was in Rochester was being the team's goaltender, but his secondary job was to be the team's movie guy. "My responsibility in the bus was to be in charge of the movies. I had to go out to Blockbuster before every road trip and get four or five movies, and I was in charge of playing them."

And Biron recalled there was one movie in particular that used to irk the team's broadcaster: "We used to always have *Austin Powers*. Don Stevens used to complain every time I put *Austin Powers* on the TV. 'We're watching this crap movie again?' he would always complain. I'm like, 'Don, the guys want to watch it. I have to put it in.' He would always complain about *Austin Powers*. He was always in the third row and [would] say, 'Marty, that's a stupid movie.' And I'd be, 'It's the only one I have.'"

With a lot of time to pass on the drives across the interstates going from city to city, Oleksy said riding the bus is an important part of the learning process. "The bus is a good time to catch up on sleep, a lot of playing cards, and a lot of team bonding."

Andrew Gordon said the AHL bus experience varies from team to team. "Some teams have fancy coach buses where you're sitting in something like a first-class airline seat," he said. "In Hershey we had satellite TV and every seat had their own set of headphones so you could listen to what everyone was watching. Or you can read a book. Other buses, the movie is just blaring in your face for seven hours."

Eric Lindquist, San Jose Barracuda broadcaster, noticed a change in the players' bus habits over the last decade. "Even when I was in Lowell, or in Long Beach in the ECHL, everyone would go back and play cards. Now, they just use their phones. Social media changed things. I think there's a lot more at stake now. I'm not saying guys had more fun back then, but I think there's a lot more focus of getting to the next level and the margin is so small, you can't afford to make mistakes."

While western teams who fly commercially don't have the bus trips their eastern counterparts do, they have to deal with the pitfalls of modern airlines.

Kevin Marshall recalled one Toronto trip that went awry trying to get to North Carolina from Texas. "We had a time where we spent 10 hours at the airport. Our original flight got cancelled; it was a Monday and we were supposed to get into Charlotte at two o'clock. Our flight got delayed, then delayed again — a classic rebooking — and then it got cancelled. So then our travel guy was running all over — I can't imagine how his day was," he said. "It was a long day, but we tried to make it as much fun as possible. We were hanging out — we're in this, might as well laugh about it instead of being grumpy."

Marshall's Marlies teammate, Brendan Mikkelson, said he preferred a long bus ride to flying commercial. "This is going to sound kind of stuck up, but commercial flying kind of sucks," he said, laughing. "So honestly, getting on a bus for five or six hours, I don't mind because you get on the bus, and being an older guy on the team now, I get two seats to myself, so basically sit back and have service and you can sit on your phone, watch a movie or whatever, so it's a little more comfortable and five or six hours later you're where you need to be."

Zac Dalpe, who spent time in Charlotte, recalled how flying in and out of the North Carolina airline hub was a challenge. "The travel [in Charlotte], we got [to] fly everywhere other than Norfolk, so that was nice. I had a lot of fun in Charlotte, I loved the city, but other than our second year, we always had to connect through Dallas. If we had to fly from Charlotte to Chicago, it'd be normally an hour and a half flight direct, but we had to fly two and a half hours out of the way, so that was a struggle at times."

John Anderson, former NHL player and Thrashers' coach, who spent 14 seasons behind the Chicago Wolves bench, doesn't hide his disdain for flying. "Since 9/11, travel's been horrid. We came back from Toronto recently, and I'd never seen this before — we got to the airport on time, but we had to wait an hour and 10 minutes just to get into line to go through customs. It's a very, very long day," he said. "Travel without a charter is like pulling teeth. It's horrible. That is what it is. Quite honestly, we have flights to Iowa, which is a five-hour bus ride, but I will go with the trainers on the bus because I just can't stand flying."

Anderson also said he had his own horror stories just based on his name. "At one point, right after 9/11, I was on the 'no fly list' because there's a John Anderson who is part of Sinn Féin — an Irish Republican political party — so I got flagged every time. I had to put my middle name on the flight list. Every time I went to the airport, even when there were 20 guys behind me, I'd let them all go in front," he said. "Travel is difficult, it is what it is, but that's the minors."

Crocker said that even though in theory flying sounds better than the bus, it isn't really so. "Everybody would say, 'Oh, it must be better, you travel by plane.' If you work in any business and use commercial travel a lot, you know that's a lie. It's not like we're running around in a charter in first class seats.

"We're just like everybody else who travels, and more so, because you have those bags you have to check in. You're there two hours — minimum — before every flight, you take a three-hour flight — in a case of going to Texas, the team flies into Dallas, then takes a three-hour bus ride from Dallas to Austin. It's a full day to get anywhere on a commercial flight."

One February, it was a nightmare trying to get the Rochester Americans to Chicago for a game. As Chadd Cassidy, former head coach of the Rochester Americans, recalled, snowstorms were raging from New York State to Illinois, wiping out flights all across the northeast.

"Up until the last minute we didn't even expect to make the trip with the flights being cancelled. Going through all the different scenarios of how we would get there, there was point where we were going to bus through the night and get there at three or four in the morning, and get two hours of sleep and then play. Then the organizations both stepped up and got us a charter plane. We still didn't get into Chicago until almost midnight. It was a long day of practice in the morning and we sat around the rink the whole day figuring out what we were going to do — but that's life in the American Hockey League," he said.

"That was a very important game for Chicago — it's one of their biggest draws of the year — so the league, we and the Wolves did everything we could to make it happen, and we were fortunate enough to go out there and win the game 3–2 and start off a really good road trip for us."

Sometimes even players who get a shot at trying out the NHL's upgraded travel face difficulties getting there. For instance, Benn Ferriero remembers one ill-fated call-up when he was playing with Worcester in 2011.

"[We were] playing in Albany against the Devils, and Matty Irwin was in his first year in the American League. We're getting on the bus to the rink, and we both get pulled off the bus and they said, 'You're getting called up,' and they left us behind at the hotel. They tell us they'll get us a flight later in the day, and a connecting flight that gets to San Jose around 11 at night. We got on our first flight to make our connection in Newark. But our flight from Newark to San Jose was delayed. Time goes by, and our flight gets cancelled. So now we're stuck in Newark on our own, and we have to spend the night, as our flight was rescheduled for the morning.

"We do that, no big deal, stay in a hotel, and the flight the next morning gets delayed a little bit more, but we finally get on a flight from Newark to San Francisco. Matty and I fly in, and as we're getting off the plane — even before we get to baggage claim — I get a call from San Jose's assistant GM. He says to me, 'Sorry, the guys who we had in pregame skate that we thought might be injured are good to play. So we have a flight for you to go back to Boston.' We think, all right, go to the baggage claim, put your bags back through security and fly back to Boston," he said. "The worst part is I felt really bad — it was the first time Matty Irwin had ever gotten called up and I had to tell him we weren't going."

Stevens recalls a trip where the players had no time even to sleep between games. "We played in Edmonton during the lockout year, and we sat around the rink eating pizza until two in the morning. Then we caught a red-eye flight to Toronto, and when we got in there it's about seven in the morning. When we got to the freight part of the airport to pick up our equipment, we got on the road at 9:00 or 9:30, and we bused to Cleveland and got there at noon, and then played at 2:00. We never went to bed between games," said Stevens.

While eastern teams don't usually get mixed up with the problems of modern air travel, there is one eastern destination teams fly to — one that isn't an easy place to land, especially in the winter months. It's St. John's, Newfoundland, home of the IceCaps. So many players and officials have a St. John's story.

Doug Yingst, Hershey's former general manager, says many of his most memorable snafus came coming to and from Newfoundland. "We had one trip recently that took us 15 hours and 15 minutes to get home. There's not too many flights to St. John's. And there's not too many flights to Harrisburg. So we got stranded at the airport. We left at 5:15 in the morning to get to the airport for a seven o'clock flight, and they kept on delaying it, and then they finally cancelled it."

The next thought was to fly Toronto to Philadelphia and then bus to Hershey. "There's a flight from St. John's to Toronto, but we'd miss our connection to Philly, so I call our bus company to see if they can drive up [from Pennsylvania to Toronto] and bus us back but they can't go over the border empty. They were very willing to do it — the time span takes about seven hours each way — but they couldn't do it," said Yingst. "So then I'm calling the Marlies and the Maple Leafs and seeing what bus company they use. And they had buses but no drivers. The long and short of it: we get to Toronto, and they delayed a flight to Philadelphia for an hour so we could get on it [and then hop on a bus to Hershey]. . . . After all that time, you're just glad to be back."

Lindquist remembers a trip with Worcester during a snowy

Valentine's Day weekend, during the same storm that left the Portland Pirates crawling up the east coast from Pennsylvania to Maine. It might be the best travel story. Or worst, depending on your perspective.

"Even according to the St. John's people, we had the trip of all trips," Lindquist said. "There was some weather issues getting there — I'm the travel guy [for the team], so I got just about everyone out to St. John's on a flight after a long delay and a sleepover in Toronto, which was unplanned. But [goaltender] Troy Grosenick [defenseman], Kyle Bigos, our video guy Charlie Townsend and myself ended up staying another night after traveling to Halifax.

"We ended up on a small flight from Halifax to St. John's without the team, and the plane's captain got on the loudspeaker and said, 'Ladies and gentlemen,' — and you look outside and it looks like a blizzard — 'I just got word we're going to be the last flight that will be able to land in St. John's. But we're expecting extreme turbulence. Get ready for a rough one. I'm going to try to land, but if I can't land, I'm going to pull up last second and try again.' So I'm sitting [next] to Troy Grosenick, and it's to the point of extreme turbulence that people were crying, praying to God. I think Troy and I were holding hands, saying, 'Dude, it's been real and if we go down, it was nice knowing you.'

"The plane was shaking and it was as scary a flight I've ever been on. We almost touched down on the runway, but he ended up pulling up last second and the captain went on the speaker, 'We're going to try this one more time.' And everyone on the plane was like, 'Hell, no. Go to Halifax, we'll stay in Halifax tonight.'"

It wasn't a whole lot better for the rest of the Sharks, who had actually landed in St. John's two days earlier. Their equipment didn't arrive until just before game time.

"Our team, in the morning skate, didn't have sticks, so they had a soccer ball on the ice. They didn't have pads on. All of our equipment got there just two hours before game time," said Lindquist. "We had to play the game, and literally, I was just able to get there and turn the on radio equipment to call the game."

To add insult to injury, the Sharks couldn't fly out of St. John's for another two days.

Travel isn't easy on the IceCaps themselves, who spend half their schedule getting off the island to play elsewhere, mostly connecting through Toronto to their eventual destinations across the United States and Canada. Andrew Gordon spent a year in St. John's during the 2013–14 season, and while he liked the town, he hated the travel. "You're on the road 12 to 14 days a month," he explained. "St. John's is a wonderful place. But the schedule is rough."

And in terms of schedules, comparing an NHL back-to-back and an AHL 3-in-3 is no contest, according to Kevin Marshall. "People don't understand how hard it is, the 3-in-3. It gets crazy. You see guys in the NHL, and they play back-to-back games and they go, 'Oh my God, this is really hard on [our] bodies.' And I lived it. I played 10 games in the NHL — not that much — but I saw the difference. You get on the plane, you have a nice meal, and you're in bed by midnight, and play the next day," he said. "But a 3-in-3? You bus maybe three hours, you get home at three in the morning, you wake up, and sometimes the games are at three in the afternoon. You have one meal in you, and you've got to go and perform.

"And you can't take nights off, because management is in the stands, either from your team or another team. If your GM isn't there, the opposite GM is there, and so the opponent's playing hard, and you have to match that level."

AHL veteran Drew Bagnall noted how usually both teams are running on empty by Sunday, which can affect the quality of play. "It's more a mental thing in the third game. You're physically drained. Mentally you just have to know to play the percentages," said Bagnall. "It's almost like you play a very safe game. The team that makes the most mistakes is the team that normally loses. You see it's more methodical, more of a chess match on a Sunday. You don't see as many guys running around and trying to make big hits because you get pulled out of position and can't recover the way you could on a Friday night."

Mikkelson says with the players in good shape, rest is the key to playing in a 3-in-3 — although sometimes it isn't the prettiest product. "It is [tough] in the sense that it's taxing the body, especially if there's travel involved. We would play Friday in Utica, come back [to Toronto] and play somewhere else Sunday. Come Sunday afternoon, you're running on rhythm. Playing three games in three nights, you're getting in a game rhythm. . . . So, you're running on that instinct a little, and oftentimes when you're doing it, the other team is doing the same thing.

"You feel a little bit bad for the fans sometimes," he said with a laugh. "But I mean, that's the way it goes for the league; you're trying to draw fans on the weekend dates, and we understand how it is."

Dalpe said the 3-in-3s were difficult for him as a younger player, but he learned to appreciate them over time. "The first couple of years it's hard, but as you move on, I like the third game the best because you're not thinking about it. I just have to go play. Sometimes that more loosey-goosey attitude works for you," he said.

Dalpe's Rochester teammate Matt Ellis said that he preferred the third game of the trifecta. "It's tough, very tough physically, and mentally as well. It's kind of funny, the third game is almost easier to play than the second. You get through that second game, and it's almost like the third game, the puck drops and you go and play hockey. Everything else is out the window. But it's definitely a grind. . . . Taking your gear off and unlacing your skates and hopping on the bus after the third game in three nights is tough. And it's even tougher the morning after when you feel all the bumps and bruises."

Goaltender Matt Hackett said even though he doesn't usually play all three games in net, it's still hard. "It's not really fun. It's pretty tough on your body, and the travel, and it gets you, and you have to get your rest when you can and be ready for that next game."

Tim Kennedy said the workload makes you appreciate what you can earn if you get to the NHL. "It is a bit of a grind, but it is good because when you do make it to the next level, you get pampered. You're flying on charter jets and going to play two games back-to-back instead of three."

Ferriero does say the league is moving toward reducing the compression of the schedule. "It's tough; the AHL in the last couple years — I played when there were 4-in-5s and 6-in-8s — I think they've done a good job getting rid of those and getting the players more rest. Everyone sees that 60-minute finished product during the third game of the 3-in-3s.

Guys are struggling, and they're tired from the games before. The AHL has done a good job showing that guys need to be rested and it puts a better product for everyone to see. It'll make us look better."

NHL veteran Troy Brouwer didn't mince words on 3-in-3s: "It's miserable. A game is tough enough as it is, and back-to-backs are difficult, and you throw a third game in there — and usually they're less than 24 hours later, too — you'll play all three games in 45 or 48 hours. It wears you down."

Bears coach Troy Mann also notes how hard it is for a coach, knowing his players aren't at their best in that Sunday game. "From a coaching perspective, you're looking on Sunday for the team to be the freshest it can be at game time. Whether it's a three o'clock start or a five o'clock start, there's no excuses with the fatigue factor — even when you know in your head there is fatigue. Even as a coach, there's a fatigue on your part, but it's mostly a mental fatigue. It's not [an] easy thing to prepare for 3-in-3, and for the players it's tough."

He also noted since the Bears draw well on Sundays, his team has one of the AHL's highest numbers of 3-in-3s. "We do play a lot of Sunday home games. . . . We're fourth in the league playing 3-in-3s because we're trying to get home games on Sundays, because you come in here on a Sunday game at five o'clock, and you have 9,000 fans, and on a lot of nights you will get 9,000 to 10,000 fans. I think that helps to some degree with the players' motivation to try and get it done Sunday at home. We've tried some different things, not bringing the guys in Sunday mornings and trying the most tweaks to get the most out of your team on Sunday, but it is ideal? No. I'd rather not have 3-in-3s."

Chadd Cassidy said he is concerned for player safety, particularly when mental and physical shape isn't at its peak. "I can tell you . . . my concern with the 3-in-3 is the development and safety of the players with the travel and everything else that's going on; to put them in 3-in-3 situations, that Sunday game if you're a scout or a coach, you can throw that game away, because it's not nearly what you want. You always are worried about injuries in those games, because guys aren't as sharp physically, not as sharp mentally, and all it takes [is] for a guy to be just off a little bit, put himself in a spot, and then he gets hurt,"

Matt Ellis, a veteran forward who has skated in the AHL for Grand Rapids, Portland and Rochester, along with playing in 356 NHL games, said he prefers the last game of the dreaded 3-in-3s. (MICHELINE VELUVOLU / ROCHESTER AMERICANS)

said Cassidy. "Unfortunately, that's the reality of our league because it's a weekend league. This isn't the National League, but it's a fine line between development and player safety."

Another unusual aspect to the American Hockey League schedule is, unlike the National Hockey League, each team isn't required to play all of the other 29 teams. In fact, it may be years between meetings, even with two teams just a couple of hours apart. Most teams play almost exclusively in their own conference, and barring a special request, a lot of teams — particularly the eastern ones — don't travel that far from home.

Monarchs broadcaster Ken Cail remarked on Manchester's quirky schedules. "One of the complaints we've had [from fans] over the years is we play the same teams a lot. So, [in 2014–15], for example, we played Worcester, Portland and Providence 12 times apiece, St. John's 10 times. That's more than half our schedule against those four teams. There are teams we see twice a year, and some teams we don't see at all. It's funny because of the proximity, Syracuse, they've been in our conference most of the years that we've been in the league — not all, but most — and we only played Syracuse twice in our entire history. The schedule is a little bizarre."

As a result, each team's AHL schedule is filled with familiar opponents, making for some heated rivalries. And according to former Sound Tiger and current New York Islanders forward Anders Lee, those games can get rough.

"Your division, you'd usually play them eight times each so you get to know those teams pretty well, and those games can get chippy at times," said Lee. "You might face a team Friday, and then again on Sunday and that carries over every game."

For all the travel stories, there is an upside, as the travails usually lead to more team bonding than you'd see at the NHL level. Instead of charter flights and rides to the hotel, the players are around each other longer, and it gives them more opportunity to pass the time together and develop chemistry off the ice.

Bagnall said the whole travel process helps a team grow closer. "Everything is so much about saving money, essentially, and balancing the cost and revenue. Busing is a lot easier and lot cheaper than flying," said Bagnall. "You get to know the guys a little bit better on a bus for eight hours. You play cards, and build those relationships on life away from hockey. I think that is important to building a good team."

Brent Regner says even though he'd prefer to fly, he can see how busing helps some teams grow. "It's fun to ride the bus, but it's great to ride a plane, because you're getting in so much earlier and everything, but everything's closer so you're riding the bus for the same amount of time. But you can play cards on a bus, and hang out with the guys, and that's also really good for team bonding."

Another aspect of bus life that some pointed out is the chatter you'd hear during the hours spent on bus trips criss-crossing across the interstates and highways. Joe Beninati said those long trips would teach you a lot about the team you were with, recalling, "The bus rides were great, lots of incredible stories. You're so close that you're hearing stories that you can't believe and your neck is snapping and breaking going, 'What? She said what?'"

Crunch broadcaster Dan D'Uva says it's an eye-opener listening to bus chatter, saying, "You overhear different conversations. Guys — especially the young players . . . you can hear them growing up. 'You hear this?' 'What state is Bridgeport in?' These little conversations are innocuous, but these are character-revealing moments you can't pay for. I would never think to ask, 'Hey, so-and-so, do you know what state we're going to for this trip?' And I'm not only talking about non-Americans," he said, laughing. "Just to overhear some of those conversations are great, some of the old guys telling stories to the younger guys. Younger guys will talk about who they know on another team."

AHL alumni reflected well on their bus time — once they experienced the easier travel of the National Hockey League, which certainly made them appreciate not having to do the same grind of the AHL.

Brouwer said he enjoyed the time riding the bus and the friendships he made. He was lucky enough to have some of them as his fellow teammates on the Chicago Blackhawks, who went on to win the Stanley Cup in 2010. "We had card tables on our buses so we could play sharps, poker, have a beer or two and just talk and enjoy ourselves," he said. "Some of the trips were pretty long, but the majority of the time, we had a good time and had some fun."

Maple Leafs forward Brooks Laich looks back at all those road trips with a bit of nostalgia, saying, "My fondest memories of the bus [are] when we used to play poker at the back of the bus, with myself, Brian Sutherby, Steve Eminger, Louis Robitaille, Dwayne Zinger and Graham Mink," he said. "We used to have a great crew and had fun playing poker at the back of the bus. It wasn't for big money — it was to enjoy each other's company and pass the hours. We really had an enjoyable time."

For the younger AHL players like Adam Comrie of the Lehigh Valley Phantoms, road trips are a chance to get to know his teammates better. "It's a lot of fun, a lot of stories and time to just hang out with each other and get to know each other. It's a lot of team bonding, a lot of meals we're eating together and having a new roommate on the road. It's nice to get to know players as people as well, not just hockey players."

Just like families on road trips in the summer, pro hockey teams get to know those familiar rest stops and fast-food chains along the way.

"I would say anywhere on the New York State Thruway, the Mass Pike or any travel plaza, there's a certain air of desperation," said John Walton.

Bears broadcaster Scott Stuccio says one particular Canadian chain is a popular stop for his club. "On our way to Binghamton we usually get a coffee stop at Tim Hortons right below the New York border. Let the guys sleep, get up, get their coffee and then it's only 20 minutes to Binghamton," he said. "If we go to Syracuse, we stop at the Tim Hortons in Cortland, and it's only 25 minutes to Syracuse, so it's not bad."

Walton also mentioned the difference some coaches had on drinking on road trips. "I remember it was funny, in Hershey, Bruce Boudreau, at one point, had an edict of no beer on the bus, and I don't know if that's a bad rule. Actually, I think it's pretty good," he said. "But Moe Mantha was a fan of beer on the bus, and I remember stopping at a Turkey Hill in Hershey for the ride back to Cincinnati, saying, 'If we're on a 10-hour bus ride back we're going to need a few pops.' There's a certain air of that too if you're walking into a convenience store at eleven o'clock at night and getting cases of beer and saying, 'We have a tough night ahead of us.'"

With all that time sitting idle, it's perhaps inevitable that pranks are a prominent feature of bus rides. And it's not just the players who do it.

Barry Trotz had a tale to tell about that. He was an assistant for Baltimore in the early 1990s when young broadcaster Kenny Albert called the games. One of the audio clips that Albert played didn't sit well with the future NHL coach.

"You spend so much time together on a bus, and all that, all the pranks come out," Trotz said with a smile, recalling how a friend named Jimmy Wiseman, who helps the Capitals with security, set one up on Albert. "I had this scheme that we'd have a rookie — it was Kenny's rookie year where he's full time with us in Baltimore — and we landed in Cape Breton, we had the local authorities when going through customs arrest him. They basically planted flour in his bag.

"They said, 'Is this your bag?' 'Yes it is.' 'We found this in there.' He was denying it wasn't his, and all that. They threw him in jail for three or four hours, and I'd go back to the hotel, and I'd unpack and that, and slowly make my way over to the police station and make a big scene. And he's trying to phone his lawyer and I'm saying, 'Hang on, I'll help you,' and sort of kept him on edge, let him sit in the clink for three or four hours and do stuff like that."

Albert, now the voice of the New York Rangers, remembers that trip well. "Early in the year, I interviewed Barry and it kind of came out funny. It came out wrong — but funny. So I played the tape for a couple of players to make fun of him. So he had heard I had made fun of him and said, 'I'm going to get you back one day — don't worry.' Kind of joking around.

"Later in the year, we fly — one of the only trips we would fly was to play the teams in the Maritimes, six games up there against the teams in Halifax, Sydney, Cape Breton and St. John's. We took three flights, one from Baltimore to Boston; Boston to St. John's, Newfoundland; then St. John's to Sydney, Nova Scotia. And the issue was going to be with the luggage.

"They had to get the hockey equipment and sticks on the small plane that seated 30 or 40 people in the regional jets. I was over-packed, for sure, as while the players just brought a small bag with underwear and socks, I had these two huge suitcases with four different suits.

"So I have two big suitcases, the radio equipment and a briefcase, and I show up, and everyone's laughing at me since I have so much luggage. We finally land in Sydney, Nova Scotia, and we get off the plane on the tarmac and go down the steps.

"There's a gentleman with a clipboard, and I guess Barry had informed the team of what he had set up, so they all knew at this point. The gentleman with the clipboard points to a name and says, 'Is this you?' 'Yes.' He said, 'You have to come with me.'

"I thought it was to help identify the luggage coming on the next flight, since the hockey equipment took priority, and I assumed he just wanted to see what kind of luggage you had and we'll look for it when it comes in. He started to ask me all these questions — 'Have you ever been arrested?' 'Do you know anyone in trouble?' 'Is your passport valid?' — and playing 20 questions. Then he says, 'You have to come with me.' He put me in this unmarked car, which is definitely some kind of police car, the computerized equipment is up front, and there's an older gentleman up front and they start driving me around, they're still asking a lot of questions. I'm thinking in the back of my mind, 'This is probably some kind of setup,' but I still have no idea at this point.

"Fifteen minutes later, we drive up to what looks like our hotel. And they finally say, 'Do you know Jimmy Wiseman?' It turns out his brother is the chief of police up there. And they got me. Barry got me back much later for the practical joke I had played on him.

"That was 24 years ago and still pretty memorable. And the only time I can say I've ever been arrested."

That wasn't the only prank, according to Trotz. "Guys would fall asleep on the bus, and so guys would tie their laces to the bottom of the seat. A guy would be reading a book, and you'd say, 'How's the book going?' 'It's the best book I ever read,' and he'd leave it on the seat and you'd go in there and take out the last three pages of the book and send it to him after he'd finished the book, and say, 'How's the book?'

"You'd put it in an envelope and wherever you were, maybe a month later, send it to him from where you were, PEI, and he'd look at it and say, 'Someone sent this from PEI and it's the last three pages of the book,' and stuff like that. There's always little pranks that go on."

The other trip Albert remembered from his AHL days was a night involving a Holiday Inn in Utica. "We get to Utica and we had played somewhere else the night before, so we get there at three or four in the morning and our room is on the first floor. It's snowing, and there's no heat, because it's not working. So we have the snow and cold coming in under the door, and we're basically sleeping in all of our clothes and winter coats in the double beds."

Trotz confirmed the story, and told his side on Toronto's TSN 1050. "It was really cold, it was snowing and it was sort of a blizzard. We get to our room and we can barely get into the room because there's a snowbank. So we go to the front desk . . . and lo and behold, I go to the front desk and say, 'Hey, there's a snowbank in our room, can we get another room?' And they say, 'We're all sold out.'

"So that night, we slept in our room and there was a snowbank in our room. You've got your sweat suit on, and you've got your overcoat on and you're under the covers because you're freezing to death. I heard this voice in the middle of the night, it's about four in the morning. Kenny goes, in this very quivery voice, 'I am absolutely freezing.'

"My response was, 'You better stay over in your bed!'"

Another aspect of the road is you get to learn about your teammates and coaches well. Sometimes too well.

Dave Starman, an analyst on Skipjacks broadcasts with Albert, remembered seeing Trotz's culinary side on one trip to Connecticut. "Ownership decided to put us up in a Residence Inn instead of a hotel so that guys could buy groceries instead of having to go out. So I remember Barry said, 'We're going out.' I thought, 'Cool, we're going out for dinner.' He said, no, 'We're going out to the supermarket and going to stock up for the week.'

"I'm watching this guy with a brilliant hockey mind squeezing melons to seeing if they're ripe and looking at bananas. It's like the scene out of the movie *The Odd Couple.* . . . I'm going up and down with him in the aisles . . . and he's price comparing," he said. "It was great. Now, every time I see Barry on a screen, behind an NHL bench or talking to Alex Ovechkin, I'm remembering him trying to see if a melon was ripe in a supermarket in New Haven."

Beninati said he developed a special skill to move around the bus. "Life on the bus was interesting, and I was kind of good at it. Because if you think about long bus trips and requiring the occasional pit stop in the restroom in the back, you had to be really good at scaling the seats to get over the bodies that were strewn across the middle of the bus. Guys were trying to sleep — these were not sleeper buses, but nice comfortable buses, but these are big guys that are stretching across seat to seat."

Beninati demonstrated a bit on the blue seats at Nassau Coliseum. "You became really, really good at — I don't know what would the verb [would] be — spidering on top of the seat and across the other seat like a low, crab-crawl spider walk to the back of the bus."

For all the bus rides, airplane rides and hotel stays over the course of a season, it's all part of the learning process for young players, according to Brad Lynn, the Toronto Marlies' travel guy. "All the bus time is part of the journey, and it is part of the experience. You have to grind that out and you see them graduate to the big team. They've earned that. It's a big team-building thing, too. You can go through those trips together and get there at four in the morning, but it bonds you with the guys you go through that with — that's the nice part of the league."

Wolves GM Wendell Young also thinks the AHL lifestyle promotes more bonding than the NHL version of the game. "You see at the NHL level, everyone's on a charter, they have their headphones on, they have their own video player. Some teams, they're given an iPad and they're watching themselves play. There's no card games, there's no conversations, there's no hanging out, because you play the game on the road, you jump on a charter jet and everyone has their own seat on the plane and they get off and go to the hotel," said Young. "Camaraderie at [the AHL] level, you're hanging out more, going out to dinners more, you're on the road the night before a game, and you can have a beer or a bite to eat, and we stay the night after a game — we don't charter out right away. A lot of friendships . . . made in the American Hockey League last a lot longer than those made in the NHL."

With days on the road, you never know what you're going to see or going to experience — and for some players, it's their first time ever to a certain city or part of the country. Even for Martin Biron, he said it was a chance to visit an iconic American restaurant chain for the first time.

"I remember my first year going out to Cincinnati and Kentucky, and having breakfast at Big Boy right around the corner. I'd never been to a Big Boy before, and when I saw it in Austin Powers a few years later, I thought '[I've] been at that restaurant chain,'" he said with a laugh. "I didn't even know what it was at the time."

The Quebec native also enjoyed seeing Atlantic Canada on one trip. "I remember going to the Maritimes and St. John and St. John's on the Rock, and in the middle of February you see the icebergs in the bay going out to the ocean. Playing in that old barn — they have a new building now. . . . I remember doing Fredericton, St. John and then St. John's — that was great. "

He also calls a team dinner with Rochester one of the best memories of his AHL career. "My second year, we had a trip to Providence. . . . We had a dinner with all the money from the segment bonuses that we had collected [from getting points in games]. And it was one of the best team dinners, everybody was laughing, everybody was enjoying each other, everybody was there; we walked back to the hotel together, I remember thinking, looking around and thinking, 'Man, if every team is like this, this is so much fun.' It was very special place in my career, that's for sure."

And there are also the bus rides after wins that makes the trip go that much faster. Eric Neilson remembered the ride home when Norfolk set the AHL record with their 18th straight win in 2012. "When we won in Charlotte and set the American Hockey League record and won back-to-back games, we hop[ped] on the bus and Jon Cooper — who was our coach at the time — said, 'The bus was at this time, but we've set it [back] to one o'clock.' So guys were able to go out and socialize, and come back to the bus, and we extended it for two more hours so the bus didn't leave until three o'clock. It's a six- or seven-hour ride back and we were pretty fired up," said Neilson. "There wasn't a whole lot of sleep on the bus with tunes blaring and team bonding and experience for us. That was a real special night for us. It was one I'll always remember."

CHAPTER SEVEN

THE CHICAGO WOLVES

Under an overcast sky, a commercial flight begins its descent, passing over the shores of Lake Michigan and skyscrapers of Chicago, and lands at O'Hare, the airline hub that's miles west of the United Center, the home of the NHL's Blackhawks.

Once you disembark and make your way through the terminal, you pass by stores displaying Cubs, White Sox and Blackhawks gear and other souvenirs, including a shirt picturing Snoopy carrying a hockey stick with "CHICAGO" written on the taped-up blade. At the main parking garage across the street, you notice each floor of the garage is emblazoned with logos known to local sports fans.

The first floor is named for the Cubs, Chicago's most iconic sports franchise, while the second floor is Bears-themed, for the city's long-time NFL team. Above sits the White Sox level, for the south side's MLB team of choice, and on the fourth level is the Blackhawks floor, with their United Center co-tenants, the Bulls, one floor above them.

The sixth floor is named for a team that isn't as familiar to as many people — particularly out-of-towners — with a black-and-red logo featuring an angry wolf over a hockey stick and puck, along with the "Wolves" name in a jagged font.

For local hockey fans, however, the Chicago Wolves are well known as the city's successful minor league hockey franchise, which first entered the International Hockey League in 1994 and quickly established a reputation for winning. The Wolves never had a losing record in their time in the IHL, and haven't had one in the AHL since joining the league in 2001. Overall, they've won four championships, claiming two Turner Cups in their seven seasons in the IHL, and adding two Calder Cups in their time in the AHL.

The Wolves were part of the International Hockey League that wanted to challenge the National Hockey League on its own turf. They certainly weren't afraid to tweak the Blackhawks. When the IHL folded under the unsustainable weight of an expensive business model, the Wolves found themselves in the AHL. Since joining, the team, which had operated most of its IHL life without an NHL affiliate (only in the last two IHL seasons did they have an affiliation with the Islanders), has had to adjust to relying on a parent club to supply players and talent to its roster.

Still, the Wolves have a drive to win Calder Cups, and the parent, the St. Louis Blues, are willing to sign veterans to help the team try and achieve that goal. In 2015–16, defenseman Peter Harrold signed a one-year, two-way deal with St. Louis worth $400,000 at the AHL level, just $175,000 less than the NHL's minimum, while Andre Benoit inked a deal worth $350,000 if he played in Chicago. Given that they play in a competitive market in the United States' third-largest city, the Wolves make sure they have some veterans in their lineup so that the team can make a viable bid for the playoffs year in and year out. And the expectations are high. Despite their streak of never finishing below the .500 mark in team history, anything short of a Calder Cup trip isn't viewed as a success.

Driving out of the O'Hare garage, you head two miles up U.S. Route 12, past the McDonald's, Sheraton Chicago O'Hare and Holiday Inn Express. Then, on the left, Allstate Arena appears in the middle of a large parking lot, right next door to a Target shopping plaza in Chicago's suburb of Rosemont.

Allstate Arena, a product of the suburban arena boom of the 1970s, is an off-white building with a church-like blue trim along the sides above its entrances that makes it look almost like an oversized White Castle. It's a large venue for the AHL, seating 16,692 for hockey.

Once you walk in through the glass doors and down the cement-wall hallways, you notice the unique architecture of the venue. The interior above the rink features a wooden roof, as well as a lower seating bowl that's at a much more gradual slope than you normally see at hockey arenas. The venue has been home of DePaul University's basketball team since opening in 1980, and with banners commemorating the Blue Demons' NCAA tournament trips and members of the Big East Conference, it has a basketball gym feel.

The arena was designed with the old World Hockey Association's Chicago Cougars in mind, and at one end of the building there are reminders that one of the more successful teams in minor league hockey now resides here: banners featuring the Wolves logo in front of the grey silhouette of the two different league championship trophies the team has won — the Turner Cup in the IHL and the Calder Cup in the AHL — as well as the team's retired numbers.

During the decade that the Wolves won four championships — from the first Turner Cup in 1998 to the 2008 Calder Cup title — the Blackhawks posted just two winning seasons and had just one playoff appearance. The Blackhawks — and notably team owner Bill Wirtz, derisively nicknamed "Dollar Bill" for the liquor magnate's perceived lack of spending — suffered from a poor reputation with the city's hockey fans during that era. Critics focused on the team policy of not showing home games on local television, one that was intended to encourage more fans to buy tickets — and alcohol once there.

Due to poor play and unpopular policies, attendance declined at United Center for games during the 2000s, dropping from 20,832 in average attendance in 1994, the first year in their new home, to just 13,253 in 2003–04. That was the same year the Wolves put up a billboard along Interstate 94 that read, "WE PLAY HOCKEY THE OLD-FASHIONED

WAY: WE WIN." The Wolves made an aggressive marketing push off the bat in Chicago, becoming known as a fan-friendly alternative to NHL games. While affordability and accessibility were originally part of the IHL's vision of being a rival league, the Wolves have carried those attributes into its AHL incarnation as well.

The Wolves' owner, Don Levin, has been a driving force, and he directly competed against the established NHL team in town. As AHL president Dave Andrews told me, "I think Don sees it as a rivalry and a challenge for him. I think he enjoyed it when he was outperforming the Blackhawks competitively and from a business point of view for a certain point in time, and that's human nature. He's a competitive guy."

The tactic worked well, as the Wolves had the third-best attendance in the league in 2006–07, averaging 7,830 per game that season, over 60 percent of the Original Six franchise's average total of 12,727.

While that particular season was a low watermark for the Blackhawks, it also led to the beginning of an impressive turnaround for the NHL team. Chicago finished with the fifth-worst record in the NHL, and a win in the lottery gave the Blackhawks the first overall pick. Years of little success for the Blackhawks helped rebuild the team. With that first-round pick they drafted Patrick Kane, and the team also picked up other promising players, such as Jonathan Toews. With some other on-ice changes, this put them on the road to being a Stanley Cup contender.

As current Wolves coach John Anderson told me, "I think the Blackhawks had to go through that to get people like Keith and Toews and Kane — all those guys were drafted because they were doing poorly. I think Chicago's done a good job of building that team and you see what they have today. There was a time, they were going through hard times, not so much financially but in the standings. But those are the growing pains you have to go through to get a championship franchise."

In 2007, Wirtz's son Rocky took over after his father's death, and he ended some of the unpopular policies — most notably, the local TV blackout. The end result was a hockey renaissance in the Windy City that saw the Blackhawks reach new heights in the city's sports landscape. The Blackhawks now are a standard bearer of hockey excellence, winning three Stanley Cups in six years in the salary cap era, and helping raise the game in a market that has become one of the NHL's best, with a strong appetite for hockey.

The Blackhawks' resurgence has changed what was a good AHL market into a unique one, with a combination of the big city of Chicago and an organization that puts a premium on winning championships at that level. The increased spotlight on the Blackhawks hasn't hurt the Wolves in attendance either, as they averaged 7,958 fans in 2014–15, sixth-best in the 30-team league.

The setup in Chicago is also unique in the fact that, unlike the other three spots where NHL and AHL teams share the same city — Toronto, San Jose and Winnipeg are the others for the 2015–16 season — the American League team isn't affiliated with the local NHL club.

The Wolves are partnered with the Blackhawks' Central Division rival St. Louis, while Chicago's AHL affiliate, the Rockford IceHogs, play 70 miles west of Allstate Arena down Interstate 90. Part of that, of course, is the competitive nature of the two teams, and so the Wolves have had AHL affiliations with Atlanta, Vancouver and now St. Louis, and never paired up with what would seem to be a natural fit, the Blackhawks. But despite that, the Wolves have held their own, and for John Anderson, who had two different tours of duty as the Wolves' head coach in between NHL coaching jobs in Atlanta, Phoenix and Minnesota, the team's status has been solid.

"We're a little different genre, but there are just as many people proud to say the Wolves are part of the Chicago sports scene as the Blackhawks. Obviously the Blackhawks get more press and adulations, but everywhere I go, people are happy to see me just because I'm part of the Wolves," said Anderson.

One thing that hasn't wavered though over two decades of Wolves hockey is the team's desire to win championships, be it Turner Cups or Calder Cups. It's part of the team's philosophy. Wendell Young, backstop for the Wolves' two Turner Cup titles, assistant coach of Chicago's 2008 Calder Cup champions and now the team's general manager, says being on a winning team is an important part of a young player's development.

"We like to get good veterans to complement our good prospects; we like to get veteran players that can go up and down, and more of the character guys to teach the guys how to be a pro. It is a lot different coming out of college or coming out of junior. It's a major grind, dealing with expectations, whether it's fitness, how to properly take care of yourself, preparation, and our vets complement that," he said. "Some teams are all about development, but I think there's a nice mix of what we can do. I think our guys develop more by winning, and if we make a run in the playoffs, I always feel one playoff game is worth five regular-season games in experience."

Andrew Gordon, who spent a season in Chicago, noticed the difference right away. "Chicago's a different breed. It's such a big city, too. I lived right downtown, and we played 30 minutes outside the city in Rosemont. You're right in the heart of Chicago, and there's such a mix of things and a thousand things going on.

"They truly run it like an NHL franchise, where your general manager's your boss. In Hershey and other teams, you don't see the general manager as much, they're in the office more. But Wendell is in your face. Wendell's not afraid to tell you if you're doing your job well — or if you're doing your job poorly — and what they expect of you.

"It truly is an organization that demands to win. When they don't — and they haven't had a ton of success in the last few years — that doesn't sit well with anybody there. There's a rich, rich history of championships and of great players coming through — some of the greatest all-time American League players in history have come through there — so that's the tradition they've built and they try to uphold.

"Everyone who puts on that jersey is expected to do the same. When you don't — and we didn't make the playoffs my one full season there — it was heartbreaking. Everyone was really upset from the minute we lost; the buzzer rang and everyone's trying to figure out what the hell went wrong. It was a 'we can't do this again, this can't happen again' attitude there. It's an organization that demands success."

Benn Ferriero found Chicago much different than his other stops in Worcester, Wilkes-Barre, Connecticut and Utica. "Chicago's a different type of franchise than a lot of the other teams I've played for in the American League, just in the fact that they want to win, and they want to win now. They don't really care about anything about what's going to happen next year; they want to compete for the AHL championships every year. A lot of the other organizations I've played in have purely concentrated on developing their draft picks and doing the best to make sure they get the ice time, and put them in situations where they can succeed," he said. "Here, it's more of a win-now, win-at-all-cost attitude, and then they deal with what will happen tomorrow, tomorrow. It's a little bit of a different attitude. They really don't care what happens next year, but just what's going on this year."

As Pat Cannone told me, the team's main focus is the Calder Cup. "They keep your mindset that way," he said. "It's one organization where that's their number one priority, so that's really good."

Mathieu Brodeur, who had stops in San Antonio and Portland, agreed. "I was in Portland where it was more about developing players, so it's fun to be around an organization where it's all about winning. It's actually fun. As a player you like it, to have an organization that wants to win."

With that expectation, however, comes extra pressure on the players. Jason Shaver, the television voice of the Wolves (Chicago is the only AHL club that televises all its games) noticed the difference. "The AHL in its current 30-team format, 10 teams are trying to build a championship team — the Hershey Bears jump to mind, the Chicago Wolves jump to mind and there are others in the mix that are trying to win a championship here and there. Another 10 teams are kind of like, 'We'll see where it is. If we get going, we want our prospects to be in a winning environment,' so I think they have their foot in the water and are going to see where it goes. The other 10, most of which are now owned by NHL teams, are in it for pure development.

"If you own that franchise and that's what you want to do, it's your prerogative — but I think a third of the league is trying to win, another third would like to win, and another third is looking purely to develop players. I think in Chicago, the mandate from ownership to general manager to the coaches to the players is: you are here to win. That is the expectation. In my three stops — not that the other two teams

Pat Cannone, who also played in Binghamton, says being in a major market like Chicago is a big plus for an American League player. (ROSS DETTMAN / CHICAGO WOLVES)

weren't trying to win, they certainly were — but I certainly notice the pressure to win in Chicago more than I did anywhere else."

Brendan Bell, who has also played for eight other AHL teams, said the Wolves have become a marquee destination for AHL veterans. "This is obviously one of the premium franchises in the AHL. It's one of the places they've always had some older guys, some veteran guys and high-quality players, and always made some good playoff runs and good regular seasons since they've been in the AHL. It's one of those spots, as a veteran guy, you hope you can end up in at some point."

The combination of being on a team that wants to win and playing near a major city is attractive, according to Cannone. "Chicago is great, top of the line, first class all the way. They treat us very well. It's a lot of fun being there, being in a great city. Compared to other cities, it definitely has its perks. It's been a great time here, and I'm happy to be here."

Ferriero compared Chicago to his previous stop out east — the much smaller city of Utica, New York. "Playing in a big city is a bit different — I played in Utica last year," he said. "It definitely makes a difference, not so much the hockey aspect, but it's the living — a faster pace, big city, stuff like that, to a small little town in the woods. The whole living aspect makes it a different situation."

For Young, the Wolves organization has been a good fit. "I think from day one the Wolves have been a first-class organization. I think that's definitely the way we're regarded with other organizations, even other AHL organizations, with our way we treat the players, and the staff too — including me. It all starts from the top; [owners] Buddy Meyers and Don Levin, they've established something from day one that they wanted everyone treated properly. Even when I was a player, a coach and a general manager, I've had players get a hold of me . . . wanting to come here. It's easy to recruit for me and the Wolves organization."

Even having the Blackhawks in the same market — and playing well — has been a boon for the team. "The Hawks are going great, and so are we. I know at one time we outdrew the Hawks on a lot of nights when we were head-to-head on the weekends, but Chicago is definitely a hockey town when you have two great franchises going," Young said.

Bell, who played in 102 NHL games, noticed the change in Chicago's dynamic with the Blackhawks' success. Even so, he still sees a good deal of community support for the Wolves. "I think it was different 10 or 15 years ago when Mr. Wirtz was running the team and he wasn't putting the games on TV, so the Wolves had a good edge there. But the Hawks have been so good the last few years, winning Stanley Cups and all that. People want to see the best players in the world, and they're up there," he said. "We still get very good fan support for an AHL market, especially when they've got an NHL club. It's kind of nice coming to a full building or a two-thirds-full building every night."

Shaver first arrived in Chicago in 2008, and he too has noticed a shift in the level of interest from local sports fans. And that's helped the Wolves. "Hockey in the city has changed greatly. The Blackhawks were not the Blackhawks we see today, which are now truly the toast of the town. You see everyone wearing Blackhawks stuff now, with huge interest in hockey. The ratings are phenomenal. And I think the Wolves benefit from that because the more casual sports fans that are into hockey, the better it is for the Wolves.

"The Wolves have been here for 21 years now, have become a staple in the community with a great fan base of their own, and I think they've [begun] to capitalize more with the groups and the family four-packs coming to games, because quite frankly, the ticket prices for a Chicago Blackhawks game are very steep. It's $100 to sit in the upper level of the United Center.

"I think from that regard, the Wolves benefit. In a city of eight million people, there's an appetite to see hockey, and some of those people will come and see the Wolves. Coming from Houston and Iowa, two other AHL stops I've been in, the size of the fan base of the Chicago Wolves when I came in was very impressive. When I first got there, I was shocked, to be honest with you."

On this early April weeknight, the Wolves are part of a busy local sports calendar that has the Cubs fresh off the plane from the Cactus League to open their new season against the St. Louis Cardinals at Wrigley Field, while the Blackhawks — en route to their third Cup in six seasons — host their division rivals from Minnesota at United Center, both within 20 miles of tonight's AHL game between the Lake Erie Monsters and Chicago.

Underneath the stands, while Wolves players head back to the locker room after warm-ups in their white-, red-and-yellow home jerseys, Young chats about the sometimes hectic world of professional hockey. "My first year with the Wolves was in the lockout year of 1994–95, as I came down from Tampa, and I kind of knew I was going to be traded back to Pittsburgh once the lockout was over. I was on the ice here at 10:30 in the morning, and I get a call — and I had a feeling it was coming — and . . . I answered and it was Penguins general manager Craig Patrick.

"I said, 'Craig, I'll see you tomorrow.' He said, 'No, no, I need you on a one o'clock flight.' I had to go back up in Pittsburgh that night. I said, 'I'm at the Allstate.' I have no clothes, I'm still in my equipment. So I call up my wife and ask her to pack me some stuff and I get on the plane. Then I walk in with a pair of jeans in the dressing room — not even a suit — and I had to [go] back up that night in Pittsburgh. It happens quickly."

Young, who played 187 games in the NHL, got a chance to win a pair of Stanley Cups with the Penguins in 1991 and 1992. He said it is always special to see players to spend even a single second in the National Hockey League.

"What's really nice is seeing the guys who are borderline players and might not have a career up there and they get into an NHL game; I usually catch them and say, 'You'll always be an NHLer now.' You play one second there — that was my thing, my philosophy. I still remember my first game I wanted to get to warm-ups, I wanted the puck to drop to say I had played in the NHL. It doesn't matter if it was five seconds, 10 seconds or 20 years, I played in the NHL. Every kid grows up [dreaming of] that, but to see kids who were not drafted by an NHL team, and eventually get signed by the NHL and play, it's a nice feeling.

"These guys are basically our kids, and that's what I say. Players are around each other more than their wives or girlfriends, so it's the camaraderie and to see guys get up there. Guys are excited to see guys go up. I come in and say to a player he's going up, the guys are pumped up and a big cheer happens.

"We're all trying to get there one way or another."

From when he first joined the club in 1994, going from the veteran-laden teams of the IHL to the developmental-league roster of the AHL, the Wolves have changed a great deal, Young said. "It got a lot younger, one year I think we had 14 or 15 guys age 30 and over, and I know the wives' room had a lot more kids around. Now there's hardly any kids around. Basically, our players are kids. It was a huge difference that way.

"The veteran rule in the American Hockey League being at five [non-development players per game] — personally, I'd like a couple more, it would be really good — but the emphasis is on development in the American Hockey League."

Young said the AHL isn't alone in becoming younger; NHL teams are also all looking to acquire less expensive talent with less experience.

"It's a different era, and even teams in the NHL now are a lot younger. The game itself, the players are much more prepared at a younger age, they're coming up with a lot more speed and can skate. I see a lot of players that go to Europe for two or three years and come back and they say, 'This league has changed even more.'

"The difference from the IHL and the American League is the veteran presence."

While tonight's crowd isn't a large one by Wolves standards — 3,525 — you'd never know it by the show they put on.

The Wolves take the ice to elaborate pre-game festivities, some that are at the top of the AHL and better than a lot of NHL teams' — and this for a weeknight game in April — with a laser show and fireworks display at one end of the ice and on the side of the scoreboard. The pyrotechnics leave a haze in the rafters as Wayne Messmer — a Wolves part-owner who is known in hockey circles for singing the *Star-Spangled Banner* at the 1991 NHL All-Star Game at old Chicago Stadium during the beginning of the Gulf War — does the honors for the Wolves this night.

Chicago jumps out to a 2–0 lead in the game's first four minutes and 11 seconds, with more fireworks after the first two goals, paired with what sounds like a car horn and police siren celebrating both tallies. The Monsters get one back before the end of the period, but the home crowd is in a good mood, with the Wolves needing points in its playoff chase.

In one of Allstate's boxes during the first intermission, Don Levin talks candidly about the team's desire to win, his own NHL aspirations, and the AHL's increase in team-owned and operated teams. Levin said the original goal was to make a Wolves game a family event. "It's back to what we were doing 20 or 30 years ago with family hockey, making it an affordable, fun experience," he said. "So that's what we want it to be, and that's what it is."

He spoke of his team's desire to win, and how Blues GM Doug Armstrong is a supporter of the push. "The idea is to win, and the idea is to feel like you want to win, and make the players feel like you want to win. Most of them do — St. Louis is pretty good about wanting to win — and they understand that winning is part of it. Some in the organization feel more strongly about that than others. Thankfully, the general manager feels that way."

Levin also discussed how some NHL teams push to use their entry-level players for evaluation. "It's tough. You sit there and look at people and figure out how much time you have to play a guy to find out if he's really going to do anything in the NHL. But if they sign him for three years, they want three years out of him. I just don't understand it."

It's also clear the high standard Levin holds for what constitutes a good season. "Any time you play the last game of the season? You've done a good job. If you win it or lose it, you've done a good job. It's better to win them, but to play the last game of the season is special."

He also mentioned what it's like to experience a role reversal with the Blackhawks and Wolves over the last decade, from when his team was winning Calder Cups and the NHL team was struggling.

"I never pretended that we were the NHL. . . . I think there was a point in time — it's reversed right now — we're not winning and they are. That's the ebb and flow of a team. In the NHL you have to get pretty bad to get good. And our problem is we're getting pretty bad and not getting good."

Levin also mentioned that he preferred his IHL days, primarily with the drop in individual ownership in the AHL. "I liked the International League a lot more. In this league, there's more and more where no one cares if you win. There's more and more NHL-owned teams, and a lot of the teams — I don't want to name names — but they want to pay the least amount of money and just make money. 'I don't want to pay for anything, I don't want to go on the road and I don't want to fly.'

"It's a couple of teams stuck in the mud. [There's] more NHL ownership, and there's more control of the AHL by the NHL, and less independent ownership, and more things being forced down your throats by a group."

Levin isn't one to beat around the bush, and when asked about the difference in owning an IHL team and an AHL owner, Levin didn't mince words. "It's cheaper this way, but it is more difficult, because they tell you [what to do]. It can make me crazy. Some people don't care. If the owner doesn't care if they win, it doesn't make a difference. There are a lot of owners that don't care. But there's a lot of owners that do."

Levin also said he's thrilled when one of his players makes it to the NHL — particularly a goaltender. "I love to see it. I really do. My son's a goalie, so guys like Kari Lehtonen and Eddie Lack, amongst others, are really special. And Ondrej Pavelec. I love Pavelec. They're good guys; hockey's a good sport. Very few of them are big-headed and jerks. Most of them are pretty good guys."

Levin showed interest in joining the NHL ranks in 2012, talking to Washington officials about possibly building an arena to bring a team to suburban Seattle. But he said the high price tag of an NHL expansion team had him wondering about its financial viability. When I asked him if he wanted to try and get an NHL team, he said yes, but not at that price.

"The answer . . . generally is yes. I think there's a [potential Seattle investor Steve] Ballmer influence and this number that they're going to get $500 million for Las Vegas, and I hope they get it. If you want to come out and say you don't want to lose a lot of money, it's almost impossible to do at those numbers, so it's probably not going to happen."

Dave Andrews remembered the challenge it was to get Chicago to adapt after the merger, but said the last decade has been much smoother. "It was difficult to bring Chicago in. It was easy to bring every other team in, including all the teams that were competing with Chicago back then, with Houston or Winnipeg. Chicago was more challenging, and Don's view of what the league should look like is different than what the league does look like, and it took a while.

"I would say there was a fair amount of friction between the Wolves and the league the first few years. They won a couple of championships so they were still doing OK. I would say that over the last 14 years, the last 10 years have been pretty good. I would consider Don a guy [who] if I needed his support on something now, I would get it."

For now, even though his NHL partner does the player signing and limits the number of veterans he can bring in, Levin does his best to run the Wolves as an organization that tries to capture the Calder Cup on an annual basis, and according to Young, it's because of his NHL-like treatment of his players.

"We try to treat the guys right. We have a philosophy that we will give the players everything they need to succeed," Young said. "Anything more than a three-hour bus ride, you're going to fly. Grand Rapids is three hours away, but we go in the night before. The guys are prepared to be on the ice. The thing with whomever our affiliate or parent team is, they know when they hand their prospects over to us they're going to get treated right, they're going to get prepared right, and not be taxed as much as every other team because we'll do it for the players."

For the Wolves on this night, they blew open that 2–1 game, scoring five goals in the third to grab a 7–3 win over Lake Erie, part of a late-season push that got them into the playoffs. And that chance at a Calder Cup run is a premium, according to John Anderson. "A lot of coaches have gone through [the league, and] they talk about development, but to me and to Don Levin, our owner, the thought process is: winning is part of the development. Just going out there and doing well and if the team doesn't do well — this is not an individual sport.

"You have to have the expectations of winning. I know that's a good thing to have going up to the National Hockey League. We're here to win. And your career is really short. You have 10 to 12 years, and you think that's a lot of time when you're 20, but when you're 32, you find it's gone like that, so it's important to win as quickly as possible."

And for Andrews, the Wolves are a competitive team, not only with their AHL counterparts but with their crosstown NHL team. "Don is the Chicago Wolves, and the Chicago Wolves will be what Don wants them to be, and he is a passionate guy about the game. Incredibly passionate. We're really lucky to have him in the league.

"He would say the same about me — I would be difficult for him, he would be difficult for me. I think there's grown a respect over the last decade of how committed he is and how badly he wants to do well there. He's invested and continues to invest in hiring really good people, and with his arena. He's a good guy. They'll continue to be a good team.

"They haven't had very many years where they weren't in the hunt. I'm sure that will continue going forward. When you look at standards of operation in our league, they would be one of those teams you look to, like Hershey in the east. Where would I send somebody to look for really strong management, hockey commitment, innovative game presentation, innovative marketing and good use of their resources? Chicago would be right there. That's a credit to Don."

CHAPTER EIGHT

AUDITIONS FOR ALL

Dan D'Uva settles into his broadcast booth atop the lower seating bowl in Bridgeport — it's almost time for the puck to drop for a Sunday afternoon tilt between the visiting Syracuse Crunch and the hometown Sound Tigers. He's called games for the last two nights and took the bus down from Albany early this morning, but he's ready as ever to describe the action for his radio listeners. The broadcaster is wearing several hats right now; he's also the team's acting public relations person (the former one having gone to the NHL), as well as his own sound engineer and roadie, ferrying the radio equipment from venue to venue, carrying it up the stairs from the team bus before games, making sure his connection with the radio station is working and the internet streaming is up and running. His primary role, however, is to call the action, and D'Uva focuses on the task at hand and opens the broadcast.

"From high above rinkside at Webster Bank Arena in Bridgeport, Connecticut, this is Syracuse Crunch hockey on ESPN Radio. Hello again, everyone, I'm Dan D'Uva, and this afternoon the Crunch go for a three-game weekend sweep."

After throwing his broadcast to a pre-recorded interview and advertisements, there's a pause for the national anthem and then the puck drops and D'Uva's visible part of the workday gets underway.

"As Cody Kunyk gets ready to square off at center with Dustin Jeffrey, drop of the puck, we're underway in Bridgeport, Syracuse from left to right."

Painting the game on a verbal canvas for his listeners, D'Uva's voice rises for a scramble in front of the cage, saying, "It looked like everyone was driving for million-dollar bills in the crease."

While the American Hockey League is a proving ground for players, they're not the only ones looking to move to the National Hockey League. There are only 30 play-by-play broadcasters across the American Hockey League, and most are looking to show an NHL team they could excel if given a chance. Public relations staffers hope to prove their worth as well, working long hours and taking those same long bus rides to try and earn their own promotion to the NHL.

In talking about the great passion people in this industry bring to work every day, D'Uva refers to Mike Emrick, who got his start with the AHL's Maine Mariners in 1978 before becoming NBC's national hockey broadcaster.

"When you watch and listen to Mike Emrick calling a hockey game, you feel there's not another place he'd rather be than at that game and telling you all about it. He brings a joy, a genuine delight in being at a hockey game and telling you what's happening," said D'Uva. "I feel the same way, and I hope that people listening hear that in my broadcast. There's not been a day since I started doing this that I've thought or felt, 'Gee, I wish we didn't have a game tonight. I wish I could stay in bed.' It's never happened. Whenever the light goes on, I still feel the same jolt of excitement. I could not imagine doing anything different with my life."

D'Uva says the key to projecting to the audience is to smile during the broadcast — even if the listener can't see it. "I try to smile even if I'm running on three hours' sleep and there's a press release that still needs to go out and the printer stopped working and the press room is out of food, video didn't work, and whatever else is going on," he said.

"It's a lot of troubleshooting and problem solving but when that light goes on, it's you and the listener, and that's the best place in the world to be."

Broadcasting in the AHL isn't an easy job — it's calling a long, grueling season on the radio, which entails the same travel that the players have — without the same fiscal rewards. Some broadcasters have second careers to fall back on, either broadcasting other events in the off-season or working in another industry. Full-time broadcasting positions usually require long hours doing public relations or other media work on top of their regular duties.

Some of the broadcasters in the AHL are fresh out of lower-level hockey leagues, looking for a chance to move up the ranks and eventually find a spot in the National Hockey League. Others have been calling games at this level for years, and have developed a strong network among their compatriots in the AHL level. With the rapid change among teams, players and coaches, these veterans sometimes become the face of the franchise as the lone constant through the seasons.

Unlike the NHL, AHL broadcasters have to be largely self-reliant. Like D'Uva, many carry their radio equipment — usually the size of a suitcase — to and from each press box, and do their own testing before games to make sure they make it to the airwaves. Sometimes, even for broadcasters who eventually go on to have long and high-profile careers, broadcasting in the American Hockey League can be a trial by fire.

Sportscaster Kenny Albert got his start with the AHL's Baltimore Skipjacks, but it wasn't a smooth first career broadcast on October 6, 1990. In fact, he worried he would be fired out of the gate.

"At that level, aside from doing the play-by-play and oftentimes doing color yourself, and keeping all the stats, I also had to act as my own radio engineer. I wasn't the most technologically advanced — and I'm still not," he recalled. "The Skipjacks had this antiquated radio equipment and someone had to teach me how to hook it up and put it together, and it was a big process before the first couple of games.

He was in the booth with former Skipjacks coach Gene Ubriaco, and the atmosphere in the Hersheypark Arena was tremendous. As Albert said, "It was great. You had the same people around you. The one gentleman on the right would have a clipboard; he would keep score so if you missed some of the assists and penalties, he would have it for you. There was another woman on the left with a cowbell, and the whole place smelled like chocolate. It was a great atmosphere.

"But it was a tight booth for two people, so I set up the equipment and we're doing the game. In the second period, I get a note handed up to me — the press box was right in front of the booth — saying, 'Call your station. You got knocked off the air.'

"So at this point, I think I'm going to get fired. It's my first game, I get knocked off the air. It turns out — we had two phone lines in the radio booth — the first one was for the equipment to be plugged into, and that's how you did the actual broadcast. The second one was an emergency number with a phone plugged in, and they would call you if there were any issues. Well, it turns out, one of us accidentally kicked the phone jack out of the plug onto the floor, and they tried to call us a number of times on that secondary phone, but it's so loud, we have our headphones on, we couldn't tell the phone was ringing."

Of course, Albert didn't get fired and survived getting knocked off the air, and went on to call the Skipjacks for two full seasons before heading to Washington to call Capitals games for Home Team Sports and eventually going back to his home of New York for a successful career calling the Rangers, NFL and MLB games for FOX.

Joe Beninati, now television voice for the Caps, first started with the Mariners in the 1980s. At the time, he had to be a jack of all trades. "You're the radio voice, the TV voice occasionally, but you're also the media relations coordinator or the public relations coordinator. You do the game notes, you do the stats, you're the travel secretary, etc.," he told me.

"I remember my first pro game in Portland, Maine. I'm in the booth a half hour before showtime, so as warm-ups are being done and concluding, I need to run from the perch to the office to do something for the game program [for] the next night. So I'm running, and I'm running from the press box facility at the Cumberland County Civic Center, and down the stairs, and I loop around on the Adirondack Red Wings' side of the building and pass their dressing room on the way to the team, to the

Maine Mariners' executive offices — and this is professional hockey to me now — and as I come around the corner, there are two Red Wings goalies — I believe it was Sam St. Laurent and Mark Laforest — out of their gear smoking cigarettes before the game.

"I wind up running back upstairs after getting final approval on the copy that needed to be adjusted around the photograph, and I made it at 6:59:40 for the seven o'clock show. 'Hey, welcome to Maine Mariners hockey.'"

The grind of an AHL season doesn't just apply to the players. Like the athletes, the broadcasters are on the bus for hours until late night, getting up early in the morning.

"It's a time that you remember fondly," said John Walton. "Anyone who asks me about working in hockey, I tell them, 'You better love it, or you're going to hate it. There's no in between.' Someone told me that when I first started. I look back on that time fondly, but the physical grind, I think, sticks with you long after you're not doing it anymore."

While you have some broadcasters that took the traditional route — coming up from the ECHL, college or juniors — you also have one that literally played himself into the job.

Scott Stuccio got his broadcasting start as weatherman for WYOU in Wilkes-Barre, Pennsylvania. Sitting in the stands in Hersheypark Arena as the Zamboni cleaned the ice, Stuccio told me about his unique road to the AHL. It all started with him playing goal in a men's league. "I was doing television weather for almost 13 years. I was also playing men's league, and the off-ice officials for the Wilkes-Barre/Scranton Penguins were our on-ice officials," he said.

The other players in the league turned out to be rather an illustrious bunch. "I ended up playing pick-up games in Wilkes-Barre's arena with them, and the people who played along were Jeff Barrett, Penguins CEO; Rich Hixon, the former president who's out in Pittsburgh now; and Greg Petorak, who's a really good friend of mine and was the controller there. All those guys played pick-up."

While it was a fun hobby, it also presented him with a great opportunity. "It was a big thrill for me to play at the arena where the Penguins played, and so it happened one weekend during the 2006–07 season,

Tom Grace, the team's first broadcaster . . . ended up getting injured and really sick somehow, and they asked me if I could come in and try calling the game," he said. "People [who] have gotten to the American Hockey League by virtue of calling college, juniors, and busted their butts are going to get mad at this, that I didn't go that route, but I ended up doing two games."

After his brief stint, Stuccio became the permanent voice of the team next season. "Tom came back, all was fine, and he thanked me to no end. And I had the most fun ever. I was around a team that was affiliated with Edmonton and Pittsburgh that year and that had rattled off a record start to their season.

"I had approached Jeff, Greg and Rich — and my family owns a pizza shop back home, so I brought them pizza to thank them for having me — and [a] few times I had filled in as practice goalie after getting to know them. So I got that close relationship with them. They knew my TV background and after a couple of times asking them, they said, 'Bring us more pizzas sometime,' and jokingly I said, 'Give me a job and I will.' And they did — they gave me a job in marketing and community relations and put me on the air with Tom to do color.

"And Labor Day of 2007, Tom put in his notice that he wanted to go back home, work closer to family and his parents. I had just gotten to know all our sponsors in two months of community work, and they said, 'He's leaving, we want you to be the interim guy, what do you think?' I honestly said, 'I will do whatever you want me to do, and will do the best I can.' He had done the first two games with me, and he had really gone to bat for me and put my name in front of Jeff many times and said, 'You need to bring him on as the next guy.' And that's how I got the job."

For D'Uva, the call to the broadcast booth came at an early age. "I grew up five minutes away from the Meadowlands in New Jersey, and when I was 10 years old, the Devils won the Stanley Cup. And nothing better can happen to a 10-year-old kid than his favorite team winning the Stanley Cup. I was hooked.

"Getting to high school, my friend and I started a show on cable access in Ridgewood with one VHS camera and two microphones, and when we finished, we were on in 280,000 homes in northern New Jersey with a Telestrator and a sideline reporter, and it was quite the show. In that period of time, going to the Meadowlands and seeing a Devils-Canucks game and calling a game from the rafters basically to practice for our first hockey broadcast at Ridgewood High School, we wanted to sound like we knew [what] we were doing before we were on TV.

"We had done football, but we wanted to practice. It's 1999, and our second hockey broadcast, Ridgewood is playing West Essex. Robbie Ftorek's son was playing and Robbie was at the game. So we had, as a second intermission guest, head coach of the Devils, Robbie Ftorek. So, being Devils fans, you go to a game, and you stalk Mike ["Doc"] Emrick and [radio voice] Mike Miller and, as a precocious 14-year-old aspiring to sportscasting greatness, you want to bounce things off him. 'Would you listen to my tape?'"

After attending Syracuse and Fordham, D'Uva said he forged a relationship with Emrick that helped him down the road. "I was walking with him to the train, the Metro-North; we talked even more, and we'd spent time at the Meadowlands, and then Prudential Center. He was more and more willing to help. I guess I was asking him questions at a higher level than maybe some other college kids. Whatever it was, I'm thrilled that I did. Bridgeport Sound Tigers broadcaster Phil Giubileo is a Fordham guy, so I had gone up there to help out Phil and called some games there and given those tapes to Doc.

"When I'm done there, the Devils have an opening in the ECHL for the Trenton Devils, and it was not long before the start of the season and [Trenton Executive Director] Jim Leahy said, 'Dan, I'd like you to come in for an interview.' I said, 'Great.'

"And I immediately emailed Mike. He called me seven minutes later and gave me a pep talk that I still relate to students to this day. He said, 'Dan, they're bringing you in for an interview, not because of all the great wonderful things you've done — they already see that and have the tapes. When you go to the interview, you want to show how hard you're going to work for them and what you can bring to the organization.'

"So I had that in mind, and I was so pumped up that Doc would call me in that situation, so I go for the interview and to make a long story short, the interview's going well, and after an hour Jim Leahy asks me, 'Do you have any questions for me?' and I said, 'When can I start?' And that was the right answer apparently, and I probably would not have said that without Doc's pep talk.

"Jim Leahy says, 'Dan, I go to and speak to a sports class at NYU that a friend teaches, and I tell students when they're interviewing for a job and the person doing the interview asks "Do you have any questions for me?" the only answer is "When can I start?"'

"Then I go up to the Prudential Center two days later . . . and Mike Levine, the New Jersey Devils' VP of Communications, comes off the elevator . . . with a smile from ear to ear and he stuck his hand out and [said], 'Why the hell do you want to get into this business?'" D'Uva said with a laugh.

Life on the road can be rough for an AHL broadcaster, and without the backup an NHL team would have with a television play-by-play, analyst and radio voice on a trip, it's usually up to one person to call games.

And for Stuccio, he recalled one trip to Syracuse that proved to be miserable. "I remember getting a chicken parm sub on the road that was ice cold, and I've got to believe that didn't agree with me. I'm feeling worse and worse the entire time. I get on the air, and after plugging into AHL Live, I had to go on the internet; I said to the board operator, 'I do not know how I'm going to make it through this game.'

"We played one period, then two periods, and the second, we scored at least three goals, so we're up 4–1 and I'm going as much as I can. My stomach, I didn't make it through the second intermission. I had to run. I came back, and in Syracuse's press box, you have to go up and come back, too. I did the third period, I'm feeling better a bit, but start to go back downhill again. I packed up my gear, I'm hunched over walking down to the bus, I remember the first thing opening the door and the first thing I thought of is, 'There's fresh air.' I felt so much better.

"Our Booster Club members were on that trip, it was awesome to see them, and I catch my surroundings and see it snowed a foot while we were playing this game. We have a four-hour day trip that's going to take six and you don't want to be the guy getting sick on the bus."

It's certainly not an easy business, and one where being able to multitask is at a premium. Working in the front office of a minor league team often requires a lot of different jobs, and usually those who can handle numerous tasks at once are the ones to survive.

Jason Shaver, who now does television for the Chicago Wolves, remembers that it wasn't his broadcasting skills alone that got him to the AHL level. "I'm fortunate; the reason I was hired in Iowa is that I was pretty good in corporate sales in the ECHL job I had. They were looking for a guy who could sell and also call a game. Houston was my first opportunity that I did have some corporate sales but I had my opportunity as a broadcaster. In Chicago, all I do is call games. We have a great PR staff, we have a great corporate sales department, so I just call games, which is my dream job," he said. "I got into this business because I wanted to call hockey games, so it's unique in that and very fortunate to not have to do the other things that most of the broadcasters in this league have to do."

Ryan Stanzel, who worked in Houston before becoming the Minnesota Wild's manager of digital media, said you learn a lot about all aspects of hockey in the minors. "You literally have to know every part of it. . . . You have to know the hockey side, but also, more importantly, you have to know everything about the business side too," he said. "Knowing how integral all that stuff is, it's far more than about just the hockey. . . . You have to know every aspect. I sat in with the finance guy, the hockey ops, PR, obviously, community relations as well. I worked in minor league baseball briefly in a ticket office, and they said, 'Bring your rain shoes with you, because we don't have a grounds crew on staff.' So it's kind of like that, you have to be ready for whatever comes your way."

Kenny Albert remembered how he even did sales in his Skipjacks days. "Looking back, it wasn't my forte. I think I made three sales the entire summer," he said with a laugh. "We would throw in everything for these folks. We would give them season tickets, ads on the boards, ads in the game program, commercials on the radio, they would get what they wanted for $500."

Maggie Walters, who inadvertently gave Dan D'Uva the extra duties with the Crunch when she jumped to join the NHL, remembers how busy her role was in the AHL. "I was doing public relations, but I was also doing team services, and advertising, and social media, and putting up dasher boards, and arranging training camp and hotel rooms. Now that I'm up [in the NHL], I'm just doing one thing. I can't say enough about [the AHL]. It's a developmental league for the players and coaches, but for someone wanting to learn about the sports industry, there's no better way to do it than working in the minors. You see everything, you learn everything.

"I think just we were lucky in Syracuse to have a great group of staff with great people. I appreciated the closeness, because you're working a lot of hours with these people and everyone knew what they were getting into, knew they wanted to be working the hours and wanted to be at the rink."

Dan Fremuth, Lehigh Valley's relations manager, said the hours are long — but worth it. "I love being at the rink. I'm not a hockey player — I can't even ice skate — but I love the game," he said. "Game days for me are 15- or 17-hour days and wouldn't trade it for anything. . . . For us, in this industry, the best day is a win and a sellout. We get that, and we did our job today."

Giubileo is a bit different than some of his counterparts. He is a freelancer for the Sound Tigers and works a regular nine-to-six job in market research in addition to calling games. While the broadcasting job isn't his primary source of income, it certainly is one he enjoys doing. The league's weekend-heavy schedule helps him avoid most overlaps with his other job, but sometimes he does have to multitask — and do his day job — while on the road.

"What's interesting is I come into an office for a regular 9-to-6 job like everyone else, and but what I'm able to do, I have some flexibility on game days where I can travel. . . . I can drive up to Hartford during a lunch break, or Springfield or Providence during a break, and get there in an hour or an hour and [a] half in most games. And in my job in market research, almost everything that I can do I can do virtually, so I can log back in my laptop and go about my normal business day. I don't have to do much on the telephone, and even if I did, we can work on a cell. Everything I do is on the computer so if email is working, I can do technical systems that I work with. I've done this since day one with the Bridgeport Sound Tigers. I'll just jump on the bus with the team or drive myself, go up the venue, and plug back in and go about the rest of my day from the venue, and at five o'clock I can get into game mode and spend the next couple of hours really hunkering down and focusing on the broadcast."

Giubileo has certainly paid his dues, having worked in the old United Hockey League before his move to Bridgeport. "I love to broadcast, but I've been in minor league front offices, and it's a hard job. That's a much harder part than the rest of it," he said. "Calling games is easy at that point. It's doing all the other stuff that really is the challenge, and you're doing the jobs of three or four people. I did that as a much younger person in life, and it's hard. It's not easy, That's not to say my job in market research is easy — it's not — but it's different kind of work and not as physically grueling at times."

Being a hockey broadcaster requires giving your all — sometimes even your articles of clothing, as John Walton found out one Boxing Day.

"We were playing the day after Christmas in Bridgeport in 2006, and because it was the day after Christmas, we bused up day-of-game. We were tied up in New York City traffic forever, and all of our guys, a good chunk of [whom] ended up playing [in Washington], we went running to the building. I've got my radio gear in hand, we're 20 or 25 minutes from warm-ups, and I'm trying to get connected to the station. . . . Doug [Yingst] came running out the Zamboni tunnel and yelling for me to come to the locker room. It was very, very out of the ordinary — and really out of the ordinary on a day when everyone was so rushed. I couldn't understand why you'd need the broadcaster in the locker room.

"I got to the door of the locker room, and the first two people I see are Eric Fehr and Dave Steckel, and they are laughing hysterically. And I have no idea why, the only clue I got was from Doug as we were walking and I said, 'Doug, what do you need me for?' He said, 'We have a problem. I think you can help, but I don't think you're going to like it.' I still had no clue, but I knew this wasn't going to end well for me.

"I walked into the coaches' office in Bridgeport and [assistant] Bob

Woods is down in the corner — almost in the fetal position — laughing. He's got tears in his eyes. It still hasn't hit me, this bizarre sequence I've been witnessing. And then I looked over at Bruce Boudreau, standing in his boxer shorts, a coat and tie, shirt and mad as all hell. I couldn't figure out what was going on. Doug said, 'He didn't pack his suit pants. He doesn't have his pants.' And I said, 'Why . . . Oh no.' I said, 'Doug, why not you?' He said, 'Waist size, my waist is two inches bigger,' — and he's the general manager, he wasn't giving them up anyways.

"I said, 'You seriously need my pants? What am I going to wear?' The whole problem is they wear their track suits on the bus, so they don't know this until they get there. So all that's left is Bruce Boudreau's track pants, which, I'll say generously, they didn't fit me very well. I went back to the press box holding onto the sides of track pants with my shirt and tie, and the beat writer Mike Fornabaio of the *Connecticut Post* is there and he looked at me and said, 'Did you lose a bet?'

"The funny part is in Bridgeport, there's no direct bench access, so in pants that are way too tight, he had to walk across the ice in my pants, and you haven't seen such tiny steps taken by a human until you saw Bruce try to get across. As he said to the *Hockey News* a week later when they wrote about it, 'I wanted to yell at the referee but I was sucking it in too much to yell at him.'

"The funniest part, it was the only time we've beaten Bridgeport all year. They've beaten us every game and as superstitious as Bruce was, I got to the bus, my pants were sitting on my seat and he said, 'I never want to wear these damn things again.'

"It was the first time I had ever made the *Hockey News*. I never thought it would be for my lack of pants."

Dave Starman, who was analyst on Skipjacks games, remembers one time he almost was called into backup goalie duty. "One game where we're in Binghamton, and somebody got hurt, and we're trying to find Olie Kolzig. Olie was down in Hampton Roads [in the ECHL], and nobody could find him. Barry [Trotz] said to me, 'If we can't find him, we're going to have to dress you as a backup.'

"I said that was fine. It's like two o'clock in the afternoon, and I'm doing the game boards, and I skated in the morning skate, and get my stuff done. Then I said to myself, 'Before I start this, I should really find out what's going on, because if I'm playing tonight, this is irrelevant.'"

While he was prepared to do whatever was needed, Starman was nonetheless relieved when Kolzig was eventually found. Starman stayed out of the crease that night.

Given all the highs and lows that they go through, the staff and players really do develop a strong bond.

"There are lots of guys who earned their stripes in different ways, and I'm not saying you didn't earn it if you didn't go the A, but you have a special kinship with the people who did," said Walton. "There are ties and stories we know, sometimes just a nod and a glance, 'I remember when we did that thing.' . . . There was that game when the glass broke in Bridgeport with [Islanders director of communications] Kimber [Auerbach] and we sat there during a playoff game, and the game was delayed for 40 minutes, and me just killing time.

"There are things if you weren't in the A where you don't share those kinds of memories, and I almost feel sorry for people that didn't. There were some nights that were tough, and there were a lot of times there were a lot of good stories and a lot of good memories."

Todd Crocker, who calls Marlies games, agreed with Walton, saying, "'Champagne Johnny' is dead on." Crocker and Walton started out about the same time — in Hamilton and Cincinnati, respectively. And they quickly got to know each other. "There is a connection point, players, coaches, doesn't matter. If you played in the American Hockey League, there is a connection point," he said. "I'll give you a great example of that. Paul Maurice went immediately from juniors to coach Carolina, and Paul then lost that job and came to coach here. And I asked him how he felt about coming to the American League. He said he felt like it was a missing part on his resume. He said he talked to these guys in the NHL and they'd have this kinship in the American League. He said, 'I never understood it. But now I do.'

"There's a level of respect you battle for, and you did have to go through crappy days, and play a 3-in-3 more than once — in fact, nine or ten times a year. You have to do some things that players who don't experience the AHL never had to do."

Bob Rotruck, who calls games for the Phantoms, shared his sentiments. "This is an incredible honor for me to get to be here and do this at this level with guys at the caliber of play that they are. The announcers, we become tight, we're going through the same thing, the nuttiness with coaches who are nice or not-so-nice, and players who give a great interview or a not-so-great interview, and the stories of the buses and traveling, and the bus breakdowns and the craziness of that, and equipment breakdowns, radio equipment.

"We're the only ones that understand where the other is coming from . . . but some of the guys who I've known more recently in this league, like [Binghamton voice] Grady [Whittenburg] and [Scott] Stucc[io] and Josh Heller in Albany, there's our own little fraternity here, and guys that have made it from the AHL to the NHL."

Eric Lindquist, who had been in the Eastern Conference before heading west, talked about the tight-knit group he was leaving behind, and how they all pull for each other. "This will be my 11th year. 'Hawk' [Bob Crawford] in Hartford, I've known him for over 10 years. I'm excited for Ken Cail calling the Calder Cup winner in Manchester this year, he's great. Mike Kelly was in Springfield for a while. We're all kind of in it together, we're all battling for the same thing. There's a lot of different personalities around the league too. Jeff Vanek is up in Portland, Phil Giubileo in Bridgeport; it's a small group, but we all kind of know what we're going through.

"The dream is making it to the NHL and [we're] excited when anyone gets a chance to do so."

And sometimes being part of that AHL fraternity comes with some pranks.

Giubileo recalls a game where he got an unexpected gift in the radio booth. "I remember playing a game in Hershey when John Walton was there, and we got crushed — it was like 9–1. And when Hershey scored their ninth goal, John had the intern — I'm pretty sure it was John, although he never admitted it — walk into the booth and drop nine Hershey bars in front of me. I thought it was pretty funny — hey, we scored nine goals, here's nine chocolate bars."

But given that the life of a broadcaster isn't easy — long hours and travel are usually the norm — the thing that drives them is the love of the game. As Crocker told me, "There's something beautiful about this league. I know some people look at it as a penalty, like you didn't make the National Hockey League so you have to play in the American Hockey League. But you also come to the realization that this league has a connection point that you don't get at the next level. You get to know the players. You get to know the coaches. We have personal relationships that go beyond, 'What's going on today? Why did you do that in the game?' There is respect between us, you don't get to be that close in the National Hockey League.

"This league, it's a personal league. You respect people's personal space, you respect their lives and you see them more as human beings and not just numbers on a sweater. And I don't know how you can't find that attractive."

According to Crocker, a season's tale is hard to pass up. "I was out of it when I left [Hamilton], I went to a TV show, and you stop being part of a journey. Every season has its own journey, and the things that happen — win or lose — [don't] matter. Every season has its own journey that you go on with the team, and the personalities and the experience and the adventure.

"When I came back to it a couple of years later and Leafs TV called me and basically needed a guy to fill in for a year . . . I said, 'Why not? I'd give it another go.' And I realized how much I missed it. Every day of it was just amazing to get back to, and so much so [that] when the opportunity arose this year, and Jon Abbott went to Vancouver full-time, they said, 'Do you want come back to do the Marlies?' It was about a 30-second conversation.

"Aaron LaFontaine at Leafs TV stopped me at a golf tournament and said, 'Jon's going to go to Vancouver and take the radio job over there, which obviously puts us in the position where we'd like to have you back to do the Toronto Marlies. What do you think about that?'

"I said 'OK.' So that's not even 30 seconds. I was excited. I love this job, I love being around it, I just love the journey."

For some, the journey leads its way to the National Hockey League, as it did for Joe Beninati. "I was motivated and willing to do those

20-hour days, and we would be coming back from those long bus trips and coming back from the Maritimes, and those were long, long trips, and I'd go right into the office and start working again. . . . That was fine.

"The person who gave me my start was Ed Anderson. Ed was the owner, operator and president of the Mariners at that time, and thank goodness he saw something in me that he believed I could be an NHL-caliber announcer.

"He gave me every opportunity, and he worked our tails off. He was stern in that sense and demanding in that sense, but always in a nurturing way, saying, 'I think you can do this. I know you can do this.' And Mike Emrick had worked in the Mariner chain in Portland, and anyone who succeeded Mike as voice of the Mariners was encouraged to 'do it like Mike.' To have that kind of dedication, and I know Dale Arnold [who succeeded Emrick in Maine] reached the NHL level with Boston. I did, but I put in all that energy and all those efforts because . . . I wanted to someday get to the NHL.

"I would never trade any of those American Hockey League experiences. It taught me the business side in a way I never thought I'd be interested in. But it taught me how to interact with media, and how to interact with professional athletes and management. It taught me a lot of things, not just help[ing] me hone my craft as an announcer, be it radio or TV.

"I can never forget those days. It was fabulous."

Kenny Albert said he loved his two years in the AHL. "It was a tremendous experience, and I look back on those two years and really wouldn't trade it for anything."

For Walton, he did reach a point where he didn't know if the Hershey booth would be the pinnacle of his broadcasting career, or if he would get his shot in the NHL. "I think no matter who you are, you never lose that dream. Even for broadcasters. There was a time, especially late in my Hershey years, you've been doing for this 10, 11, 12 years, you start to wonder; and you're in a place that's comfortable, you think maybe this is it."

But Walton's call to the NHL did come, during the summer of 2011 while driving on the Pennsylvania Turnpike. "I was in the car, I was outside of Pittsburgh in Somerset, Pennsylvania . . . when my now-boss called. On that stretch, for 20 miles after I got the call, I was emotional. I actually broke down for a few minutes. It was like all of those hopes and dreams for 15 years realized.

"I was actually passing through Columbus near my parents and could tell them in person instead of on the phone. And I got to tell my son and daughter in person and they didn't know either, so it worked out perfectly.

"I had to keep it quiet for a few days, and I knew that late in summer and it put a lot of stress on my boss in Hershey to find a replacement, but they were wonderful to me. The fans, I still remember a lot of nice things that were said by a lot of people who I knew for a long time, Facebook messages and Tweets and email messages, and it was overwhelming. It was a couple of weeks I'd never forget.

"Before I got out of the business of learning to be an NHLer, it was wonderful. One of the greatest moments of my life, without a doubt."

Giubileo, who enjoys his time he's spent in the Bridgeport booth, says that he'd love the chance to take on a full-time broadcast job in the NHL. "It's a blast. I really love doing it; if I didn't love it, I wouldn't do it. I do it on a freelance basis and it doesn't bring me a lot financially. It's more of a labor of love, and just like anyone else I'm chasing the dream and would love nothing more than to work in the National Hockey League on a full-time basis.

"I've been blessed to work some NHL games with the Islanders, whether it's been color commentary with Chris King at the time — I've done some play-by-play during the preseason and filled in during the regular season [in 2014] — and of all the games, I got to do a game where John Tavares had five points and a hat trick as they blew out Dallas 7–3. And they came back from 2–0 in that game to do it."

He also pointed out that that was part of a very memorable week, not only for calling his first NHL game. "That was my first regular-season game play-by-play, and it was the same night Kyle Okposo wasn't there because his wife had their first baby, and three days later my wife and I would have our first child. My wife was six days overdue on the day I got asked to fill in and I was totally assuming during the game I would have to drive back to Connecticut. It was a crazy week for me.

"I've been to Pittsburgh several times, gone down to Carolina to do some work with the Islanders, so I've been blessed to be able to do that as well, and I do some regular voice-over work for the NHL on an arena highlights project that they do over the course of the season, so it has opened some opportunities for me. But I'm like everyone else in the league. I want to work full-time in broadcast and call games. I don't even keep count, but I've called a lot of minor league hockey games, but it's still great to be able to show up at the arena a few hours before the game and just kind of hang out with the coaches and chit-chat with the players and the rest of the media.

"For lack of a better word, that's my social life. I work, I spend time with my wife and my daughter and I broadcast hockey.

"But I really love doing it, and a lot of the broadcasters around the league I've been around for a really long time, and I value them as friends and colleagues, and it's one of those things in this league and in the minor leagues; and you do have to get some closer relationships than up in the NHL where it's a different world.

"You want to get to that level, you want to get to the best hockey league in the world, but some of the relationships you create, watching these kids come up and develop and learning — and they're not NHL guys yet. There's something different about hockey players; they're so down to Earth, which is why I like calling the sport, more so than others. And there's something that changes when you get to the NHL, as you're only human.

"You get those big contracts and you become a different type of player and person, and a little bit more guarded at that level than when you're a young kid riding the bus and starting to learn. You can have a little bit more fun. And it's really great watching that type of development, which is why I like the league so much. And you get better relationships with the coaches and the staff because you see them more often and it's different than the regimented, structured world of the NHL — and it really is regimented and structured. It has to be. I really do enjoy working in this league."

D'Uva, who looks forward to telling his listeners the stories of the Syracuse Crunch at least 76 games a season, says he still enjoys it. "I care very much about the quality of my broadcasts and that's not because I think I'm the broadcaster, it's because I think the fans deserve it. My job is to tell the story of each game, of each player, and of a season, and of a franchise, and of a league, and reveal the characters that make it happen.

"If it's the linesman, the star center, the guy selling peanuts, the fans care about these teams because they care about the players. There's a certain connection that's born when you see yourself identify with the athletes and trials and tribulations, successes and failures. You feel a bond with someone and you want them to do well. The more I can create that bond, the better I'm doing my job. . . . It's a human interest and you try to provide that entertainment.

"I'm not a car salesman, I'm a journalist. There's a bit of showman in it, but I'm a journalist. That's why I say telling a story is an essential part of the job, accurately, objectively and in a way that keeps people listening. I simply take the principles that I have, and what I've been taught and I've always applied to every area of my work. If I'm doing that, I'll be satisfied. Because if I'm listing everything I'm supposed to be doing, I'll cry myself to sleep. But I enjoy it thoroughly.

"Steve Yzerman was here and asked me a similar question of 'how are you getting by, and with more and more responsibilities' and I said, 'Steve, this is hockey. I love this.'"

CHAPTER NINE

THE TORONTO MARLIES

Driving up the Queen Elizabeth Way, once you pass the blue wel-come sign marking Toronto's city limits, you merge onto the Gardiner Expressway, the main artery into the heart of downtown. As you follow the shore of Lake Ontario eastward, the urban skyline of Ontario's capital city, with its iconic CN Tower, dominates the horizon. You pass the many condominiums that have popped up in recent years and see Exhibition Place, the site of the annual Canadian National Exhibition. On prime acreage along Lake Shore Boulevard, the fair-grounds is home to the city's deep sporting roots.

The Hockey Hall of Fame's first permanent home was built on these grounds in 1961, and housed the Stanley Cup, Calder Cup and other hockey artifacts. While the space was one of the more popular spots during the CNE's run in August, the attendance numbers were low the rest of the year. The space was also becoming antiquated — especially compared to other major sports Halls of Fame that had developed into compelling tourist destination spots for fans. In an effort to remedy that, a new Hockey Hall of Fame was built in an old bank building on the corner of Yonge and Front Streets in the city's downtown at the cost of C$27 million. The Hall left the CNE for good in 1993.

Not far away from the original Hall was Exhibition Stadium. It was built in 1948, and, starting in 1959, it was home of the Canadian Football League's Toronto Argonauts, and the first home of Major League Baseball's expansion team the Toronto Blue Jays in 1977.

The "Ex," however, proved to be a bit problematic for the Blue Jays. It didn't offer a lot of shade and, perhaps even more pressingly, some of the seats were more than 800 feet from home plate. Its close proximity to Lake Ontario wasn't ideal in either the spring or the fall. Tellingly, the first game in Blue Jays history was played in snow; in fact, the Jays had to borrow the Maple Leafs' Zamboni to help clear the field. High winds and pesky seagulls were common. After football fans were left drenched by the elements after the Grey Cup game in 1982, it was decided a dome would be needed for the city's outdoor pro teams. A C$570-million retractable-roof stadium was built right next to the CN Tower. When the SkyDome, as it was then called, opened in 1989, the Argos and Jays moved downtown.

Eventually, both the original Hall of Fame building and Exhibition Stadium were demolished to make room for BMO Field, home of Major League Soccer's Toronto FC. You can still see part of the original Hall of Fame façade with its white, angled roof — it now serves as Gate 4 for the stadium right across from the Queen Elizabeth Exhibit Hall.

There's another key sports venue on the Exhibition grounds, however. Once you pass the blue highway exit sign for Rogers Centre — the current name for the SkyDome — you can see the Ricoh Coliseum on your right. The low, brown brick building with its characteristic green-topped turrets was built back in 1921 for the CNE's agricultural shows. At the turn of the 21st century, there was a concerted effort to bring a hockey team to complement the NHL's Maple Leafs and to give the city a more affordable — and accessible — option for professional hockey.

While Toronto had the Leafs playing in the new Air Canada Centre (which opened in 1999 on the site of an old Canada Post building), as well as several Ontario Hockey League teams in the area, the city hadn't had an alternative professional hockey team since the World Hockey Association's Toronto Toros in the 1970s.

At one point, the International Hockey League was considered an viable option, as there were plans to move the Phoenix Roadrunners franchise, but that fell through when the team wasn't one of the six teams the AHL absorbed when the IHL folded in 2001. Plans to purchase the AHL's Louisville Panthers and move them to Toronto also fell through — the Hamilton Bulldogs wouldn't allow a new franchise within its 50-mile territorial radius. But the Bulldogs themselves agreed to move to Toronto for the 2003–04 season, and after a C$38-million renovation and expansion of Ricoh, the relocated team took the name of the IHL franchise they originally wanted to bring to Toronto — the Roadrunners. However, the Roadrunners' stint in Toronto was short-lived; the team relocated to Edmonton for the 2004–05 season, filling the void the parent Oilers left as the NHL season was wiped out by a lockout.

Once the NHL returned in 2005–06, the Maple Leafs moved their AHL team from St. John's to Ricoh Coliseum, and put their top affiliate just over two miles away from Air Canada Centre. It was seen as a fairly novel move, but indicative of how NHL teams and their AHL affiliates increasingly collaborate with each other.

In today's American Hockey League, more than half of the clubs are owned and operated by their NHL parent clubs, which creates a different focus and organizational philosophy. Individual owners, who generally want to see a good return on their investment, prioritize winning and getting into the playoffs. Teams that are owned and operated by the NHL tend to be run differently. These teams are usually seen as part of a larger financial picture, where winning and filling stadiums is often less important than developing players for the big leagues. These AHL clubs are seen as part of the support structure for the parent team. By putting the farm team in the same market as the parent club, it gives players and management of both teams some added flexibility.

If an NHL player gets injured and their AHL affiliate is across the country, it can pose a logistical problem. They have to get the AHL replacement on a flight to wherever the NHL team is playing, which sometimes can be an all-day process. The recent trend in the league is to have the AHL affiliate close to the parent club so that, barring a team being on a road trip (though teams sometimes pre-emptively call up players in case of an injury on a lengthy, distant journey), a player can arrive at the team facility in just a few hours and, in some cases, be able to suit up when a player is deemed unfit at the team's morning skate.

When the Leafs' farm team was based in St. John's, Newfoundland from 1991 to 2005, if a player was called up, he would need to pack up and fly to wherever in North America the Leafs were playing. And getting out of Atlantic Canada is often a dicey proposition in the winter months. The relocation of the Marlies franchise put the NHL and AHL teams just miles apart, meaning a call-up is now just a short drive to the Air Canada Centre. It also allows the Leafs to have players on hand just in case someone isn't available for a particular contest.

The two teams even share the same practice facility, the MasterCard Centre, in the west end of the city. That means a call-up can literally walk down the hallway — if both teams are at home — and fill in immediately for a practice. It also means there's much more interaction between the players on the two clubs. (Typically, once training camp breaks in September, players on the NHL and AHL clubs rarely see each other outside of call-ups and other unusual circumstances.)

The arrangement also works nicely for the players. One of the logistical headaches for a player on the bubble of an NHL roster is arranging for housing for the season, as he usually has to wait until the season's opening night to determine whether he needs an apartment in his NHL or in his AHL city. But a player who signs a two-way deal with the Maple Leafs can go ahead and get an apartment in the Greater Toronto Area, knowing either way, his workplace will be close by. As veteran forward Keith Aucoin told the *Patriot-News*' Tim Leone when he signed with the Marlies in 2012 as a free agent, "If I don't make it, then I don't have to move anywhere. It makes it a little easier."

The close proximity also means that the team personnel is present at AHL practices and games. And in terms of potential call-ups, being in sight is being in mind. As Brendan Mikkelson, who spent 2014–15 with the Marlies, told me, "For the guys going up and down, it's very convenient, and for the management it's extremely convenient as far as the last-second moves other teams can't do, so I'm sure there's huge advantages with that."

Toronto's model was adopted by two Western Conference teams in 2015, when the San Jose Sharks and Winnipeg Jets moved their AHL affiliates to their NHL rinks, mostly for convenience of having their AHL club essentially in-house.

For Brad Lynn, director of hockey operations for the Marlies, it's an advantage for the Leafs' organization to have their affiliate that close. "That's a huge advantage. It's massive, not only for the financials and stuff, but you can send a guy down on paper and he stays in the same city. Of course in training camp, guys don't know which team they'll be on but they know if they're a bubble player, they get an apartment in Toronto. . . . Veteran guys with kids in schools, and it's a huge advantage. And it cuts down half the logistical nightmares when the guys are down the street, or at MasterCard Centre; they walk down the hall from one room to the next. That's cut down the headaches."

Brendan Bell, who was part of the inaugural Marlies team back in 2005–06, recalled the ease of getting called up — particularly compared to what it would have been like the year before when the Leafs' farm team was based in St. John's. "Toward the end of my third year as a pro, I was getting called up and down, and I would go to the rink at the Ricoh Coliseum in the morning, and get a call to go to the ACC. I'd take my bags and make the three-minute drive for the morning skate. Then I'd get a tap that I wasn't going to play tonight, so I'd go back over to Ricoh and drop my stuff back off," he said. "It was a unique situation."

After getting off the highway and driving around Exhibition Place, you pull up to the parking lot outside Ricoh Coliseum, with a large Canadian flag in front of the building and the CN Tower looming behind it. Walking toward the ticket office and the Heritage Court entrance of the building you see a red sign with the Marlies and Ricoh Coliseum logos, and in front of it is parked a blue Ford Explorer with the team's logo and "TORONTO MARLIES HOCKEY CLUB" along the side, with a white-tinted back window with the Marlies and Maple Leafs logos that proclaims "EVERY GAME IS A TRYOUT."

Through the doors, you see a large hallway, with the Marlies' season schedule and logo hung on the walls. Once you enter the seating bowl, you can see how the heritage building was redone over a decade ago. Essentially, a modern one-deck arena was installed on top of the older infrastructure to create a nice, retro feel. Grey and blue seats make up the now-7,830 capacity venue, with a large sign at one end proclaiming it "Home of the Toronto Marlies" and a blue flag with a Maple Leafs logo and "AHL Affiliate" next to the United States flag at the other end.

Chicago Wolves announcer Jason Shaver, in town to call the upcoming Wolves-Marlies game, says he loves the redone barn. "I love that it's an older building with the now modern amenities," he said. "I think they've done a great job here and [have] the right capacity for this marketplace."

In the hockey-mad city of Toronto, the winter months revolve around the Air Canada Centre. The familiar skyline featuring the CN Tower is a staple camera shot on *Hockey Night in Canada* — the Maple Leafs regularly appear on the popular Saturday-night program broadcast across the nation. Yet within the Air Canada Centre — the center of the hockey universe for many Canadians — there is still a connection to the team's AHL affiliate. Across from the entrance gates to the arena, there is a Molson Canadian countdown clock ticking down to the Marlies' next game. And on one of the glass doors underneath the clock, a Marlies advertisement shows a group of players celebrating.

According to Jason Chaimovitch, the AHL's VP of communications, the Marlies' owner, Maple Leaf Sports and Entertainment, does a good job at putting the AHL club on an even playing field with the NHL, NBA and MLS teams they also own. "MLSE does a good job with corporate branding," he said. "All their signage, wherever you go, it's the Leafs and the Marlies and the Raptors and Toronto FC. They treat everyone equally."

The next morning, just a few miles west, the Marlies look to earn a chance to skate onto the bright stage of the frozen surface at Toronto's downtown arena. Players are able to take a huge jump in the organization.

"I love there's not just the two measures of success, of winning and losing, but it's also the development league," said Lynn, the Marlies' director of hockey operations. "It's just as exciting as winning the big game, as seeing one of our guys grinding it out and getting better at his game, to see him get called up, and on Hockey Night in Canada the next night, there he is. To see him have success, that's just as exciting as winning games. That's what I really like about the league."

While the team isn't necessarily at the top of the league in ticket sales — during the 2014–2015 season, Toronto was in the middle of the pack with an attendance average of 5,347 — the fan interest is still high in the future Maple Leafs, particularly given the rebuilding the team is undergoing.

As Marlies broadcaster Todd Crocker told me, "People in Toronto, the fans are like general managers; they all want to have a voice and a say and an opinion on how the team is growing. If you ask a hundred fans of most other NHL clubs, 'Who's on your AHL team?' . . . they may not have a lot of answers. But there are more than a few people, and I'd say a majority, who know [2014 eighth overall pick] William Nylander, [2012 pick] Connor Brown, Matt Frattin — they know names here. They know these guys.

"The fans are so involved that they keep you sharp, they're thirsty for that information, and you have to keep giving it to them, and by keeping [giving] it to them, you keep the wheels greased," he said.

Crocker also noted the large attention paid to the team by independent media and fans. "Because there are so many different demands, media-wise, for the hockey team, and especially in a hockey-mad market like Toronto, where I could liken the fan coverage like Leafs Nation and Pension Plan Puppets and things like that, those guys probably cover the team as much as I covered the Bulldogs before — and they're fans.

"They're fans, they're not paid big dollars to cover the team — they're doing it because they love it. And they're doing as much work as when I started. Now, of course, you've got to fill a very hungry fan base in Toronto that is Maple Leaf-oriented. And that includes the Marlies."

Under new head coach Mike Babcock, the Maple Leafs are in the midst of a rebuilding phase. And as part of that effort to give the Leafs' development a quick start, the Marlies have been undergoing an experiment of their own. Babcock had the Marlies implement the same system as the parent club, a puck-possession style that emphasized quickness over grit, and one that would allow players to play seamlessly between the two clubs.

The Marlies began the 2015–16 AHL season as the third-youngest team in the league, undersized and with an average age of just 23. They kept a key player of their rebuilding process, Nylander, in the smaller rink down the road from the ACC. While the Maple Leafs stumbled out the gate, the move paid dividends for the Marlies, as the team's prospects finished with the best winning percentage in the AHL, and reached the Eastern Conference Final, with Nylander, defenseman T.J. Brennan and goaltender Garret Sparks playing big roles.

This rebuilding phase brings its own pressures, especially given how hockey-mad Toronto is. This isn't an easy place to play — especially for young players — as the spotlight and hopes of a team that hasn't won the Stanley Cup since 1967 weigh on its AHL players, too.

Derek King, a former Leaf from 1997 to 1999 and an assistant coach for the Marlies from 2009 to 2015, knows how the demands on AHLers in Toronto vary from other cities. When I asked him if, for a player, being in Toronto was like being in a bit of a fishbowl, he agreed. "That's a good way to put it. Kind of a fishbowl. They know the players and a lot of them have played up with the Leafs, too, so people know who you are; even if you've played one game with the Leafs or 30 or 40 games with the Marlies, they know who you are."

One aspect that's a positive for the players is the number of local products that end up playing for the Marlies, making it a special place to play. Connor Brown spoke about what it meant to him to play in his hometown. "Obviously, growing up in Toronto, it's a good hockey city, a hockey mecca. There's a lot of interest in the Marlies and the young guys in the system for the Leafs, so it's a lot of fun."

Jerry D'Amigo, who spent from 2010 to 2014 with the Marlies — and 22 games with the Maple Leafs —remembered his time in Toronto fondly. "It's great. The good thing about it is you know where your dream is. You know where you want to be, and that's a cab ride over to the rink," he said. "I had a great time there. It was a great hockey market, and there's 7,000 fans there during the playoffs and some of the games there.

"It's a good fan base; they care about their hockey there, which is good. And it's hockey crazed. It's a lot of fun there. It's a good town."

For Mikkelson, being in a major city is a plus. "Toronto, honestly, we play in the best city in the league. We get spoiled that way," he said. "It's one of the biggest cities in North America, there's lots of things to do."

The ownership umbrella also helps the Marlies players enjoy some perks that other AHL teams may not enjoy. According to Marshall, the Marlies players are treated very well. "Being in a big market, and owned by MLSE, budget-wise, for us players and staff, it's a lot easier compared to lower-market teams. Sometimes [on other teams] it can almost create conflicts between the players and the trainers — sometimes you need a new piece of equipment, but they're running on a budget, they don't want to bust the budget.

"But here, it's great, we have everything we need as players. I know there are a lot of other good teams out there, but Toronto, minor league–wise, it's way up there. The way they treat us . . . we get food — a lot — before games for pre-game meals and everything. It's pretty nice here."

Mikkelson agreed, telling me, "Toronto and the Leafs, I don't think there's ever any expense spared, and from that standpoint, as a player, everything you need is right at your fingertips. For the young guys, it's a great development tool and for someone like myself, it just makes coming to the rink enjoyable and you just strive to get better."

Crocker said with the Maple Leafs' prospects being sizeable investments, and their importance to the team's future, the organization takes good care of them. "A lot of people say, 'They should languish in the minors and have to battle their way out. You have to hate where you're at in order to get to where you want to be.' I put this to people who think that way: if I said to you, 'If you go out and buy a car, would you treat that car horribly so that it didn't last or maximize its potential?' No. You would wash it and wax it and take care of it and put the right gas in and everything you can do to make sure that car would last you and run great for you.

"You don't take an investment — and especially the amount of money they're investing in players now — and do that. That doesn't happen. That's one thing I will say about Toronto, they have been great as far as what I've seen. They have skills coaches, player development people, nutritionists, even yoga people.

"They don't miss a trick in trying to develop these guys into NHL-caliber players. I think that's one of the things [about] this organization [that] impresses me most. Lots of people make jokes about the Leafs and how they don't do very well — but from inside the organization, I don't see it. They have put these guys in a position of not being able to offer an excuse. And I love that style of thought process."

For King, while some AHL teams look to win, the Marlies' focus is on developing prospects. "You run into those teams, and that's what they want to do. I find, being here in Toronto, they've really built a structure where they develop these kids, and give them whatever time they need. And I think that's great," he said.

"Looking back at my career, I wish maybe I spent a bit more time in the minors. It might have helped me instead of having that slow start. . . . I'm not complaining," he said with a laugh.

On an April evening, the Maple Leafs are playing out the schedule of a forgettable season, while the Marlies host Chicago at home. The big club, following a win at the Air Canada Centre over Tampa Bay, are down in Buffalo facing the Sabres at First Niagara Center. The team got there the night before, as the NHL's CBA rules require them to arrive in the city the night before the game, even though the two arenas are less than 100 miles apart — or less than a two-hour bus ride.

According to King, a parent club that struggles — particularly when it's the Leafs that dominate the local sports scene, win or lose — can sometimes create angst among some Marlies players. "It's tough. We're in the same town as the big team, and when they're struggling, you as a player may think, 'I might get a shot here,' and when they don't, sometimes you see . . . they get a little upset or a little down. At our level, the staff we have with [former coach] Gord [Dineen] and [former assistant] Benny [Simon], we tried to keep everyone on an even keel and talk to them for how it was for us when we were playing.

We were up and down, or sent down and called up. It's not easy, and you find that happy medium."

According to AHL president Dave Andrews, the Marlies struggled business-wise when they arrived in Toronto. "We had a challenging start with the Marlies early on. The building is phenomenal. It's a great facility. I think early on there was a belief in MLSE that the Leafs brand and a building like that couldn't fail. And they were wrong," Andrews said. "Selling in the American League requires a different strategy than NHL teams."

But then a former GM and a future NHL coach helped make the team more relevant in the crowded hockey marketplace. "When the Marlies really turned around is when Brian Burke came in and Dallas Eakins came in as the coach and created a culture in Toronto where Brian really put a lot of focus on the Marlies. . . . [I]n arena and on television at the ACC, it was about kids developing with the Marlies," Andrews continued. "Brian started putting a big marketing push on growing the Marlies and putting the attention there, and Dallas, I think, did a fantastic job coaching there and got the team playing well and got his profile to grow in Toronto. The league benefited from the attention Brian and Dallas created for the Marlies."

The Marlies' 2012 run to the Calder Cup Finals has been the Marlies' highlight since arriving in town a decade ago, the first time a Toronto pro hockey team reached a championship round since the Maple Leafs' last Stanley Cup in 1967 — and the first time a Toronto pro hockey team ever played a game in June.

Despite the sweep by Norfolk, the run gave the team a wave of enthusiasm, boosting the team's profile.

"They had the good playoff run, and the Leafs didn't, and you had full buildings there. National media attention way beyond we had before, plus Leafs TV, they began to work with us, and Sportsnet started to produce more game[s] and we got more national TV games in Canada," said Andrews.

Andrews added that his duty of handing out the Calder Cup in Toronto — or any other Canadian city — is special to him. "We're in the center of the hockey universe where we're in the first couple of stories. . . . When the Cup goes out in those places, it's special. It's an honor to be part of it, when you grow up in Canada and play the game and read the *Hockey News*, and the American League is the American League up there."

And for Jason Chaimovitch, the AHL's VP of communications, the media attention for a Canadian final series always is good. "It's rewarding when Toronto or Hamilton or St. John's is in because, for me, it's more rewarding to see the media's response and full press box and highlights leading off [TSN] *SportsCentre*. It's different up there."

Before the game against Chicago, the Marlies gather behind the glass doors of the locker room that is just off the Ricoh Coliseum hallway. The only thing separating the team from the fans in the concourse is a thin black rope and a security guard checking media credentials, but players coming in and out of the locker room and the team's backdrop where the post-game interviews are filmed are all in full view of the fans in the hallway. To reach the ice, the Marlies walk through the fans in the hallway, underneath an archway into the seating bowl, then walk several steps down through the crowd in the middle of the rink before stepping onto the surface.

With a turbulent season at the top level, the Marlies used more than 50 players in 2014–15, some on Professional Tryouts. Nylander, the Leafs' prized prospect and perhaps the biggest name in the Toronto lineup, is still with the Marlies despite the Leafs' struggles. The Leafs are resisting the temptation to have him give the team a kick — perhaps at the expense of the Swede's development.

On this night, in front of a crowd of 2,892, the Marlies strike first, just four minutes and forty seconds into the contest, but the visitors answer 44 seconds later. Chicago scored again with two minutes and thirty-two seconds left in the period on a power play, and that was all they needed to grab an important two points in the playoff chase.

For the Marlies, it was another learning experience, one the management hopes will help build the team's players. There is a lot of optimism about this team.

And as for Andrews, who was leery of possibly failing in Toronto when the team left what he felt was a good situation in St. John's, he

Kevin Marshall noted during his stint in Toronto that the Marlies, as part of the Maple Leaf Sports & Entertainment group, usually have access to equipment some other clubs may not offer. (GRAIG ABEL VIA TORONTO MARLIES)

is happy to see the Marlies succeed in the spotlight. "If I think back to when we first had the Marlies, I was of two minds. 'If this doesn't work, we're going to fail in the center of the hockey universe.' This is not good. If you ask me if I would have rather been in Toronto or not, I probably would have said I'd rather not be in Toronto and not take the chance of failing there," he said. "But if you ask me now, it's worked out. It's helped to build our brand in Canada. . . . I think the future is bright there."

CHAPTER TEN

FIGHTING'S FADING ROLE

In Allentown's brand-new PPL Center, Hershey and Lehigh Valley square off in a battle between rivals separated by just 76 miles of roadway. While the Phantoms took the early lead in the contest, the Bears rattled off three goals in a three-minute-nineteen-second span to hold a 3–1 lead as the clock winds down inside the first period's last minute of play. The home team is trying to get some momentum back on their side.

Phantoms forward Jason Akeson puts a shot on Bears goaltender Philipp Grubauer. Then Bears defenseman Steve Oleksy collides with Lehigh Valley's Brandon Manning. The two lose their balance momentarily before chasing the puck into the corner. Manning delivers a big hit on Oleksy, sending the blueliner into the boards, causing him to stumble again. Once Oleksy gets back on his skates, he takes a swipe at Manning. The pair drops their gloves, getting a cheer from the sizeable midweek crowd of 7,433.

Phantoms broadcaster Bob Rotruck's voice rises while relaying the tilt to his audience via the radio, local cable television and internet broadcast. "Oleksy has had a couple of big penalty-minute seasons

before and Manning throws a right and Oleksy's helmet comes off! . . .
Oleksy's jersey is tangled up high on him, and now Manning is pinned
against the glass and the linesmen will come in and separate those two
players. Steven Oleksy has been somewhat of a rough-and-tumble cus-
tomer before, a 28-year-old defenseman who has played a fair amount
with the Washington Capitals as well."

Welcome to the rough-and-tumble AHL. With a final tally of three
fights, this Bears-Phantoms game is above the AHL average. Both teams
would go on to finish the 2014–15 season in the league's top five of fighting
majors, according to HockeyFights.com, a site that tracks that data.

Following the game, Oleksy looked worse for wear, a big a shiner
under the brim of the Michigan native's black knit "DETROIT BAD
BOYS" hat. He hasn't always been a fighter. Oleksy skated with Lake
Superior State University, where, as part of the NCAA, fighting in
games is an automatic misconduct. Oleksy only added fighting to his
game once he turned pro; he wanted something that would help dif-
ferentiate himself from other players.

After three seasons in Las Vegas, Toledo and Idaho of the ECHL,
Oleksy got his first taste of the AHL with the Lake Erie Monsters in
2010–11, recording 39 minutes of penalties in 17 games. The following
season, he worked his way onto Bridgeport's roster with 98 minutes in
50 games. He then earned his way onto Hershey's roster in 2012–13,
where he racked up 151 PIMs (penalty infraction minutes) in just 55
games — 11 of them via fights, according to HockeyFights.com.

While Oleksy's toughness had put him on track to move up the
pro hockey ranks, at the same time, he knew that he couldn't rely on
that alone. When he was called up to Washington for his NHL debut
on March 5, 2013, there was some expectation based on his stat line
that he would simply be a tough guy to face the rugged Bruins. But
he recorded an assist in his first game and recorded a goal and three
assists before his first NHL fight, five games in. Oleksy became a regular on Washington's blue line for the remainder of the 2012–13 season,
notching nine points and 33 penalty minutes in 28 games, as well as
appearing in seven postseason games, picking up an assist and just two
minor penalties in those contests.

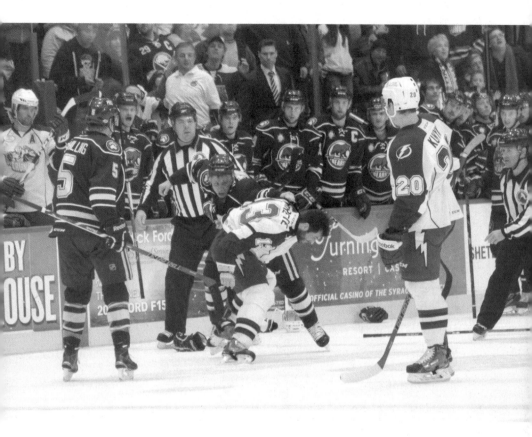

Steve Oleksy, a defenseman who came out of NCAA's Lake Superior State, decided to add the element of fighting to his game to help give himself a better shot at a professional career. (SYRACUSE CRUNCH)

Oleksy played in 34 games for the Caps the next two seasons, recording two goals, eight assists and 53 PIMs, proving to be more than a one-dimensional defenseman, and to be one that could offer finesse as well as toughness. As a result, in 2015 he signed a one-year deal with the Pittsburgh Penguins, who offered him $250,000 to play for Wilkes-Barre with a chance to earn $575,000 at the NHL level. Olesky, as one of Pittsburgh's "Black Aces," also got a chance to skate with the Stanley Cup when the Pens closed out San Jose to end the 2015–16 season.

The game is changing and Oleksy was able to adapt along with it. This style is even starting to trickle down to the AHL as well. "It's definitely changed over the course of my pro career, that even at this level the fighting isn't what it used to be. The guys that do fight, and even the guys who are considered heavyweights, have to be good hockey players. That's the way it has to be. . . . You can't strictly be an enforcer anymore. Those guys are kind of extinct in this hockey league, and the fighters have developed and worked on their game, including myself," he told me. "I was [a] guy who tried to add fighting to my game to set myself apart. The in-between guy isn't going to make it on skill alone, and the other isn't going to make it on strictly fighting. You have to be able to put the two elements together in this business."

Rugged players in the Milan Lucic mold have come into vogue around the NHL, players who can not only throw a punch but also are able to play the game with skill. An enforcer who could only really play to help protect his teammates — and not much else — isn't much called for anymore, even at the AHL level.

NHL roster spots are just too valuable to used up by a one-dimensional enforcer, and using a sixth defenseman or 12th forward spot for someone who hardly plays puts a strain on a team's ice time — particularly if there is an injury or penalty that makes another unavailable. You don't want any weakness your opponents might be able to exploit.

Reflecting the needs of the NHL, the AHL has also begun phasing out the role. When the contracts of enforcers expire, they aren't renewed. Those players are then forced to look for AHL-only deals or find work in the lower minor leagues or Europe.

As Chadd Cassidy, former AHL coach for the Rochester Americans, told me, teams can't afford to carry an enforcer on their rosters anymore. "I don't think that we're deemphasizing fighting per se, but we're [emphasizing] that if you're going to fight, you still have to be able to play. And there's a big difference. For a long time, there were guys that that's all they could do, is go out and fight, and didn't have a lot to add to the game itself. If you look around our league now, and the National League, those players are gone. You have to be able to play," he said. "Those roster spots are too valuable. Your fourth-line right wing has to be able to play in his own zone and quality minutes. Your sixth defenseman can't be a goon. He's got to go out and move pucks and he's got to be able to defend, can help you on the penalty kill, so I just think there's more of an emphasis on being able to play."

That's not to say there's no fighting. There are still spontaneous bouts in games as certain teams do try to keep an element of toughness in their games, but the days of staged fighting between two players seem to be just a memory at the NHL — and soon to be AHL — level. Players who drop the gloves have to keep their roster spot by virtue of their play, not their fighting prowess.

"I never was a fan of the staged fights or two guys lining up and you just know from the bench it's going to happen. I like where the game has gone; you can have toughness, you can fight, but you want to make sure the guys can play the game as well," said Bears coach Troy Mann. "I look at our lineup and we've got a number of guys who can do it: Oleksy can do it, Garrett Mitchell can do it, Dane Byers did it, Kris Newbury too. We have six to 10 guys who aren't afraid to do it — but they can all play and for me, that's ideal."

J.P. Côté has noticed a big change in the league since he started with the Hamilton Bulldogs in 2003–2004. "There's less fighting than when I started. Most of the fighters now, they can play. Back when I started, I'm not going to name names, but there were guys that couldn't skate and [were] just there to drop the gloves and go at it and hit each other's faces. To me, that's crazy," he said. "[Now,] you don't have to fight, you just have to be willing."

The statistics back up just how rapid the decline in fighting in professional hockey has been over the past decade. The decrease began when the NHL returned from the 2004–2005 lockout. While there were about 0.37 fights per game in 2005–06, according to HockeyFights. com data, that number dropped to around 0.32 bouts per contest in 2014–15. In the 2015–16 NHL season, that figure dropped to just 0.27 fights per game. The Toronto Maple Leafs did not having a single fight in their first 26 games, which would have seemed inconceivable even a few years ago. The Stanley Cup champion Pittsburgh Penguins had just 10 fights in 106 regular-season and playoff games, tied for fewest in the NHL in that span.

By comparison, the NHL's fights per game in 1974–75 was roughly 0.42 per game, and rose up to 0.86 per game in 1984–85 before starting to head back down to 0.55 per game in 1994–95.

Though the prevalence of fighting is still higher in the AHL, as the league has traditionally featured more fights than the NHL, the drop has also been significant. In 2005–06, there were about 0.90 fights per game in the AHL, and the number went up to a fight-per-game pace in 2008–09. But by 2014–15, the number had fallen to a 0.79 fights-per-game average, and according to HockeyFights.com, that number was down to 0.62 fights-per-game in the 2015–16 season.

One of the reasons fighting has decreased so markedly in the AHL is a change in the rules. Before the 2014–15 season, the league decided to make two fighting majors in a game an automatic game misconduct — meaning players who had a fight early in the game would have to avoid getting into another brawl to stay in the game.

According to former Pirates coach Ray Edwards, that's had an impact. "We've seen some scraps but the staged fighting is really gone, which is good. But you can tell the two-fight rule has had an impact," he said. "I'm still glad it's in there, because it keeps people honest."

Wolves general manager Wendell Young said the rule helped cut down the bouts. "After the first fight, the guy isn't going out and going back trying to start a second fight. I'd be surprised if there are many guys in the league who have had the two-fights-in-a-year rule, because once they have one, they watch themselves after that."

You can see the ripple effect this change in style is having on the league. As Rotruck said, "They're getting sent to us from the NHL. And now, some of those guys, the AHL enforcers are getting sent down to the ECHL because they're not finding an opportunity to play. Tim Spencer from Hershey goes down to South Carolina, Steve MacIntyre got sent down to Utah. This is the changing face of the game."

Eric Neilson is an AHL enforcer who has amassed 866 penalty minutes in 284 AHL games, including the first two months of the 2015–16 season, and has racked up 108 fighting majors according to HockeyFights.com. For him, the change has been swift. He remembers that when he first came into the league, playing for the Rivermen in Peoria, Illinois in 2007–2008, they'd go up against teams whose fourth line was all enforcer-type players. "Now, you see some teams don't even have an enforcer. It's more of a skill game, and you have teams that have maybe one, two max. In that respect, the game has changed," he said.

"But that's not just in the American League, that's in the NHL, too. The game totally has changed, that's what I've noticed. The toughness of a *Slap Shot* mentality, the goon stuff — you rarely hear goon in professional hockey now. In the ECHL, AHL, NHL, there's no goon, per se. There's tough guys and enforcers, and those guys have to run around and be able to play the game."

Neilson found out first-hand how tough it was to be able to keep playing after the 2014–15 season. When the Lightning opted not to bring him back to Syracuse, he signed a deal with the ECHL's Manchester Monarchs to start the 2015–16 season. After a Professional Tryout contract in mid-October, he did eventually earn a spot with the Montreal Canadiens' AHL affiliate in St. John's — but he might have been picked more for his off-ice influence than his on-ice toughness. He appeared in just six games for the IceCaps before being released to make room for former Arizona enforcer John Scott.

Rotruck has noticed the change with the Phantoms, the affiliate of the Philadelphia Flyers that has long been known for its toughness. The Phantoms had helped usher in a much tougher brand of hockey in the 1970s, and from 2012–13 to 2014–15 the club was in the top five in the AHL in fighting majors, according to HockeyFights.com.

As Rotruck said: "We have an enforcer, Derek Mathers, and he can barely get a sniff of playing time because other teams aren't dressing their enforcers. And you don't want to be down to 11 forwards with a twelfth forward that is not out there as much as the others. You've got to have some depth to your game."

Rotruck isn't a fan of this change in rules. "Let's say you have your first fight where two tough guys go, but they don't really settle it and it ends early because someone fell and touches his knee to the ice and the linesmen break it up.

"In a regular situation where they don't have that rule, they can come out and settle matters and have an encore where they didn't get to [finish the] fight the first time. . . . Now you can't do that; it'd be a game misconduct. Maybe the only time you could do that would be in the last minute of a game where the score is already decided, and you don't care about getting a game misconduct. So I dislike that rule."

Bridgeport broadcaster Phil Giubileo noted that players now have to add value to justify an AHL roster spot. "You have to be able to play. If you're going to get to the NHL and stick, you've got to be able to do something other than drop the gloves," he said. "Very few American League teams have that kind of player, and if they do, they have to contribute."

Buffalo Sabres assistant coach Terry Murray, who has coached in the AHL and the NHL over the past four decades, said one-dimensional players are on their way out. "You saw a dramatic change in the NHL [in 2014–15] with the so-called tough guy and most teams have sent that player down to the minors or he's gone to Europe to play. It's just a philosophical change in the game. I think everyone was a little bit tired of seeing, two or three shifts into a game, two guys get on the ice and fight, and nothing's happened. That's a big change.

"There's still room for players who are hard and gritty, and battle hard and instinctively drop their gloves and fight. That's part of the game I don't think will ever go away. . . . As we move through the process of what the NHL did, it'll work its way down here. Over time, you'll see less of the heavyweights [in the AHL] too, in my mind."

Retired AHL veteran Drew Bagnall thinks less demand for enforcers will result in fewer of them coming from juniors. "I think it's a reflection on how hockey has changed with guys coming up. Obviously, the lack of one-dimensional fighters in the National Hockey League deters that role in juniors, so when . . . that's a feeder league into the American Hockey League, you just don't see that much of it.

"I still think fighting has its place in the game in certain situations, but it's definitely not fighting for the sake of fighting. You're not fighting because that's what you have to do every night to stay in the lineup, you're fighting because the consequences of something that the ref dished out wasn't fair or enough."

In the last few decades, the AHL had a reputation for being a wilder brand of hockey than the NHL. And some are nostalgic for the old days. Don Stevens, longtime voice of the Americans, remembers what he was told when he decided to head from the IHL to Rochester in 1986. "I was in Salt Lake City and I said I was going to the American Hockey League, and they said, 'You don't want to go there. It's a goon league.' I said, 'No, it's not.'

"My first game was in Rochester against Binghamton, and it was a big brouhaha on the ice, and people were yelling at the Whalers, and Shane Churla came off the ice, climbed up onto the stage and went after some fans on the stage and I'm thinking, 'What did I get myself into?' It was an interesting start, but really wasn't indicative of what it was about. The game overall is a lot different.

"There's no more *Slap Shot* and except maybe the [Ligue Nord-Americaine de Hockey] in Quebec, there's a certain degree of professionalism I think that goes down through the East Coast League and maybe the Central League and whatever other leagues are below that.

"At times I'm a little disappointed it's not more of what it used to be. I'm old school and I know the reasons for the rough stuff, and to me it's a necessary part of the game. Players are better at policing themselves than the officials ever will be."

Brian Willsie remembered the wild fights in his first few AHL games in 1998–99. "I had a bench-clearing brawl in my sixth game in Hershey against Kentucky. Troy Crowder and Scott Parker got in a bench-clearing brawl and we were 1–5 at the time. We were getting booed at home by our fans, and a guy named Garrett Burnett sucker-punched Troy Crowder, and Scott Parker jumped the bench to go after him. Then I look and the coach is sending everyone out there, and we had a bench-clearing brawl. Parker was on a rampage, beating four or five guys, and I was holding a guy — I didn't really fight — and he was going around punching guys, even the guys who were holding because the referees couldn't get a hold of him."

For some of the league's announcers, fighting's fade isn't what they like to see. Giubileo, for instance, said he wasn't happy with the decrease. "The fighting thing, it's disappointing to me, because it's something I really enjoy. If you ever go and watch some of my calls on YouTube, you'll notice that I really do enjoy calling hockey fights and a lot of that does go back to my time with the [UHL's] Danbury Trashers, when you spend more time calling hockey fights than hockey games. To me, fans get into it . . . the minor league fans like to cling to that, liking the rough, physical hockey that results in punches thrown and altercations. I would see a fair amount of in my first three or four years in the league. You don't see as much of [it] now."

Lindsay Kramer notes that there are still AHL markets where fighting remains popular. "Syracuse is a funny market. They like their tough guys. The only banner is of John Badduke. It's not retired, but it was a fan vote after year five. They didn't vote for Scott Walker or Mike Peca or anyone like that. They've always had a soft spot for an Eric Neilson, that sort of guy.

"It's not just fighting — fans are savvy and tell when a team isn't sticking up for one another. . . . It's not like there is a constant presence of a brawler, but there are 10 guys on the team who will drop the gloves. [Crunch owner] Howard [Dolgon] loves that. He's a boxing promoter, and he loved the days of the Brandon Sugdens, the John Baddukes, the Jon Mirastys, the Zenon Konopkas, and I don't think he would stand for a parent club that completely ignored that.

"I don't [think] he thinks he can sell a whole bunch of tickets to see a fight, but I think he knows he can't sell tickets to see a softer team or a team that's not going to stand up. Angelidis, Konopka, they're perfect examples of guys who can play but can drop the gloves."

Kramer noted that the game still has changed with the absence of line brawls and more theatrical fights that sometimes showed up in the AHL even just a few years ago. "Clearly, hockey has gone that way, and . . . early on you had a lot of line brawls, you had guys climbing from one side of the penalty box to the other, you had guys jumping off the bench. It was a zoo. There was a lot of staged stuff off the opening faceoff. I think a lot of the acrobatic, unnecessary junk is gone. But come to any game in Syracuse, or Rochester, or Binghamton or Utica, you're not going do without that."

Rochester Democrat & Chronicle writer Kevin Oklobzija says Rochester is certainly a spot where pugilism is popular. "There's never been anyone in Rochester who's complained that there's been a fight during a game. They love Andy Ristau, who was barely here, but he's a legend. Bob 'the Hammer' Fleming — one year here, and people still talk about him. In 1991–92, Barry Melrose was coaching in Adirondack, Fleming and whomever [from the Red Wings] fought. His skates must have been 15 years old. He really didn't need them," he said with a laugh. "They were some old CCM Tacks."

He added that with the increased NHL ownership in the league, fighting is likely to drop off further. "The more NHL teams that own AHL teams, the more that will become the rule. Eventually, I think they're going to end up banning fighting. Or it'll be a game misconduct. It's so close to that already. Very few NHL teams put that type of player on their roster in the American League."

AHL president Dave Andrews says the league is seeing less fighting and fewer enforcers in the league, with the league introducing rules to discourage their place on a roster. "We still have per-game average more than the NHL does, which is a product of our players trying to make a statement and get a chance in the NHL. What's happening with the game, the most recent rule changes have been to reward speed and take away clutching and grabbing, and some types of hits have been taken out of the game. I think it's harder for a one-dimensional player to get ice time. Our league has become so fast, and the NHL has become so fast, it's just hard for coaches to see a role that's one-dimensional in that way.

"My own personal view — and we have made some subtle rule changes over the last few years trying to position our game in a way that [a] one-dimensional player doesn't have a role — we're not going to see players getting three fighting majors before they're thrown out of a game. We're trying to say, 'Look, if it happens in the heat of the moment, OK, there's rules to deal with that.' I'm not all in favor at all of guys who that's their only job. And I think as the game progresses, you're not going to see that anymore."

According to Yingst, the AHL is changing at a rapid pace. "I think it's happening now quickly, and going to fade even more, and you're now looking for the tough fighter who can actually play a little bit," he said. "It's leaving the game."

Bridgeport coach Brent Thompson said that he saw the tougher element as a way to protect younger players — but that the element is slowly disappearing. "I think fighting in the NHL has definitely dropped. In the American League, I think it's a different animal, I think it's a bigger part of the game and you need the tough guys to police and help the young guys be a little bit more confident and play knowing someone's got their back," he said. "But I do see the trickle-down effect. . . . I'm sure you ask me in five years, I'm sure it'll be dropped down to what the NHL standard is now."

CHAPTER ELEVEN

BRIDGEPORT SOUND TIGERS

Getting out of New York City can be quite a challenge. You leave the Islanders' new home at Brooklyn's Barclays Center and drive up the Brooklyn-Queens Expressway, passing near LaGuardia Airport and Citi Field, home of the New York Mets, crossing over the Whitestone Bridge into the Bronx before hopping on I-95 — one of America's busiest highways — toward New Haven. The New England Thruway heads out of the city, through Westchester County and over the Byram River into Connecticut and Fairfield County one of the United States' wealthiest counties. Along the shoreline, the bedroom communities of Greenwich, Cos Cob, Stamford and Norwalk pass by, but once the elevated interstate winds toward Bridgeport, remnants of that city's industrial past, with factories, warehouses and smokestacks, slowly begin to dominate the view.

Off Exit 27 for Harbor Yard, a large red-and-white-striped smoke-stack sits on your right, and the off-ramp brings you down from the ele-vated highway to street level in the midst of the industrial city. South Frontage Road runs next to the interstate wall and the city's sports complex is on the right.

Harbor Yard Ballpark, home of the independent Atlantic League's Bridgeport Bluefish, and Webster Bank Arena, home of the Bridgeport Sound Tigers, are paired up right off I-95. The arena, a red brick structure with some off-white concrete, is located right next to a multi-deck parking garage, a $56-million structure owned by the city to revitalize one of the tougher areas of the city's South End. The Metro-North — New York's commuter rail — and an Amtrak station, as well as a ferry that goes across Long Island Sound, are nearby.

Like the arena they play in, the Sound Tigers have been the center of a rebuilding process for the NHL's New York Islanders, as the team has looked to a return to prominence through smart draft picks and young talented players — most of whom are funneled through Bridgeport.

It's by design that several players who have made up the core of the Islanders, such as Kyle Okposo, Anders Lee and Frans Nielsen, have spent time with the Sound Tigers, learning the Islanders' system and developing before coming up to the NHL. A team that traditionally hasn't made as big a splash in free agency that some of its other Metropolitan Division rivals have, the Islanders also aren't usually a team that bumps against the salary cap limit, relying more on home-grown prospects rather than importing other players from signings.

The infusion of young players has been beneficial to the Islanders, who qualified for the Stanley Cup playoffs in 2013, 2015 and again in 2016 after a drought that stretched back to 2007. The club is now regarded as one of the league's up-and-coming teams, with a talented roster but one that certainly has roles for AHL products to step up and fill.

The Sound Tigers have been owned and operated by the Islanders since their inception in 2001, playing just across the Sound from the NHL's team's former home of Long Island. The Islanders' move out of Nassau Coliseum to Brooklyn in the fall of 2015 has left some questions unanswered about if the franchise will remain in Connecticut, or if it will eventually move to a refurbished arena that used to house the NHL parent club.

Walking through the glass doors into Webster Bank Arena, you see a modern one-deck facility with the suites atop the seating bowl, sitting 8,525 for hockey. Besides the Sound Tigers, the arena has hosted a number of college hockey games, including several NCAA tournament games, as well as Sacred Heart University and University of Connecticut contests.

Bridgeport is a good location for an AHL club, not only for its relative proximity to Brooklyn — one can hop on the Metro-North and be in Manhattan in 90 minutes — but also its location is far more central and convenient for away games compared to other teams in the AHL. Hartford is about an hour bus ride up Interstates 95 and 91, and Springfield is just a half-hour further north on I-91. Providence is a two-hour ride east along I-95, making a good portion of the Sound Tigers' road trips short jaunts of two hours or less via bus.

As Brent Thompson, the Sound Tigers' coach said, "[AHL travel] is a grind no matter how you cut it, but you're on a bus, you're playing a game against Hartford, and you're back home and then maybe jump up to Providence. The travel isn't that bad. But it is still a grind. But that's one of the advantages of Bridgeport."

Thompson says the spot along the Connecticut coast is an asset for the Islanders. "The location of Bridgeport is what I think is so special," he said. "It's a great building. It's a first-class facility. We're fortunate that our locker room is one of the top locker rooms in the league, great weight room, and every tool is at your fingertips to develop these players into NHL players."

Like many of the league's owned and operated teams, the proximity of the AHL club is one of its biggest assets, as players can be sent down or called up with relative ease, and Islanders officials have easy access to scout some of the club's top prospects.

Thompson said being close to the parent club is a plus, and with former Bridgeport coach Jack Capuano now in Brooklyn — and Thompson is a former Islanders assistant — the two share a common thread. "It's a special relationship with the coaching staff in New York and our staff, and just the fact it's so close, that it's an easy situation for guys to be called up for an emergency or if it's long-term basis."

Former Sound Tiger Colton Gillies said the location near the parent club is an asset for players. "The big team is only an hour and a half away, so you have a lot of guys coming to watch, especially with

Colton Gillies, a former first-round pick of the Minnesota Wild, who spent time playing for Houston, Rochester and Bridgeport, was signed by the Sound Tigers to add veteran leadership to the team for the 2014–15 season. (COURTESY AHL)

our division being really close. There's no flying, and you have a lot of scouts coming to every game."

Sandwiched in between the major media markets of New York and Boston, Connecticut represents a strange dividing line between the legions of the two cities' fans. Those in Fairfield County and the western part of the state largely pledge allegiance to some of the nine combined NHL, MLB, NFL and NBA teams New York has to offer. The further north and east you go toward Massachusetts, fans tend to gravitate more toward Boston's professional teams of the Bruins, Red Sox, Patriots and Celtics.

According to broadcaster Phil Giubileo, the dividing line also makes its way to the AHL with two teams in the Nutmeg State. "Connecticut's really an interesting hockey market. You go back and have the history with the NHL's Whalers, and obviously up around Hartford there's a rich hockey tradition. Fairfield County, where Bridgeport is situated, is really unique. As a city itself, it isn't a hockey hotbed by any stretch of the imagination, all around the area it is. Fairfield County, it's a newer hockey tradition and growing, and I think our proximity close to Long Island helps.

"We have a growing number of Islanders fans, and a lot of that comes with being affiliated with the New York Islanders since day one. But you also have pretty rabid Boston Bruins and New York Rangers fan bases as well, and they all kind of meet right around here. It's fun when you have a Bridgeport-Hartford game and there's a lot of Rangers fans there [to see the Wolf Pack, the Rangers' affiliate] as well as when Providence [Boston's AHL affiliate] comes in and you have the Boston fans that seem to really travel really well and come in.

"In my nine years with the team, it's been really great to see the fan base grow and see a really great group of loyal fans stick around with the team for such a long period of time. Being close to Long Island and having a close relationship with the Islanders organization is special, because you see some of the other AHL-NHL affiliations — to have your NHL team in your backyard, your NHL team owning you, I think it is helpful with player development, some of the things the two teams have done together to build a brand and a tradition that we have been able to in Bridgeport the last 15 years."

Paul Ryan, communications and community relations manager for the Sound Tigers, said the location is also an attraction for the players. "Players like it because you're an hour out of the city and you're not too far from the Island, and now even closer to Brooklyn. It's a real interesting spot right on the water here. It's a cool little spot."

On this night, playing out the schedule of a season that hasn't gone the way they planned, the Sound Tigers took on the Providence Bruins, who brought some fans wearing black-and-gold to go with the blue-and-orange color scheme favored by the home fans. While the Islanders had a good 2014–15 season — mostly thanks to the Bridgeport products who skated in this arena on their way to the NHL — the

Sound Tigers struggled. Bringing in a few AHL veterans at the start of the season didn't help.

According to Giubileo, it can be very tricky for a broadcaster to call a long season like this. "It's never as much fun to call a team that doesn't win very often. It was such a unique and strange year because we got off to a really good start and then everything kind of fizzled after January," said Giubileo. "You look at the small things of player development and you try to tell the story in a little bit of a different way, looking at how [Islanders prospects] Ryan Pulock and Griffin Reinhart developed over the course of the season, seeing some of the younger guys coming in the tail end.

"Bridgeport, they didn't win a lot of games, but they were competitive, they would hang in and get a lot of one-goal losses. . . . But you could see them building and becoming better hockey players over the course of the year and culminating [in] seeing a couple of those players in the [Stanley Cup] playoffs."

With the Sound Tigers falling out of the Calder Cup race, management opted to ship off the more veteran players and fill out the roster with some players just coming out of college and on Professional Tryouts. This made it more of a chaotic job for Thompson to manage a roster very much in flux. Thompson, who had also coached in the ECHL, felt his experience there helped him navigate the season.

"It's a challenge managing bodies, especially the call-ups, the injuries. You have to have a good pulse on the East Coast League to manage and maintain consistency," he said. "The priority in the American League is to develop, and it just gives more opportunity for other guys. It is a challenge to manage that kind of movement, but it's also fun because you're involved in trying to bring a guy up to fill a role, and also giving that player another opportunity."

With such a high turnover — in 2013–14 they had 66 players, and 45 in 2014–15 — Paul Ryan joked that he didn't get a chance to even introduce himself to some of the new players. "It was insanity. I didn't get to introduce myself to some of the guys. They knew who I was, and I knew who they were, but it was like, get on the bus and we're off, and the guys are playing before I get a chance to introduce myself."

Capuano, who coached in Bridgeport from 2007 to 2010, said the

Sound Tigers make sure prospects get the time they need to learn the Islanders' system and improve their skills. "There's no question Bridgeport is crucial to our success. We share a lot of the systems they play; we go through training camp and show the same video, their coaching staff uses the terminology we use here. There's a lot of important ingredients that go in there."

Capuano also said the team's compressed, weekend-heavy game schedule does allow time during the week to work on development and get ingrained with the Islanders' system down at the AHL level. "They almost play like a college schedule with Friday, Saturday and weekend games, so they're off ice conditioning and they get to work a lot at that, and on the ice, they practice quite a bit too. Not only do they implement the systems, they get time to work on their game, and that's what they need."

With the Islanders' concentration on rebuilding the team from within by development and draft picks, the AHL affiliate has a huge role to play. As general manager Garth Snow told me, "It's organizationally the lifeblood to have a quality coaching, teaching program in the AHL, and it feeds the NHL team when you need players, either from a lack of performance or an injury. We'll keep going the route we have the last few years and we have some good prospects in the system in Bridgeport, and some good young prospects that are too young for the AHL."

Indeed, Giubileo, who has called Sound Tigers games for nearly a decade, has seen the core of the Islanders' team come up through the system. "It's amazing, going back and thinking about some of the players that were there in my very first season with the team in 2006, and remember[ing] guys like Frans Nielsen — he was a key contributor — and guys like Kyle Okposo came in the following year. Even more recently, if you look at the key players, the younger players who [came] up in the last handful of seasons, guys like Brock Nelson, Ryan Strome and Anders Lee, those guys spent significant time with the Bridgeport Sound Tigers. Calvin de Haan spent considerable time with Bridgeport.

"Garth Snow has structured and rebuilt the organization, which began when he started as the GM, you look and see what he's done with the team. Many of these players they've drafted have come through

Bridgeport. If you're John Tavares, you're going right to the National Hockey League, but most of these players have filtered through Bridgeport at one time or another."

Okposo, a right winger who played in Bridgeport from 2007 to 2009, said his time in Connecticut was a positive one. "I really learned how to play a pro game. It was definitely a good experience," he said. "I've known [Nielsen] for a long time, we've known each other since I got drafted [in 2006] and we had rookie camp that year. It's been neat to see [picks] come up through the system."

Ryan Pulock, the Islanders' first-round pick in the 2013 NHL Draft, said despite the Sound Tigers' tough season in the standings, the experience was personally good for him. "It was a good development for me. We worked every day on little things, which I needed to do. I think my defensive game has improved from last year, and that's a big area I have to focus on if I want to make that next step and [be] an elite player in the National Hockey League."

One of the aspects of life that a lot of fans don't realize about young AHLers is that it is usually their first time on their own. A junior player coming out of Canada usually lives with a billet family that takes care of the player, and a college player in the United States is housed in dorms and fed by the university. But once you turn pro, you have to find your own housing and make your own meals, and even while a first-round pick like Pulock would earn $925,000 if he had a spot with the Islanders, he only gets $70,000 while playing in the AHL, along with other performance and signing bonuses.

To help ease the transition during the 2014–15 season, Pulock found a place to live with other young teammates Adam Pelech and Jesse Graham. "It's different. Playing junior, you have a billet family and come home after practice and you have supper on the table," said Pulock. "We helped each other out with that — cooking meals and whatnot. It's good to have someone that's in the situation as you to work through that."

Graham said it was a good season to learn the ropes with some fellow young players. "We all adjusted together," he said with a smile. "It was good. It was a lot of fun coming in and being the rookie again, going through that experience.

"Pro hockey is obviously a lot different than junior. You have to be a lot more focused and it takes a lot of dedication to bring it every night. It was a tough adjustment at first, but you know, it was pretty fun."

Alan Quine, who led the Sound Tigers in points in 2014–15, developed a lot over the first two years he spent in Bridgeport. "You learn a lot from older guys, and in the first year, the coaches were good with me. You're just a sponge and try to get used to playing against older guys who have man strength and are bigger and stronger than you coming out of junior," he said. "The coaches were all good with me and let me develop and took my defensive game seriously and I think that helped."

One of the products of the Bridgeport pipeline was Matt Donovan. He played parts of four seasons before making the jump to the NHL. In the Islanders' locker room at Nassau Coliseum, he talked about what he learned as a young player out of college. "I learned a lot not only hockey-wise but as a person. You come out of college or junior, and you turn pro and play 70 or 80 games, it's a lot different."

Donovan also said it was special to come up to the NHL along with several players from the Sound Tigers. "You're growing as a person and a player, and it's with most of these guys in this locker room. It's fun to grow together as an organization and play with these guys not only in the A, but it's fun to look at the guys, at how you were in the AHL together and now you're where you want to be in the NHL together."

Donovan eventually signed a one-year, two-way deal with the Buffalo Sabres for the 2015–16 season, one that would earn him $825,000 with Buffalo, but also $400,000 if he played in Rochester.

For the Sound Tigers playing out the schedule at the end of a long season, they were able to hang with the Bruins for the first period, but fell behind 2–0 in the first 137 seconds of the second. Captain Aaron Ness — Bridgeport's All-Star representative for 2014–15 — brought the majority of the crowd of 5,731 to its feet with his seventh goal of the year, but in the end, the Tigers didn't quite have enough to get the win and fell 3–2.

After the game, Ness talked about what it was like to play in Bridgeport. "It's been great. It's my fourth year now, and I've had a blast since day one. It's second to none, and first-class everywhere."

Bridgeport had struggled, but he was happy that former teammates were doing well for the Islanders as they headed toward the Stanley Cup playoffs. "I played with a lot of those guys, so it's fun seeing them doing well."

Giubileo talked about how some of the Sound Tigers got a taste of the Stanley Cup playoffs as the Islanders faced Washington in a tight seven-game series. "Watching Griffin Reinhart playing in an NHL playoff game — even Scott Mayfield playing in a playoff game as well, . . . it was interesting to see that down the stretch, and those were some nice little opportunities for them.

"I've been through my share of losing seasons with the Sound Tigers so this one wasn't tough as some of the others, because there was still talent there. At the end of the day there were some good players that stuck around."

After the Sound Tigers' season came to an end, Pulock packed his bags and headed down to Long Island, as he joined the team as a "Black Ace," one of the players who keep skating after their AHL season comes to an end, in case a player on the NHL roster gets injured. As a result, he got to experience the playoffs close up.

"I was able to watch the playoffs [at the Coliseum]. The fans were phenomenal. It gave you chills just watching. It was a cool experience, but it was good learning as well, watching how, come playoff time in the NHL, every play is so crucial. You can't take a shift off or you'll get burnt. There's too many elite players that will take advantage of you if you aren't ready to go every shift."

Even though he didn't get in the lineup, he had to keep preparing as if he might — particularly with the injuries the Islanders had on the blue line. "You go to stay focused and put the work in every day and prepare yourself, in case injuries happen," he said. "You have to be ready to go, and I was fortunate enough to get a chance to be around there and be that close."

For his part, Anders Lee, who won the NHL Rookie of the Month in February, enjoyed his time with the Sound Tigers. He believes a big part of the chemistry the Islanders now have is due to the strong focus the organization places on player development.

"As a young guy coming from college, it was a great way to learn the pro game. Understanding the structure and how important it is at both the AHL and NHL level, to go down there and spend some time, focusing on my game and getting used to the pace. Every step along the way gets faster and faster," he said. "You build that camaraderie and chemistry playing with guys and when you get up here you know you're closer as a team and spent more time with each other, so it's nice to have a lot of home-grown guys throughout the organization."

Colin McDonald also got a shot at the NHL lineup as well. Paul Ryan, the Sound Tigers' communication officer, told him, "I don't ever want to see you ever again," when McDonald left to go to the Islanders in February. "A lot of people have said, 'That is the most cliched thing you can say for a guy in your position.' He was on that yo-yo and kept going up and down," said Ryan. "And he didn't come back."

Ryan saw him two months later during the Islanders' playoff run. "I saw him after Game 6, and it was cool because I thought he was genuinely excited to see me. And right after the game, I was like, 'I told you I didn't want to see you,' and he said, 'I know. I worked hard and stayed here.'"

Another Sound Tiger, Scott Mayfield, who didn't score a lot of goals, got his shot to experience the Stanley Cup playoffs as part of the Islanders. With the Islanders' injuries, Mayfield got his chance to dress against Washington, which surprised Ryan.

"I was shocked. I found out two hours before the game that he was getting the chance. Not that I didn't believe in him, but I wasn't sure the coaches were going to use him. It's a big decision, and everyone was talking about putting Ryan Pulock in, but Scott had had some NHL games before.

"To see a guy like Scott Mayfield, he works so hard all year long, he couldn't score ... [but] he scored in the second-to-last game [for Bridgeport], he scored an empty-netter," said Ryan. "I'm filming the game for our coaches and I'm jumping up and down because I'm excited for Scott. He's such a good kid, but he couldn't find the back of the net.

"He got to play in Game 6 in what is probably the last game in the history of Nassau Coliseum — at least for now — and a Game 7, and just seeing the look on his face, that's the coolest part. As much as I hate seeing those guys go up because do I like them and like to hang out with them, that's what they want to do. That's the coolest part for me."

From a season that was mostly forgettable on the AHL level, the Sound Tigers had made their impact elsewhere, as part of an Islanders team that was able to reach the postseason. And like many of the owned and operated teams, the AHL team's success is largely determined not only by their on-ice record, but also what they are able to contribute to the parent club.

For Pulock, he said his time in Bridgeport makes it easier to fit into the Islanders' future plans by learning the system used by the parent club and also getting training for just learning how to be a part of the NHL. "They stress the same things there the Islanders do up here. They work the same systems, that sort of thing. So you know the system that they like to use by playing in the A. Having Brent Thompson there, he's been up and he knows what it takes and [is] good [at] helping us prepare to be ready to play in the NHL."

For Ness, who after the season signed a one-year, two-way deal for $575,000 at the NHL level and $300,000 at the AHL level to join the Hershey Bears, playing with the Sound Tigers was a good experience. "I loved it there. I always felt I was a great fit there. It's a great organization, great people. Nothing but great things to say. It's been a great [few] years for me, and I've enjoyed every minute of it."

According to AHL president Dave Andrews, while the Islanders may eventually decide to move their affiliate closer to home with the renovation of Nassau Coliseum scheduled to be completed in 2016, the city has done a nice job of earning itself a place in the American Hockey League — with or without the Islanders' team in town. "I think Bridgeport will probably continue to be in the American League for quite some time. Whether it will be in the current incarnation is another question.

"From a business perspective, if you look around our league and say, 'What would happen if the Islanders moved them to Nassau?' If that was to happen, Bridgeport is a much better location than a number of other places in our league."

CHAPTER TWELVE

LEHIGH VALLEY PHANTOMS

If you head toward Allentown, Pennsylvania, on Interstate 78, you will eventually set your sights on one of the AHL's newest arenas. Getting off at 54, the U.S. Route 222 exit, a left reveals the sign for Allentown. You pass by Dorney Park amusement park's roller coasters, then begin toward the city center. Past the strip malls, there is a residential area that features an electronic billboard for the Lehigh Valley Phantoms, the newly relocated AHL franchise.

As you enter the aging downtown core and pass by the storefronts on Hamilton Avenue, you will see the brand new PPL Center, the $177-million arena that seats 8,420 for hockey and is part of a larger redevelopment project for the city. The building opened in September 2014, giving the Phantoms a permanent home after years of leading a nomadic existence.

The team began as the Philadelphia Phantoms, an expansion franchise purchased by the Flyers in 1996 that played at the Philadelphia Spectrum, across the parking lot from the NHL club's brand new rink, the CoreStates Center — now known as the Wells Fargo Center. The Phantoms won a pair of Calder Cups in 1998 and 2005, Philadelphia's first professional hockey titles since the Flyers last won the Stanley Cup in 1975. But the Spectrum became slated for demolition, and the team was sold and moved to the Glens Falls Civic Center after the 2008–09 season.

The move wasn't intended to be a permanent one, as Glens Falls wanted to prove it was a viable AHL market and the renamed Adirondack Phantoms looked to secure a permanent home. The 4,794-seat arena had seen four Calder Cup titles in two decades, but the city had been without AHL hockey since the Adirondack Red Wings left town in 1999.

In 2011, the plans for what became the PPL Center were announced, and in 2014, after five seasons in New York, the Phantoms moved south and looked to establish itself in a new market.

Bob Rotruck recalled what it was like in Glens Fall at the end of the Phantoms' run there. "My wife and I lived there for four years and our daughter was born there, and we had a lot of friends in the town. It was emotional and awkward . . . because when we were leaving, Adirondack didn't know if they were going to get a new pro team or not, so we didn't know if this would be the last game or not. By the end of the season, there were rumors that they likely would get a new team, but for much of that stretch, we were just working hard trying to help that loyal and traditional hockey market secure a new team — which they deserved with the fan support that they had been giving the Phantoms up there," he said.

"The Phantoms were completely honest with the town and the market and they weren't, like, packing up their bags and sneaking out of town like the Baltimore Colts. Right from the very beginning, they said, 'Hey, we're a temporary team, we're building a new arena in Allentown, we're going to give you a chance to show what you've got because you've been so nice and generously welcomed us in. You've wanted this team here, albeit temporarily, so we're giving you this chance to show your ability to support.'

"So for me, I didn't know what the fan response would be at the end of the season, and if fans would be throwing stuff at us and saying, 'Get out of town.' But instead, the crowds just got bigger and bigger and it was more a matter of fans just saying, 'This might be our last chance to see the games here and see the team.'

"It was more overwhelming with love and support for the team and what [they] were able to bring them — and [that] was neat for me to see as well and to be a part of that and bring the last Adirondack Phantoms broadcast. I was amazed. They kind of overwhelmed me with their showing of support and appreciation, is the best way you can describe it. They're doing the wave, saying, 'Thank You Phantoms,' and doing cheers, saying, 'We want the Flames,' because there were rumors they would get the Adirondack Flames.

"It was a celebration. We had our largest crowd we had for five years there. Glens Falls seats 4,800, and they had 5,400 their very first game, and had 5,500 for their very last game. It was packed. It was electric there. We weren't going to the playoffs, and the players wanted desperately to get the fans a win for their last game there, and we didn't. We lost in overtime, and it was an emotional night there too."

Shane Harper, who played off and on for the Adirondack Phantoms from 2009 to 2013, recalled his Glens Falls time fondly. "I actually really liked it there. My girlfriend is from there, so I still go back. I haven't left the Adirondack area yet," he said with a laugh. "I go back there every summer, even went up there for Christmas this year. I really liked playing for that organization. It was fun; I had great times and great memories there. And it's nice to go back — the summers are beautiful there," he told me.

However, Kevin Marshall, part of the Adirondack teams from 2009 to 2012, said some players found the transition from Philadelphia to New York state tough. "I didn't like it. I came out as a junior guy, you came in, and [then] the relationship between rookie and veterans changed a lot. I came in there and was not talking much and doing my thing, and the atmosphere was just not good. They were in Philly before, and so they go to Adirondack, way smaller city, smaller rink, everything went from being pretty nice to being kind of rough.

"Guys sometimes were negative about it; they were complaining a lot, and it was kind of heavy in the room. We didn't do well, didn't make the playoffs and we went on a stretch the first two years and were out of the playoffs by February, so the atmosphere was just not a good environment."

The bit of limbo the franchise was in finally came to an end in 2015, when they were able to settle into a new arena, and one that was on the edges of the Flyers' footprint in eastern Pennsylvania. A gritty industrial city that was most known for Billy Joel's 1982 song "Allentown," it was a town looking for a team as well as a team looking for a place to play.

Brandon Manning, who spent three years with Adirondack, talked about the transition to his new home. "The three years we spent in New York [were] good, we had good fan support there, but just to see how many Flyers and Phantoms fans there are in Lehigh Valley and Philadelphia is overwhelming for sure. You spend three years, so it's home, and you're kind of comfortable with everything," he said. "But you can't beat a brand new rink and facility, and how close you are to Philly and to New York City. There's a lot more accessibility for us. You can't beat going in front of 8,500 fans at every home game. . . . I think the guys who were in Glens Falls are re-charged, and I think it'll pay off for us.

"When you're playing 3-in-3s, you can come into your own building and jump in the hot tub and just be more at home. Going into an older rink in Glens Falls, you were just trying to kill time, whereas now we have a setup."

According to the team's relations manager Dan Fremuth, who grew up outside of Philadelphia, while it was a challenge to enter a new market, it helped that it was an area where hockey was already well-known. "Obviously coming into the market, we're doing things for the first time. . . . But the amazing thing is there were already hockey fans here. Some expansion teams, some teams that relocate to a market that's never had hockey, you have to educate them about hockey — this is what icing is, this is what offside is, and that kind of stuff. The very first hockey event we had here was the Battle on Hamilton, a mixed-squad game between the Phantoms and the Flyers, and we sold that game out.

"As a staff we were blown away by the amount of orange-and-black in the stands. What that told us was there were hockey fans here. There were Flyer fans here, there were Phantoms fans here, from the

Phantoms' days at the Spectrum and the proximity to Philadelphia and Wells Fargo Center and the Flyers. So there were people who wanted hockey here and obviously came and supported hockey right away."

In fact, a photo session the team did early on in its tenure for the local newspaper took longer than expected due to the interest.

"We did a shoot for the *Morning Call*, the newspaper in town; they were doing a 'Welcome to Allentown' kind of centerpiece, right before our opener. We had a couple of guys go out to the corner at 7th and Hamilton in their gear and their jerseys, standing at this monument that people here would recognize as downtown Allentown, sort of the new guys meeting the old," Fremuth recalled. "It was a simple enough photo shoot, but it took us 45 minutes because people would stop and want to take pictures with our guys and [want] autographs. We couldn't shoot for more than two minutes before someone would roll into the intersection, put down the window and yell, 'Go Phantoms!' This is before we ever played a regular-season game."

Terry Murray, Phantoms coach in the last years of Glens Falls and first year in Lehigh Valley, talked about how his Adirondack team would visit its new home under construction on road trips. "We, as a group in Glens Falls, stopped in Allentown once every year the past couple of years to take a look as construction was going on, had walked through the building, and everyone was excited. To see the finished product is pretty amazing.

"I'm really pleased to be able to be the first coach in Allentown for this Phantoms team. It's a good challenge, a great group of guys and the fans have been absolutely terrific. They've been selling out the building and got a lot of support with Philadelphia being so close."

Former Flyer Keith Jones, commentator for Comcast SportsNet Philadelphia and studio analyst for NBC Sports Network, said the move closer to Philadelphia was good for the Flyers and their players. "I do think it's extremely convenient, and I also think it gives the players down there even more incentive to try to make an impression — at least in every home game — when you have an opportunity. Sometimes on the road you can feel a little bit isolated from your own team and your own scouts and general manager," he said.

"I think, geographically, when it's so much closer, you always feel like there's a connection and, at nights when you have a great performance, that you catch the eye of the general manager and give yourself a little bit [of] opportunity to get up a little bit quicker than you anticipated when you first joined the club."

While Glens Falls was a bit off the beaten path for scouts and management, Philadelphia general manager Ron Hextall was no stranger to PPL Center, making the short ride north from Philadelphia to check out the team's prospects.

He also felt that Murray — Jones' first NHL coach — was good at helping the Phantoms learn the system implemented by the NHL club. "He's a great teacher, and that's really what playing in the minors is about. It's not necessarily the head coach doing all he can to get to the next level. In some cases it's about him implementing the system that's put in place by the head coach in the National Hockey League level," said Hexall.

Walking into the brand new arena, you pass by the Tim Hortons near the entrance and look out on the facility. The lower bowl of black seats is topped by rows of three decks of suites atop them on the sides, with one upper deck section behind one goal, and another with advertisements on a yellow wall on the other. The Phantoms have hung up six banners from their time in Philadelphia, including two marking their Calder Cup championships as well as a pair of regular season and conference championship banners each.

Allentown had been hard-hit with the decline of heavy industry in the last half century, and as Fremuth said, the team is playing a role in the revitalization efforts. "With our players, our mascot or our staff, that's a collaborative effort, whatever it may be, to get out there and inform and educate people about this special thing that's happening in downtown Allentown. It's not just the Phantoms, it's the PPL Center and the revitalization of downtown Allentown that comes with this building and what it means long-term for the city," he said. "Hopefully this is the first step of a much larger plan to build up downtown Allentown and make it great again. We're just a segment of that."

The larger goal of the arena — to get people into downtown Allentown, is working well Rotruck said. He compared the Phantoms' arrival to the city's AAA baseball team, the Lehigh Valley IronPigs. "The IronPigs are one thing, and they're important to have established that professional sports can work in this town after years and years of a lot of naysayers saying it wasn't the right fit or really doesn't work for us. The IronPigs proved those naysayers incorrect, and [the Phantoms] downtown are proving that this can work. With naysayers saying this can't work downtown, well it is working," said Rotruck.

"You have the revitalization going on and all these restaurants all around this block and the brand-new hotel, and people are coming and flocking in from around the area, and from outside the area. They're coming back to Allentown and saying, 'I can't believe this is downtown Allentown,'" he added.

For Andrew Gordon, who came to Phantoms after playing for the IceCaps in St. John's and the Chicago Wolves, the transition to a brand-new AHL town made his transition to a new team easier. "It feels a little bit of a fresh slate. I didn't know anyone in the organization, first time coming into a new city. Every city you play in, guys have been there before, and guys know what apartments to live in, know what restaurants are good, what hotel your parents should stay at when they come in to town," he said.

"But we all came in here completely blind. Everyone's trying to figure out where's Target, where do I have to buy bed sheets and such? So for the first little while it was a real feeling-out process with the city. Having a building like this changes everything. When you have the ability to come into a rink like this — coming to a weight room that makes you want to work out and a dressing room that makes you want to hang out with your buddies, things like that — it changes your day. This has been a great experience."

Murray agreed the new building was a boost for the team, particularly with the ability for players to hang out more in the locker room. "It's been a very positive change from the coaching aspect. You spend five years up in Glens Falls, I was there for two of them, and we're coming into a new state-of-the-art building, which has a lot of energy and emotion. The fans are really into the game, and [we're] selling out the building every night," he said.

Veteran forward Andrew Gordon was part of the first Phantoms team to play a season in Allentown during the 2014–15 season, experiencing both the pluses and minuses of arriving in a brand new AHL city. (PUCK STOPPER PHOTOGRAPHY VIA THE BRIDGEPORT SOUND TIGERS)

"As a coach, it's nice to see the players come to the rink early, stay late, they have a lot of room to do their off-ice workouts and are committed to do it. It's not that they weren't willing to do it in Glens Falls — there just wasn't the room. You could only get three or four guys in there at a time. So this is a nice team setup, for team bonding and team play."

Gordon said also with the team not winning a lot since the move from Philadelphia, it was important to try and establish a new tradition in their new home. "I know the Phantoms as an organization have struggled the last few seasons, so we're overcoming a bit of history here. Guys don't know how to win yet, like some guys do in Chicago and they know in Hershey. We're sort of battling our own history at the moment, and trying to write our own in the new building," he said. "It is sort of a fresh start for everybody, and trying to improve upon the past."

The city's proximity to the parent club — it's just 76 miles from PPL Center to Wells Fargo Center — is helping build enthusiasm for the team. It's part of the recent trend to have the AHL teams close to the parent club for the ease of calling up players and being able to see the club's prospects on a regular basis without a long trip. It does benefit the AHL club as well, as sometimes the right fit of a parent club helps build enthusiasm and sell tickets. And with the Flyers brand being a big selling point in this part of Pennsylvania, financially, the Phantoms could cash in.

"The city itself has been great — 8,000 fans a night, the proximity to Philadelphia is wonderful. You meet some fans from Philly who might not be able to afford the $80 tickets or whatever they are in Philly, and come up here and see some of the prospects and feel like you're part of the organization and part of the franchise. That's a real key to the success in the American League, is [to] have the fans feel able to support both franchises," said Gordon.

"When I was in Chicago, we'd go into Abbotsford, and we'd pack the place and create a rowdy building; it was awesome — but because we were Vancouver's affiliate. But when Blair Jones played for them [from 2012 to 2014], he said it was the most dead, quiet building — you could hear a pin drop 90 percent of the games. And here I thought this place was always unbelievable," he said with a laugh. "If Vancouver had a team up there, they'd always do very well, I'm sure, but it's just the luxury with the proximity we have — they can watch us on Tuesday night and watch the Flyers on Wednesday night. It's a real special added bonus."

Adam Comrie, who also played on that first Lehigh Valley team, said the fan support was tremendous. "I've actually never been a part of team that's had such a good fan base. They've been awesome. Even though we're not winning at home as much as we should be or that we potentially could be, we keep on selling out and keep on breaking records for attendance and it's awesome having such a good fan base in a new city for a new team."

Rotruck agreed the affiliation helped the connection. "It helps [that] it's the Phantoms brand, and the Flyers affiliation. Rob and Jim Brooks, over a decade ago, they had an idea of putting a team here in Allentown. And initially, they said if we can get into the American Hockey League with the new team, we'll be rivals with the [Philadelphia] Phantoms, the Hershey Bears and the Wilkes-Barre/Scranton Penguins. That triangle of rivalry around us.

"But they were able to purchase the team when they couldn't play at the Spectrum anymore, and bring them here. But the original plan was to have the Lehigh Valley Something Elses. The team was going to succeed and thrive in this building no matter what, but to be able to carry over the Phantoms history. . . . We do get some fans who come up from Philadelphia who say, 'Hey, we're so glad the Phantoms are back in Pennsylvania, we missed them for the last five years.'

"But the fact of the matter is, most of the fans here had never been or rarely been to a Phantoms hockey game. It really is a new element. It would have succeeded had it been the Rangers or the Sharks or anything else. To be able to bring in that Phantoms identity to this market, that meant something to a few people here and people closer to Philadelphia and gave us a nice head start running here."

Rotruck said the mix of informed fans and a new town gave the Phantoms a unique setup. "What's amazing for this market [is] that it has this feel of an expansion market; you have a lot of fans, but you have a traditional base of the Phantoms, which have won two Calder Cups.

"You have all the fans who are loyal to the Flyers and who were excited because it's a Flyers team, but also a lot of fans who don't know a whole lot about hockey who are coming here and checking this out for the first time. I've talked with a lot of fans who said this was their first-ever professional hockey game. You'd think, being an hour and change from Philadelphia and a couple hours from New York that people had been to an NHL game before. It's not true.

"Allentown is its own identity and its own market, and Lehigh Valley. There are a lot of families bringing their kids to their first-ever pro hockey games."

AHL president Dave Andrews said the arena was key in the effort to revitalize downtown Allentown — while the move also rekindles some rivalries between the Bears, Penguins and Phantoms. "I think it's been a testament to Rob and Jim Brooks. They had a dream and it wasn't [an] easy dream to bring to fruition. They're good guys and they were persistent.

"I think they were able to forge in Allentown in terms of the political and the business leaders in the community, and what that building is going to mean for the community is an awful lot. It's an expensive project. . . . When they put the shovel in the ground, it's a tremendous transformation of their downtown.

"When you think about the Brookses having ownership with the team coming out of the [old Philadelphia] Spectrum when it was going to be knocked down, and going through the years in Glens Falls — which were much better than anyone thought they'd be, either for the fans or the organization — that's a long road to go down.

"It's a good public-private partnership. And for us, putting another team in Pennsylvania with Hershey and Wilkes-Barre, and we had lost Philadelphia, and to go back there was really important. It's a successful part of the American League and has been for a long time."

A good weeknight crowd files in for a game against Hershey, and as the brightly colored yellow Peeps Zamboni smooths out the ice (Peeps is the iconic marshmallow treat that was started in nearby Bethlehem), the fans, mostly clad in the orange-and-black, head to their seats.

While the home team doesn't give the fans a lot to cheer about — they suffer a 7–2 loss to the Bears — the large crowd still is enthusiastic and into the game. They have a very loyal fan base. In fact, despite not qualifying for the playoffs in 2014–15, the team was fourth in the AHL in attendance with an average of 8,163 per game, and had 22 sellouts.

The Phantoms' on-ice performance was hampered with injuries sustained by the parent club, requiring several call-ups through the season. It can be a challenge to adjust to a fluctuating roster.

"It makes it interesting," coach Murray said with a smile. "It's what coaching is all about: change and little adjustments. We're here for the NHL team. We're here for the Flyers. It's our job to get the players ready and keep them ready if there's an emergency call-up and to develop players to play full time for a long time."

Rotruck noted how the enthusiasm increased as the team's first season progressed. "What is incredibly interesting, our crowds at the beginning of the season were OK. But then we had a Saturday night that wasn't a sellout, but it was a good crowd, and we're getting fans out the second time and buying into it.

"Now the whole thing has snowballed, and you can't keep them away. We're getting these 8,900-person crowds in a building that seats

8,400 and we have to turn people away. It's been amazing to see that develop and this market latch on. This Phantoms team is giving this whole community our identity.

"It's more than just a hockey team. It's a venue and [it's] bringing 8,000 people every night for a hockey game on a weekend night to a downtown that was a lot more desolate and deserted on a regular weekend night before this."

CHAPTER THIRTEEN

THE CALDER CUP

It's June and the finale of the 2014–15 AHL season is under way, with the Calder Cup matchup featuring one team that is relatively new to its city against another that is playing its last games for its town.

The Comets arrived in Utica in 2013, and they are the city's first AHL franchise since a 21-year-old Martin Brodeur played goal for the Utica Devils in 1992–93. A year later, the town wants to prove that it belongs back in the American League.

It's been a special year in "the Aud," a 3,815-seat venue with a cable roof that evokes the "The World's Most Famous Arena," Madison Square Garden. The venue hosted the AHL's All-Star Game here in January — back when temperatures were just 20 degrees. The snow outside the Aud has long since melted away, and so have 28 other AHL teams' Calder Cup hopes. And while the Calder Cup playoffs are played on a smaller stage than the NHL's postseason, it's not small for the fans and players involved.

The Monarchs are looking for Manchester's first AHL hockey title since the team entered the league in 2001 — but these are the last games of the franchise in New Hampshire, as the team is slated to move to Ontario, California next season.

Calder Cup tickets are a hot item in a city that has taken to the Comets, as after selling out 26 of 38 home games during the regular season, fans camped out to buy tickets for the finals, with all three games selling out in just over two hours.

And the locals are loud, much to the appreciation of Comets coach Travis Green. "This is a great place to play," said Green. "We've got amazing fans — in our minds the best in the league — and they give our guys a lot of energy. It's a good place to play."

Utica's Nicklas Jensen said the crowd gives the Comets a boost. "We're playing at home in front [of] the best fans in the league. It's easy to get ready for these games and we know how important it is."

Manchester coach Mike Stothers said he knew how the atmosphere would be a boost for the home team. "A few of us had the luxury of being here during the All-Star Game and they were that loud at the skills competition, and following it up with the same kind of boisterous [atmosphere] in the game. So we knew [what] to expect."

The Comets and Monarchs are battling for a two-foot-tall, 35-pound, solid silver trophy on a two-tiered Brazilian mahogany base that was first awarded in 1938 — a year after the Syracuse Stars won the International-American Hockey League's first title in 1937. The actual silver cup is a foot tall, while the wood base that carries plaques with the roster of each of the last 20 Calder Cup champions is another foot high.

It doesn't have the mystique of the Stanley Cup, but for many players, it may be the only hardware they win — even if they go on to have successful NHL careers. Some of the biggest names in the NHL today have been able to hoist the Calder Cup in recent years, including Carey Price, Patrick Sharp, Tyler Johnson, Mike Green and Ondrej Pavelec. For veterans who have spent most of their time in the AHL, it can be the ultimate challenge of their career.

While the Stanley Cup requires a bit of luck, skill and good health to win, the Calder Cup may require even more good fortune, with the dynamic of the Stanley Cup bringing in an added factor. A good team in the regular season could be broken apart if the parent club goes on a playoff run, robbing the AHL team of its best players at the crucial part of its season. Or a team might get a sudden influx of talent when the parent club gets eliminated, changing a playoff series, even in mid-stream.

Thanks to the Stanley Cup playoff factor, the best AHL teams don't always reach the finals. While Manchester and Utica were able to do that rare feat in 2015, it was the first time since 2000 the two conference's top seeds met for the hardware.

The challenge to win a Calder Cup is no less grueling for players and coaches, and for those who are able to win one, it is a highlight of a hockey career.

Barry Trotz has been an NHL coach for nearly two decades, but when asked about his Calder Cup championship in 1994, a big smile crosses his face. "It was pretty special in Portland — that was our first year. They went from the Maine Mainers and we came up from Baltimore and became the Portland Pirates — and we broke a lot of ground. We went on to win the Calder Cup. I'll always remember that till the day I die. . . . The different series, the different players you had to go through. And the way the smaller communities like a Portland, Maine, embrace a Calder Cup championship. We had a ticker tape parade.

"I said, 'They're having a parade; I don't know how many people are going to show up — it's not big place.' We came around the corner and it looked like New York City. There were so many people, cars could barely get through the line on Main Street. There were papers coming down from the buildings and it was unbelievable. I don't think there's anything that can replace . . . the purity of winning in the minor leagues, I don't know if that can be replaced. Winning the Stanley Cup is the ultimate — but the purity of winning in the minors, I don't think that can be duplicated. It's guys living the hard life, doing something great in smaller, blue-collar towns. It's not New York City, it's Albany or Utica or Baltimore. I think there's a lot of purity to that."

When Trotz went to a reunion for the Pirates' title team in 2014, he said it was like the clock had turned back to their Portland days. "It was funny. When I got there, 20 years later we aren't as fit, and I don't have any hair anymore and stuff like that and we all looked different. But it all felt like we were apart for only a couple weeks or a month."

AHL president Dave Andrews won the trophy as the general manager of the Cape Breton Oilers back in 1993. He compared it to being part of Edmonton's last Stanley Cup celebration in 1990. "I was fortunate to be with the Oilers for a couple of Stanley Cups — on the periphery as being the general manager of the American League team, but I was there. I remember being in a limo with [Edmonton general manager] Glen Sather in Boston after we won in 1990, and it was probably two in the morning at the team party and I thought it was time to head back to the hotel — when the general manager heads back, it's a good time to head back.

"So I hopped in a car with Glen, and he said, 'So what do you think? Pretty great, huh?' I said, 'I'd never dreamed I'd be around it.' I said, 'There'd be only one thing better.' He said, 'I know what it is.' He said, 'It's to win for yourself in the American League.' I said, 'Yeah, you're right.'

"He was there when we did win in 1993 and he was at the game sitting with me, and the clock was counting down and it was out of reach in the first period, and he says, 'What you doing here?' I said, 'Watching.' He said, 'No, you've waited a long time for this.' We had a lot of long painful years before we got there, and weren't expected to win it either, so to win it was very exciting.

"It was terrific. I kept in touch with a lot guys from that team and George Burnett, our coach, and we had a heck of a good run. We did it in a place that it meant so much, like Sydney, Nova Scotia, a place with high unemployment and not an inferiority complex, but a tough place for people to live. They always feel like they're badly treated by the federal government of Canada or the city of Halifax — they're the poor cousin.

"For those fans, it was a big deal, and we probably sold our building for five years before we won, and it was really special winning it there. It was very cool."

J.P. Côté, a veteran defenseman who won the Calder Cup with Hamilton in 2007 and Norfolk in 2012, said those two wins are the highlights of his career. "It's not the Stanley Cup, it's not the most-wanted trophy in the world, but you go through the same things. You go through four rounds of just grinding and just the fact that everybody together elevates their game, game after game after game, and then you reach the final," he said. "I lost in the final once [in 2013 with Syracuse] and won in the final twice. You realize there's 28 teams sitting at home and 29 that won't be the winner, and you realize this is as good as any trophy. I've never won the Stanley Cup, but just the fact you're working to that goal, the camaraderie that surrounds it, to me, that is an achievement that I'm most proud of."

Chris Bourque won three Calder Cups with Hershey in 2006, 2009 and again in 2010. "It's great. It's the best thing that can happen if you're a player in the AHL, winning a Calder Cup," he said. "To win three of them is something really special and something I'll remember for the rest of my life, and probably the best memories I have in hockey. It's a hard thing to do; it's not easy, but once you get it done, it's really special."

Mike Angelidis, who won the 2012 Calder Cup with the Admirals, relishes the memory of raising the trophy overhead as Norfolk's captain. "It was unbelievable. It was like a dream, the way we won," he recalled. "You win the Calder Cup, and get to see all the past players that won it and have gone on to the NHL, and great AHL players that played. It's something special. You can feel the history in it. It's something I'm excited to tell my kids about and my grandkids about. It's an honor to win it — and it's a special honor to win it as a captain and get to hoist it."

Graham Mink won the Calder Cup twice with Hershey, in 2006 and 2009, and when he looks back over his hockey career, the championship was the high point. "Winning a Calder Cup — obviously winning a Stanley Cup is the ultimate — but from a Calder Cup perspective, I couldn't have been any more excited to win that than anything else. It's extremely hard to win, the grind you're going through is the same. It's [the] same long season as an NHL team, same playoff structure — but you're not flying private jets and having catered meals all the time, too.

"It's a very long season, and kind of a war of attrition, so to come out on top is a tremendous feeling. It was an honor. I was privileged to be on the two teams that did win Calder Cups, and certainly my best years in hockey, I'll always look back at that, it was a great time.

"You don't win it and think, 'Oh, it's just the Calder Cup.' It's a tremendously hard thing to do and very gratifying win when you do win it."

Wendell Young has a unique perspective of the Calder Cup, having won North America's four major hockey championship trophies, winning a Calder in Hershey in 1987–88, along with the Stanley Cup, CHL's Memorial Cup and IHL's Turner Cup.

"It was huge, it was the pro cup I was part of, especially in Hershey way back in 1987–88; I don't know if I can remember that far back," he said with a laugh. "It was special, and I grew up in Halifax watching the Nova Scotia Voyageurs back in their heyday when they won the Calder Cup four out of five years, and I had those heroes growing up. I watched practices and all that. To be part of that, I never thought I'd be able to play in a league that high, and [to] get to play in it was quite special."

For all the glory that goes to the winner, there is the other side, the team that falls just short of their goal. Colton Gillies was a player on the other side of the handshake line, reaching the 2011 Calder Cup Finals with the Houston Aeros in a series they lost to Binghamton — a loss that still stung years later.

"You form a bond with everyone, and I know I was fortunate to go to the Calder Cup Finals my last year in Houston. I got called up [to the NHL] toward the end of the season, but for me, I was looking toward the [Calder Cup] playoffs. That's what we were there for. We wanted to win, and unfortunately, we lost to Binghamton."

Asked how important winning the Calder Cup was to him, Gillies spoke of how much he wanted another shot at the championship. "It honestly is a great accomplishment. A lot of people don't really hear about the Calder Cup. It's a hard thing to win, too; it's the same layout as the NHL. You really have to battle, and at the same time, that's the best part of the season," he said. "Honestly, I wish if I could go back in time and put more of me into that series we lost, I would, but I'm hoping someday I could get back there to play."

Martin Biron vividly remembers Rochester's run to the Calder Cup Finals in 1999, and although they lost to Providence, that spring was memorable for him. "Buffalo beat Boston in the first round of the playoffs, so [Providence] got all their guys back. For us, Buffalo was still in the playoffs, so we played [the Bruins] and they were really good. They beat us in five. Game 3 was a three-overtime game, and Game 4 we ended up winning, and then went to Providence to lose. But the whole playoffs from the beginning, we beat Adirondack, we beat Hamilton, we beat Philly . . . Domenic Pittis scored a goal in Game 5 at home against Philadelphia to go up 3–2 — he basically kicked it in the net with his skate — but with no video replay and the referees pointing at the net.

"Brian McCutcheon was telling everybody to go to the showers — 'Don't celebrate. Go get your gear off in the locker room,' — because he didn't want to . . . have to get guys back out there to play. We were down 2–0 in the series but came back to take a 3–2 lead. And they allowed the goal. And we ended up winning Game 6 in Philly to go to the Finals."

The Calder Cup isn't just a pinnacle for the players to play in, however. It's also a special moment for the broadcasters and employees who work a long season with their teams — sometimes waiting years for a taste of a championship.

Don Stevens, the "Voice of the Amerks" warmly recalls Rochester's 1986–87 Calder Cup title. "It's one of those things that you don't realize exactly what's going on until it's over and you have a few days for it to sink in. I remember my first year here, we won the championship, and won it in very dramatic fashion. We won the regular-season conference championship on the last night of the season in a shootout in Binghamton. That was absolutely huge. We couldn't get to our building with fans lining up across the bridge and couldn't get the bus through. Then, we ended up winning the championship in Game 7 in Sherbrooke, and we got home at 3:30 or 4:00 in the morning. It was cold out and we landed our charter at the airport and there were four to five thousand people just waiting for us," said Stevens.

"Two days later — I call it my best birthday present ever — we had the championship party at Blue Cross Arena and probably 10,000 or 11,000 in the building for that, then the parade earlier that day, the streets were lined with people. It was absolutely fabulous. I don't know if you can ever have a better feeling than that. Obviously, it's not to the scale of winning the Stanley Cup or NBA championship or Super Bowl or anything like that, but in Rochester it was huge."

Todd Crocker fondly recalled Hamilton's 2007 Calder Cup title, and a future Hart Trophy winner's first professional championship. "Stunning," he said with a smile. "I remember that first round against Rochester, Hamilton had just lost Jaroslav Halak to the Canadiens, and then they put in this kid Carey Price. Fans were livid about it — they were like 'Jaroslav Halak was our one chance to get to the Calder Cup' — and then they let him go to the World Championship. It was bizarre. I remember going to the first round and thinking they weren't going to get by Rochester. And they did. You start to believe a little bit, but then you realize they're going to face Manitoba next. Manitoba was a good team — and that battle was more impressive than any other that took place.

"They faced Chicago after that, and that's when you started to believe in this kid Carey Price. He was going to carry them the whole way, and they made sure they gave him a chance to win every night, and when they got to the finals, that was the first time playing Hershey, and I was calling TV games at that point. That was the first point I said to myself, 'Hershey hasn't got a chance.' This team is the team of destiny here. Price is great, they have Ajay Baines, who was an amazing leader. When they won the Calder Cup, it was the highlight of my career to call that win in my hometown."

John Walton called the AHL's most recent dynasty in Hershey, with the Bears claiming three Calder Cups. To him, each holds a different memory. "It's like trying to pick between your favorite kids, probably. There really isn't one. In 2006, we had missed the playoffs altogether [the year before] — the first four years that I was in Hershey we didn't get out of the first round in the postseason. . . . I'd never won a playoff series. The demise of the [Colorado] affiliation, we had nine player tryouts at the end of their last year there. And here comes Washington, and they hadn't done anything in the postseason either [with Portland], but they had a lot of first-round picks, and there was hope. We needed a coach, and there's this guy [Bruce Boudreau] who won a lot of games, but he didn't get out of the first round either, but he came to Hershey and it was just a magical experience. To have a team that surged in the second half of the season — we didn't win the division, we finished second — but to get in the postseason and win 10 straight games in the playoffs.

"Norfolk four straight, Wilkes-Barre four straight, then against Portland, in the best series of hockey I have ever seen — Washington-Boston [in 2012] would be close for me now, the way we won in a 2 vs. 7 and had little business doing it the way we did it — but to be able to go seven games [against the Pirates], and see on the eve of Game 7, Corey Perry, Ryan Getzlaf and Dustin Penner all assigned [to Portland] when we had a 3–1 lead and lost two in a row. 'How the hell are we going to win this thing now?' And we did.

"Eric Fehr and I in Hershey, maybe not so much in Washington, but in Hershey, Fehrsie and I will be tied together forever, because I screamed my head off and the building went nuts [for Fehr's Game 7 overtime winner]. That call has been replayed on YouTube I don't know how many times."

After losing in the 2007 finals to Hamilton and getting knocked out in the first round in 2007–08, the Bears returned back to the AHL's pinnacle with a vengeance in 2008–09.

"We were a machine." said Walton. "Bruce had been gone for a year, it was Bob Woods's first year coaching, we won 49 games; it was just a solid year. Two of the best teams in the league met that year, Manitoba and Hershey. It was a great series and the Bears won."

The next year, Hershey repeated as Calder Cup champions, and did something a Bears team hadn't done since 1980 — hoisted the trophy at home, rallying from 2–0 down to beat the Texas Stars.

"To me, maybe most special [was 2010], to be able to see the reaction of the people I'd been around eight years. I had one more year in Hershey before I came to Washington." said Walton. "Winning it at home, the only time we did, and the first time in 30 years that had happened, the moment that I remember — more than the clock hitting zero, because I'd seen that before — but with the one minute to go, our public address announcer Don Scott: 'one minute, one minute remaining in the period.' But the volume, it was incredible.

"It was the loudest building I've ever heard, and just was this release. Even when the clock hit zero, it was more . . . a sigh than it was a cheer, with the one minute to go, it was going to happen, and it's going to happen in this building. I opened Giant Center, and when people moved in [we] said it wasn't the old place until you win a Cup in the new place. We did, and that was some unfinished business out the door."

And for Walton, as the Bears celebrated on the ice below in front of their fans, came a special memory. "My son got to lift the Calder Cup in my place when we won at home in 2010, which was the greatest moment in hockey to me in my life, to be able to watch that. I had tears coming out of my eyes for 30 seconds just watching it."

Ken Young, who owned the Norfolk's 2012 title team, vividly remembers how the clock wound down on the decisive Game 4 at Toronto's Ricoh Coliseum. "The game in that last 15 minutes wasn't that close — it's not that there was a huge amount of anxiety, but there was a huge amount of pride, and the fact is, Jon Cooper had prepared that team so well, so as an owner of the franchise . . . you say, 'This is what we play for.'"

He also recalled how special it was to win the Cup in the hockey-mad city. "If you couldn't win back in Norfolk, Toronto [was] the next best place to win, because their fans are so, so knowledgeable of the game, and that was a lot of fun. We ended up taking the players out after the championship, and there were so many Toronto fans ended up in the same pub we were in and wanted to drink from the Cup, and talking to them and that was a thrill too."

Even though he sold the AHL's Admirals in 2015, Young said he still wears his former team's Calder Cup ring. "It's a memory of very good times," he said.

Sometimes the journey is just as special for those along for the ride. For Dan D'Uva, who called the 2013 Crunch team that reached the Calder Cup Finals, just seeing the team rallying from a 3–0 deficit to force a Game 6 with the Griffins back at home was a special moment.

"We played the first two games here and lost first two here, and we get on two sleeper buses out to Grand Rapids. We would have flown but the timing was wrong, and it was too tight. Detroit loaned the Griffins their private jet. We did not have that luxury. We had two sleeper buses and we're down two games to none. We'd only lost one game the entire postseason, and then we lost two in a row. We get on the sleeper buses, get out there, lose Game 3 and are down 3–0, and thinking, 'Oh my God.' But you know what, we come back, and won Game 4 to force Game 5, and forced Game 6 back here," said D'Uva.

"First of all, after Game 5, when they had won, I never before had wanted to get from the press box to the locker room as quickly as after that game. It was so fun to be a part of that team and go into that building and shut up 11,000 fans who were expecting the Calder Cup to be given out that night and forced a game in Syracuse. Getting on the bus after that experience, the jubilation, the excitement. It wasn't a celebration, but it was like, 'Here we go.' That intensity and that fervor for winning and for the game, the camaraderie was awesome. Then you've got that long ride knowing the next game would be in Syracuse. And we also know, in the world of minor league hockey, the broadcaster has a lot of other things to do, so I hardly slept on the way back. I tried to get a nap here and there but I was getting emails and text messages from the booster club, from the local media, from our staff: When could we do an interview? When is the bus going to arrive? When are tickets going on sale?

"Well, as it turned out, we . . . timed almost perfectly the arrival of buses. The booster club we had a couple hundred people outside at seven o'clock in the morning to welcome the team back, and tickets went on sale immediately. So after calling the Game 5 in Grand Rapids, the bus ride, handling the press and the fans that were here, I came up to my desk where the phone banks lit up, and I answered phones and people buying tickets for Game 6.

"I didn't go home until about 7:30 p.m. I was in the office, answering phones, with people buying tickets all day. All day. The capacity is 6,399. We sold standing room only for that game. While it was draining, and I was exhausted from broadcasting the game, updating game notes, chaos and everything, it was exhilarating."

While the Calder Cup doesn't quite have the "Keeper of the Cup" like the NHL does — the trophy can sometimes be found in a car trunk — some traditions of its more famous counterpart are alive and well in the AHL. Like the Stanley Cup, champions can have their day with the Calder Cup, although unlike the NHL, it's a little more low-key. There are no "keepers" along for the ride.

Former Hershey general manager Doug Yingst explained the protocol when they had won the trophy. "We keep the Calder Cup in the office for a couple weeks, and we FedEx it with the players back to their homes and where they live, and share it with all the sponsors. It's at our convenience, so we get plenty of time with it." Players can get their turn with the trophy, and usually put it to good use when it's in their possession for a day.

Mike Angelidis remembered his day with the Calder Cup fondly. "I had a big ball hockey tournament with all my family and my relatives, and all the kids came out. It was just special. I shared it with my family and everyone there. When you get it, you don't really know what to do with it at first, but just sharing it with your close family and friends is something special."

Eric Neilson took the trophy around his native New Brunswick. "I had 24 hours with it; it got to my house at 8:30 in the morning. So I had breakfast with it, sat it down, talked to it, cleaned it up a bit, the fellow before me — I'm not sure who it was and I'm not going to name any names — he had some fun with it, so I cleaned it up," he said with a laugh. "I took it to the gym, did a little workout with the Calder Cup. I actually made a video with it, so you'll be able to see it on YouTube. The first-ever Calder Cup workout, I knew we were going to have a big day. I took it to a radio station, and took it where disabled kids go for rehab. There's a kid back home who a couple of years prior went into the boards and was paralyzed, so he's in a wheelchair doing his rehab close to home. I had just met him, he's a hockey player and a hockey fan, so we ate ice cream out of the Calder Cup, and hung out with it a little bit.

"Then I took it home, had a little road hockey match for the Calder Cup with my buddies that I grew up with and then from there we had a little shindig back at my parents', a lot of friends and family came over. We had a good time with it there, and then took it to downtown Fredericton — Freddy Beach — and we'll leave it at that," he said with a laugh.

The players also get a souvenir that's a little more permanent than a day with the Cup; the teams issue championship rings to commemorate the title run. While they aren't quite as diamond-studded as a Stanley Cup ring, that doesn't mean it wasn't just as well-earned over a long season and grueling playoff run.

"I think every player is different, but [Steve Oleksy and Andrew Gordon] have a compete mode for the sport, and are huge, huge competitors. In many cases, the Calder Cup is their Stanley Cup. They're playing for a ring. The rings we give out for the Hershey Bears are outstanding, so to win a championship at every level . . . You have 30 teams, one winner," said Yingst. "It's not the NHL, but it's close, and it means a lot to them, and to everybody."

Back in Utica, while the Comets — down 2–0 in the series — were able to grab Game 3 to give the white-clad fans a reason to cheer, the Monarchs took Game 4 and were in position to lift the Cup with a 2–0 lead late in Game 5.

Comet fans did get to celebrate one last goal for the season to make it 2–1 with just 14.3 seconds left. But then the Monarchs got a key faceoff late after an icing with 6.5 seconds left, clearing the puck down to the Comets' end before the home team could touch it. With the buzzer came a joyous rush of black-clad Monarchs off the bench to celebrate the team's first-ever AHL title and becoming the first since 1982 to win a title in the franchise's last game of existence.

Gloves and sticks went flying through the air as the Monarchs celebrated en masse behind their own goal in front of the Aud's stage area, celebrating a year's worth of work culminating in the historic silver trophy. Utica fans chanted, "Let's Go Comets," "U-TI-CA," and "Thank You Comets," for the season that came up just short, but also gave their appreciation to the Monarchs for reaching the pinnacle of the league.

The two teams took part in the traditional handshake line, culminating two months' worth of extra work, and capping nine months of play since the two teams reported to training camp in British Columbia and California in September before being sent east to play their AHL seasons.

The Comets saluted their fans and headed back to their dressing room for the season, while Andrews presented the trophy for Most Valuable Player of the playoffs to Jordan Weal and then gave Monarchs captain Vincent LoVerde the Calder Cup.

After posing for a photo with the Cup, he carried it over to his waiting teammates, then showed it to the crowd, and one by one, he began a procession of teammates passing it on to other teammates to take a skate around the ice. Andrew Bodnarchuk, Josh Gratton, Sean Backman, Brian O'Neill, then David Van Der Gulik all took their turns going down the ice with the Cup aloft. Jeff Schultz — who won the Stanley Cup as a King the year before — carried the trophy for a quick spin, then handed it to Paul Bissonnette.

For Ken Cail, who called the entire history of the Monarchs' AHL franchise, the Calder Cup–clinching game — which was his last for the AHL club — was bittersweet and emotional. "The evening was great, and it was very, very emotional for those few who had been with the team since day one," said Cail. "It was the culmination of the 14 years of a terrific franchise in the American Hockey League. I had difficulty making it through the end of my broadcast, reflecting on those years from when I was first hired, the people that I'd worked with in the booth, and the team, so it was [a] very emotional broadcast, but I did manage, somehow."

Unlike the Stanley Cup champs who hop on a charter home with the trophy, the Monarchs took buses back home with the hardware in tow, arriving in New Hampshire early the next morning.

Just days after the Cup was hoisted, Cail recounted what the trip home was like. "We had two buses going to Utica and coming back. What happened on the ride back, I was on the bus with the staff and coaching staff, trainer, equipment guys, a few media guys that the Kings sent out, as well and our PR guy. We were one bus — which was a relatively quiet bus. The other bus was where all the fun was. I know the guys had an amazing five-and-a-half-hour ride back from

The Manchester Monarchs won the 2015 Calder Cup championship, taking the trophy back to New Hampshire to celebrate with their fans before the franchise officially relocated to Ontario, California, in the summer of 2015. (AMERICAN HOCKEY LEAGUE)

Utica, just judging by the way they looked when they got off the bus in Manchester at 5:30 in the morning on Sunday. I know their bus trip was more spirited than ours was. And it looked that way," he said with a laugh.

"I know they had a great time, and [they're] a terrific bunch of guys and worked hard from day one in training camp and never let up to make this a possibility. It was very resilient, very few stretches where we went without a victory. They had the best regular season record, they had home ice advantage throughout the playoffs and we didn't have that many long-term injuries at all. And we only had one major call-up to the Kings, and that was Nick Shore, who was our leading goal scorer at the time, and he stayed with the Kings till the end of their season. They sent [him] down to us after their season was over, he stepped in and didn't miss a beat.

"We were fortunate in that way; we were not ravaged by call-ups, or by injuries. You have to have those things working for you if you expect to win a championship."

Since the team wouldn't play another game before heading to

California, the Calder Cup banner was raised at Verizon Wireless Arena before breaking up for the summer.

"There had been some question to where the banner would be hanging, in Manchester or Ontario, California, but I think the Monarchs made it clear that banner is going to stay in Manchester, where I think it should stay," said Cail. "Most of the players were on hand, having a great time, and a lot of interaction between the fans and the players. I had a chance to emcee it and got to talk about each player individually a little bit, and then they showed an 18-minute video, and there were a lot of oohs and aahs during the video, so it was just a spectacular night, and don't think the fans ever wanted to come to an end."

According to Cail, the 2014–15 Calder Cup was another important accomplishment for the Los Angeles Kings, who had won a pair of Stanley Cups in 2011–12 and 2013–14. "It really just shows what kind of organization [Kings general manager] Dean Lombardi has put together with the Kings. I hear from other people that their parent club and the AHL club don't always hit it off. I've never experienced that. The Kings and all of their organizational coaches, and Dean and Rob Blake, you wouldn't believe how many times they see them in person. They're actively involved in watching their prospects first-hand, and as are the organizational coaches. . . . I think it was a great rapport with the Los Angeles Kings and the Manchester Monarchs that trickled down to the players.

"The first Stanley Cup for the Kings, there were 13 former Monarchs on that team, and the last one, there were 14 former Monarchs on that team. It tells you how well the Kings have drafted since Dean Lombardi took over, and they have made a tremendously deep organization."

For Andrews, who as AHL president is the person who stands at center ice with the Calder Cup champion at the end of each season, it's always a thrill to hand out the Cup. "It's great. It's way more fun if the home team wins, and we haven't had that in a while," he said with a laugh. "I've had a lot of fond memories handing it out. I remember Philadelphia when they won it in the big building against the Wolves in the lockout year [in 2005], great players on both sides, really good games. It was a sweep, but every game was a really good game, and it was the fourth-largest crowd to see a game in Philadelphia at that game. It was fantastic.

"Finally handing out in Hershey [in 2010], they had won three times on the road when I was the president and we handed it out; there had been an awful lot of road presentations, which aren't really quite as much fun. The Wolves won it at home [in 2008], and that was cool as well.

"It is fun when the home team wins, just because the atmosphere is electric."

CHAPTER FOURTEEN

ROCHESTER AMERICANS

Rolling westbound on the New York State Thruway, past the Finger Lakes and travel plazas featuring Roy Rogers and Dunkin' Donuts, you get off at Exit 45 and pass through the toll booths and then head onto Interstate 490. From there, you drive by Rochester's affluent suburbs of Victor, Pittsford and Brighton, cross the Erie Canal and pass St. John Fisher College, the training camp site of the Buffalo Bills. The wooded suburban landscape then turns into concrete barriers and overpasses as you approach the downtown core. Cross the city line and at Exit 16, you take the exit for Clinton Avenue and Downtown.

As you make the curve, you see Rochester's skyline, and as the expressway ends, you see an elaborate green iron sign above the roadway proclaiming "WELCOME TO ROCHESTER CENTER CITY" in white and gold letters. With the Xerox building on your right, you make a left onto Court Street, pass the popular Dinosaur Bar-B-Que and then cross over the Genesee River. Just off the banks of the river is the red brick of the Blue Cross Arena, home of the Americans.

The Amerks have played in this building since they came into the AHL in 1956 — predating their current NHL affiliate, the Buffalo

Sabres, by 16 years. When the Amerks first entered the league, their rivals were the old Buffalo Bisons. The Rochester team, celebrating its 60th season in 2015–16, has won six Calder Cups and is a winter sports staple in this Western New York city.

This part of the Empire State is pretty much known for both its harsh winters and its passionate sports fans, revolving mostly around the Bills and Sabres, and while Buffalo is an hour down the Thruway, those two teams are the de facto choice for the top level of professional sports in town.

The Rochester Americans were able to capitalize on that connection for years as the Sabres' top affiliate, and hockey became a way of life during the snowy, windy winters just off the shore of Lake Ontario. But while the Amerks enjoyed a high profile in town, some missteps involving an expansion of their sports empire cost them their relationship with Buffalo, temporarily. The team went through a dark period and the league was concerned for the future viability of the Amerks. Only once the two teams reconnected was Rochester able to get back on its feet.

Past the brick and white concrete back of the Blue Cross Arena on the river, the main glass entrance features a large image of "Mr. Amerk," Jody Gage, who joined Rochester in 1985 as a player, winning four Calder Cups before retiring in 1996 to become the team's general manager.

The arena was renovated in 1998 and has a 10,669-seat capacity for hockey, with a two-tiered deck of blue seats. It still has an old-school feel. Behind one goal there is an unusual setup; there is a stage beneath the long string of red banners commemorating the building's hockey history, and the deck breaks into a small lower deck and upper deck. The Blue Cross has a video board hanging over the far blue line — old-time scoreboards behind each goal are a bit of a throwback to arenas, such as Boston Garden, that had the basic time and score that fans now would be more accustomed to seeing at their community rink.

The history of hockey in Rochester is a big part of the experience, as this building, the former Rochester War Memorial, was where legends such as Johnny Bower, Gerry Cheevers, Don Cherry and Al Arbour all skated wearing the classic red-white-and-blue sweaters.

When you ask Gage what makes Rochester a special place to play, the answer is easy — the city's long hockey history, with an all-time hockey great scoring in the building's first game between the Canadiens and Bisons in November 1955. "It's got a great tradition, a great history; it's the second-oldest franchise, behind Hershey. It's got a great fan base and it goes back to the old days. The first game ever played here was the Montreal Canadiens with Rocket Richard, and he got four goals in the first game that was ever played in this building. The first franchise here was a combination of Montreal Canadiens and Toronto Maple Leafs. I know in the Calder Cup years they beat the Toronto Maple Leafs in an exhibition game."

Starting in 1959, the Amerks were Toronto's affiliate. The Leafs won four Stanley Cups in the 1960s (there were only six NHL teams until 1967). According to Gage, the Maple Leafs' farmhands were among the best teams in North America.

"The Rochester Americans were the fourth-best team in pro hockey back then because they had the Toronto Maple Leafs prospects and great teams in [the] 1960s. A reason I know a little bit about the Rochester Americans is they were my dad's favorite team growing up, because they were the Toronto Maple Leafs' team, and he used to follow the Americans games on the radio with Bronco Horvath, Dick Gamble, Al Arbour, Don Cherry, and all those great players who are now in the Hockey Hall of Fame [who] were here," he said. "It was almost like that hockey was like the NHL today."

When the NHL put a team 76 miles west in Buffalo in 1970, hockey in the area took a regional feel, especially in 1979 when the Knox family — owners of the Sabres — purchased the Amerks.

"It goes back to the first year of the affiliation in 1979–80; they won a Cup in 1982–1983 and we won it 1985–86. I think that team that won in 1985–86 had six or seven young kids who played in Buffalo," said Gage. "There's been a great tradition of the development of players here — not just in the 1990s — because everyone talks about the Jason Pominvilles, the Ryan Millers who developed here by a great system and great coaches. There's a great family thing here and we tried to bring players here like [Randy Cunneyworth] and Doug [Houda] before they got into coaching. They knew their responsibility was to be depth for Buffalo but also be veterans and help develop players in a winning environment. . . . It gives our fans someone to relate to when you bring up a player like that."

Every year, the Amerks and Sabres try to find a way to both develop players for the NHL and have an AHL team that can win games, Gage said. "I remember [talking with former Sabres GM] Darcy Regier, we like to say it's a two-part question in the American Hockey League — how do you develop players in a winning environment? That takes care of the NHL partner, but it also takes care of part of our market, the fans?"

Given the team's storied history, it's a fun place to coach, said Chadd Cassidy, who coached the Amerks. But there is also more pressure than some other AHL stops. "It's an honor to coach here because of the history and tradition of Rochester and the American League, one of the oldest franchises, and all the great coaches and players that have gone through this city and won so many Calder Cups. But there's a lot of pressure too, because people expect you to win," said Cassidy. "Now there's 30 teams in the league and people commit more to winning at this level, and the playing field has evened out with the veteran rules, and there are high expectations."

According to Gage, there is a strong connection between Buffalo and Rochester, and part of the allure of the Amerks has been their affiliation with the team down the Thruway. There is a rivalry but also a great sense of loyalty. "Let's face it. I think Buffalo-Rochester-Syracuse, we're all upstate, and I'm putting it a way that makes sense, we're very competitive when it comes to the cities. We can pick on Syracuse and Buffalo people, and vice versa, but no one else can. It's a close bond, and the great thing about it is the fans do go to Buffalo for the Bills and the Sabres, and the Pegulas have really have come in and saved upstate New York with the buying the Bills, the Sabres and the Amerks and putting a lot of money in the thing.

"I want to say a brother-sisterly thing where our fans love the fact when a Ryan Miller goes up to the National Hockey League and [get] to see him here, and they still can follow him. They like following them when they're in Buffalo, but not necessarily somewhere else," he said with a laugh. "It's strange, the best way to say [it is] it's a brotherly thing, because my son plays youth hockey and I'll help coach, and we play a Buffalo or Syracuse thing, it's a rivalry. It's a battle. But no one else can say bad stuff about upstate New York. If anyone else says something bad about Buffalo, we'll be the first ones to defend them and vice versa.

"It's great our fans can go down the street to watch their players, but a majority of our fans are Sabres fans — they don't sometimes like it when they bring our players up, because they're Amerk fans, but they understand it, and they're very, very educated. It's also nice that Buffalo fans, when the Sabres aren't playing, they can come down and watch some of the prospects. It's that close, and that's why it works."

Don Stevens recalled that when he first arrived in town in 1986, the Amerks were the thing to do in town. "When I first came here, Seymour Knox the fourth, the son of [Sabres and Amerks] owner Seymour Knox the third, picked me up at the airport. 'You'll love it in Rochester, and it's the social event of the community.' And that's what it was. That's what you did. Wednesday, Friday, Sunday it was Amerks hockey. That's what you did in this community."

Kevin Oklobzija, who covers the team for the *Rochester Democrat & Chronicle*, remembered the team's Calder Cup runs in 1987 and 1996 vividly. "[In 1987,] they had a great rivalry with Binghamton. They played a six-game series with them and then played Sherbrooke in the final. And won it on the road. They get back at probably three in the morning on a charter flight from Sherbrooke, and depending on who you talk to, as the years go on, the crowd gets larger and larger. But there had to be 1,000 people at the charter airport terminal when the players walked off the plane. The little terminal at the side of the airport, there were people everywhere welcoming the team home.

"[In 1996,] I remember Rochester won in Game 5 in overtime on a Scotty Nichol breakaway goal to go up 3–2, that was a Monday and Game 6 was a Wednesday. The next morning on Tuesday, the box office opened and the line was out the door, up the street and across the bridge to the library.

"Portland blew them out, 5–1 in Game 6. That same thing on Thursday morning — Game 7 was on a Friday — but the line was even longer. You would have thought it was the Stanley Cup Finals.

"The building was smaller, but a smaller building with 7,300 people screaming, it was as loud and crazy an atmosphere as I've ever witnessed — the noise and the excitement and craziness and anticipation, and no one is sitting down for the entire third period, it was tough to hear anything."

He also remembered the enthusiasm carried over to the road. "In 1993, they knocked off Binghamton in the semifinals. Rochester fans in Binghamton, after Game 7, they carried Olie Kolzig out of the arena on their shoulders out to the bus. In the visiting rink. That's how nuts the fans were."

However, bad financial decisions by the club began to take a toll on the team's reputation in the 2000s. Under Steve Donner, the ownership group built a soccer stadium in Rochester, and looked to elevate the city's soccer team, the Rhinos, to Major League Soccer. Donner looked to acquire an indoor and outdoor lacrosse team, and built what became Sahlen's Stadium. But by extending his finances, he put the crown jewel of the city's sports scene in peril.

"We got into a bit of trouble. As an organization, we tried to expand with indoor and outdoor soccer, we had indoor and outdoor lacrosse, we had women's soccer, a rink complex, we built a soccer stadium and all sorts of things [were] going on and the organization became mired in quicksand and began to sink economically," said Stevens. "We totally ruined our reputation in town, and owed everybody money. People didn't want anything to do with the organization. As parts were sold off, things started to turn around and got better and better."

The Amerks' affiliation with the Sabres was one of the casualties. Buffalo decided to pair with Portland in 2008, and the Amerks affiliated with the Florida Panthers, a team that had shared the Amerks since 2005. It was an arrangement that didn't work well for either parent club or affiliate, according to Stevens.

"It should have never happened in the first place that the affiliation went anywhere. I don't know if it was a good thing in showing us all what it means to this community to have that close proximity to the Sabres, but the experiment with the Panthers — which we didn't want in the first place — the Rochester Americans didn't have anything to do upon that decision. It was forced upon us. It was just awful," said Stevens. "It did not work for us, it did not work for the Panthers. It was not a good marriage at all."

The situation was bad for the Americans: Buffalo was upset over Rochester's situation and Florida was in flux.

"Florida was in such disarray at the time. They were changing GMs at the time — they had four GMs during the time they were in Rochester. So just between no money in Florida as an organization and a scouting system and development program, that is never going to be good when the GM is always changing every year. There's no continuity there," Oklobzija recalled.

"They didn't have much for talent, they didn't have money to spend on prospects. They shared with Buffalo in the first three years — and Buffalo was mad at the ownership in Rochester, so they wanted to do nothing. And Florida didn't have enough input and they were willing to get a goalie or a player but Buffalo would only give them so many slots; they basically said no, we need our guy to play. It wasn't good."

Losing a connection with a Sabres team that had really captured the region's imagination with a pair of conference finals appearances in 2006 and 2007 in exchange for one that struggled to make the playoffs was hard for the Americans. Their new parent club carried little weight in this part of the country, especially compared to the Sabres. And after the marriage with Buffalo dissolved, enthusiasm for the team waned.

But the natural gas magnate who helped solve an uncertain ownership situation in Buffalo also stepped in to restore the partnership. Curt Styres, a self-made millionaire from Ontario, purchased the team in 2008 from Steve Donner for around $6.5 million, along with the National Lacrosse League's Rochester Knighthawks for $5.6 million, according to Oklobzija's research at the time.

Styres brought some stability back to the franchise that even had the AHL concerned. But being a lacrosse enthusiast and likely requiring a sale to restore the relationship with Buffalo, he sold the hockey team in 2011 to new Sabres owner Terry Pegula for an estimated $5 million. Pegula promptly spent $100,000 to break the Sabres' affiliation with the Portland Pirates three years early to restore the Buffalo-Rochester relationship.

Stevens said the sale was a big step forward for the franchise. "When [the Sabres] repurchased it, it really . . . helped advance Rochester and bring the hockey back. We're not to where we were, but we're climbing back. We led the league in attendance the first 10 years I was here. And we have a long way to get to that point."

AHL president Dave Andrews said the move allowed him to get some peace of mind now that one of the league's flagship franchises was secure again in Western New York. "I was thrilled when the Sabres contacted me and said they would have an interest again to make this work and move from Portland," he said. "Having the Sabres back in Rochester was crucial. That's a flagship franchise for us. It's so important in the community and the Sabres relationship had to be. To get that back on track — that was a big day for us to have Mr. Pegula, and his wife, Kim, is from there, so it's a good story. It's been much better; it's taken a little time but it's getting better and we're not worried about the future of the Rochester Americans any more. For many years, we were.

"We were lucky to have the guys step up and buy when they did. . . . Any time you have teams that are having financial difficulty we're pretty involved behind the scenes. We're pretty involved in trying to get out ahead and find solutions and deal with some of the issues. There were quite a few years where I was spending a lot more time dealing with Rochester than some of [the] other teams. The relationship between the Panthers and the ownership was bad. When the relationship goes bad, I've got both sides coming through me trying to deal with it. With 30 teams you're going to have two, three, four kinds of situations going on all the time. Put one fire out and go to the next one.

"Not everything we've done has been a success story. We've gone to some markets and failed and moved on. But Rochester's not one you can fail in. That requires attention because it's the Rochester Americans. To me, they're in the same breath with Hershey. You can't have the failure in Rochester. It's not what we do."

Graham Mink, who spent the 2009–10 season in Rochester during the Panthers' affiliation, recalled the city's fans, and how a good run could bring the team back toward its heyday. "I liked Rochester; we had a really good team there. We started out the year well. There's a lot of history there. [Styres] wanted to win. He purchased the team and put a lot of money into it and wanted to bring the team kind of back to where it was in its heyday. We started to do that and turn it around," said Mink.

"We didn't have the finish that we wanted to — we had some call-ups and some injuries take place — so it was kind of disappointing in that sense, but I enjoyed playing there as well. The fans there are very passionate. I think if they could have some sustained success they could get a lot of their fan base to come back."

Oklobzija said the fluid nature of AHL rosters makes it a tougher sell in Rochester than it used to be. While in the old days of the Amerks, fans could count on several players spending years with the team. Now, it's more of a short-term stay. "The way the league has changed, I almost look at the American League now as the International League of baseball. Guys are just here a very short time, and if they're not going to play in the NHL, the parent team usually doesn't bring them back. There's one or two guys — the veterans. When I got here in 1985, there were six or seven veteran guys who signed for Rochester. And while they may go up and play for Buffalo, they knew that wasn't their goal. They were there to play in Rochester; they signed with Rochester because they knew they wanted to be here and the team was going to win, and winning was a priority.

"While there may be opportunity in Buffalo, they also wanted to be in a place where hockey was important in the community and winning was important to the team. They were stars in town. I don't think that's the case anymore because largely people don't know who half of them are, because they aren't in town long enough to create an identity.

"It's a much tougher sell now. During the summer, with baseball, on a beautiful night in Rochester, people want to get out. If you don't have a good product on the ice in February, [it's] pretty tough to get people to leave the house in a lake effect snow event. I see a major change in that regard, and I don't know what brings it back. Not that people don't want to go to games — this is a big hockey area [considering] the number of guys who have gone to play pro hockey, the number of kids who play youth hockey and how big the Sabres are here. But the Amerks are not the team anymore, and for a long time they were."

Brian Gionta, who is one of the city's NHL products and now captains the Sabres, said he was a regular at games when he was growing up in Rochester. "I went all the time; you catch the Amerks or games up here [in Buffalo]," he said in his locker stall at First Niagara Center. "It's the team to follow. It's a great hockey city, a great hockey town. I think Western New York has a strong program and hockey roots — much like a Canadian city."

He also is happy the Sabres and Amerks are back together as affiliates. "The affiliation makes sense. It makes sense for the fans, all the way around. It was tough to see them be lost for a few years but [I'm] glad it's back."

David Leggio, who hails from the Buffalo suburb of Williamsville, recalled his time playing in Rochester fondly. "[All my AHL stops have] been great — but for me Rochester was really special, being close to home," he said with a smile. "I had a lot of friends and family see me all the time, and I honestly got a boost off of seeing friends and family there."

Martin Biron, who spent two full seasons in Rochester, said that the proximity of Buffalo had definite advantages. There was a strength and conditioning coach who was living in Buffalo and would come back and forth, and if players had equipment issues, Buffalo trainers could help with that, he said. Plus, Jim Corsi, a goalie coach who later became famous for being the namesake of one of hockey's advanced stats, would come down to Rochester and work with the team.

"Just the fact [that] on a Saturday night if we didn't have a game, we'd get in the car and go out to Buffalo and watch the game from the press box. The Sabres would make that available, and we did that a few times," said Biron. "All of that really helped really keep us in the loop."

During his tenure in Rochester, one of his teammates had the chance to play a unique double-header. On March 28, 1999, Domenic Pittis skated in both in an NHL and an AHL game on the same day. He was called up for an afternoon game in Buffalo against the Penguins, and then drove back to Rochester to play against Cincinnati that night.

"He was chasing the scoring title, played maybe seven minutes in Buffalo in the afternoon and in Rochester played the power plays, and in the third period played a regular shift," said Biron. "That was a real possibility because we were so close with just an hour driving, and you were there. That really helps."

During the Sabres' 1998 and 1999 Stanley Cup runs, Biron was a "Black Ace," one of the players called up for the extended season. In 1998, Biron and five other Americans got to experience Buffalo's improbable ride to the Eastern Conference Finals, where they fell to Washington in six games — three of them going to overtime.

"That was the year of the Olympics, and we lost in the first round of the playoffs against Philly, and we ended coming up right at the beginning of the playoffs in Buffalo. We were with them for the whole shebang against Philly, Montreal and Washington in the Conference Finals. That's when I think we did develop a different relationship with [Rochester coach] Brian McCutcheon. There were six of us in a room; we were on the ice on our own, not part of the regular morning skate, never part of the regular practices and we got to explore. We were together for six weeks. It was a lot of fun," he said. "We used to play 3-on-3 for an hour, work on our skills and see what the NHL was about."

The Americans' bid for the Calder Cup ended in defeat on June 13th, and Biron arrived in Buffalo for Game 4 of the Stanley Cup Finals on June 15th. He said learned a valuable lesson from one of the toughest moments in Buffalo sports history.

"We lost to Providence, and we got called to Buffalo just in time to get there for Game 4, and the Sabres tied the final at two. We went into Game 5 in Dallas where we lost, and then back for Game 6 and the Brett Hull goal. I remember the guys' faces after they lost Game 6 in the locker room, and just being crushed, defeated. They worked two months to be there and were just a shot away from Game 7," he said.

"All of those things, being a 21-year-old, you don't realize it. But you look back at your career and the agony and sadness, that's what the

Goaltender Martin Biron, who played 508 NHL games with the Sabres, Flyers, Islanders and Rangers, fondly recalled his time with Rochester in the late 1990s before his career began on the big stage. (ROCHESTER AMERICANS)

game is all about. That's what sacrificing and wanting to win the Cup is all about. Those were really good lessons."

As many of the players develop in Rochester before heading to Buffalo, those kind of lessons are learned every year. For instance, Jason Pominville, who was with the Americans for three seasons before becoming an integral part of the Sabres teams that went to the Eastern Conference Finals in both 2006 and 2007, really appreciated the coaches' focus on development.

"At the time, a lot of the guys from Rochester — especially in the lockout year [of 2004–05] — I feel like [Sabres coach] Lindy [Ruff] and his staff were able to come down to Rochester quite a bit — it's only an hour drive — and got to see a lot of us play. The year following the lockout, me, [Thomas] Vanek, [Ryan] Miller, [Paul] Gaustad, [Derek]

Roy, [Daniel] Paille, quite a few guys who were playing on that team. It really gave them a chance to get a feel what every player was about, and believe in us and brought us up at the same time," he said. "It's a great development league, and a great year for us too since the league was so strong."

Pominville said it was great to experience that season of AHL, which was stronger than normal given the NHL lockout. When he arrived in Buffalo in 2005–06, there was a good mix of players. "Obviously there were great players in Buffalo already, great leadership, great depth of the team, and we were big pieces of that, carrying in and helping out wherever we can. That led to us having back-to-back conference finals. It was a nice run. Winning is always fun and being part of that is great," he said.

"We had a great group of guys, we all kind of came up at the same time, so good team, good coaching — Randy Cunneyworth was our coach, Doug Houda was there, our staff was awesome — and [we] made a lot of good friends. That was the best part. Most of those guys in the AHL, I ended up playing with in Buffalo for quite some time. Quite of few of those guys, we played in Buffalo for a long time, and all kind of came up together, so those are friendships that will last for a long time."

Gage recalled how special it was for him to see Pominville get his NHL shot in Buffalo. "Pominville, it was very rewarding to see him finally get his chance — but not only get his chance, [he's] now succeeding in the National Hockey League. He spent four years down here in the minors."

Rochester is a good place to develop, many players say. And as Drew Bagnall told me, part of the appeal is city's long history of hockey. "We've had really good fan support, and I think part of it is the marketing. They take hockey very seriously here, and it's part of the culture. It's fun to get recognized around town, for an American League guy to get recognized at the grocery store and have someone say, 'Good game last night against Hamilton,'" said Bagnall.

"Guys realize they may be a little more in the spotlight here that they would in other places and I think they try to act as they can when they're out in public eye. It's nice to know that people care about the game that you're playing. Some games, it's tough when you don't play well, but that's part of the game."

Matt Ellis talked about the city's hockey resume. "It's a great hockey town. Great support, great history and fan base. It's an unbelievable place to play. I've been fortunate to have a couple of great stops in the American League. Grand Rapids was great, Portland treated me well and Rochester's a first-class hockey town."

Zac Dalpe also talked about Rochester's history. "They're passionate, and there's a lot of tradition and history in Rochester. No matter what, when things didn't go down there the way we wanted it to go down — there's still fans in the stands every night, so they support us for sure."

Jerry D'Amigo also talked about his time in Rochester glowingly. "I've had the luxury of playing in Toronto where the hockey market is good in the AHL and NHL. Rochester is right there, good fan base, and they care about their farm club. That's the main thing, when you have good support from your NHL parent club and they believe in producing guys from the minors. That builds confidence for us."

With a rebuild on in Buffalo, the end of the 2014–15 season wasn't what Amerk fans had hoped. The parent club recalled a number of Amerks players to finish out the season at the NHL level after shedding players at the trade deadline. Before a game against the Marlies, a promotional video for the team showed how dire the situation was. Nearly half the players were actually down the Thruway in Buffalo and skating for the Sabres instead of this late-season game against Toronto.

Bagnall said he was thrilled for his Rochester teammates wearing the blue-and-gold in Buffalo rather than the blue-and-red in Rochester. "You always want — especially at the stage I'm at in my career — you want those guys to go up there and stay. As much as you love having them around the room and know how much they can help you win down here, you want them to succeed and reach their end goal, and seeing those guys up there and sticking and playing as well as they are. Phil Varone, those other guys have put their time in the American League and all they needed was their opportunity to showcase what they had, and they're getting their chance and the opportunity to play a lot of minutes and play a pivotal role on the Sabres, so it's awesome to see."

The Amerks hit the ice to the team's long-standing signature song, J. Geils Band's "Freeze Frame." The Rochester roster features a lot of new faces, including the starting goaltender Anthony Peters. Less than a month before, he was playing with St. Mary's University in Halifax. Peters looked a bit out of place wearing the Huskies' maroon-and-white pads with the blue Americans' uniform. Another Professional Tryout (PTO) player, Jayden Hart, signed a contract just five days before. He scored to put Rochester up 1–0.

While the Amerks played a decent game against the playoff-bound Toronto club, it wasn't enough to give the home team the win. Rochester fell 4–3.

Oklobzija said even with a lineup filled with players on PTOs, if the players put forth a strong effort, it's appreciated in Rochester. "When you have that kind of lineup, everyone is looking for their chance to prove they can play in the American League; you get an effort anyways. Some fans and people I've known for a long time appreciate that. It's not necessarily the talent that can play in the NHL that these guys have. But in Rochester — a very blue-collar town, similar to Buffalo — if guys work, they're going to be more appreciated than a guy with amazing skill but does little with it."

According to Stevens, it's not quite like the old days when visiting teams used to hate to play in Rochester — although he says that's the case in a lot of places around the AHL. "The winning teams are the ones that other teams hate to play against. That's the way it used to be, and now, you just don't mind playing against teams. When teams used to come here, their locker room was down in the basement, and it was 120 degrees down there and there were rats and they had to walk up these flights of stairs — or take a freight elevator that was so slow you could have climbed a rope and gotten up faster."

"So, they absolutely just hated coming to Rochester. Not only that, it was a very physical game, and you went home . . . black and blue. And you knew you had been in one heck of a hockey game. So players hated to come here. But now they love to come here. Years ago, if you lost double-digits in home games, you had a bad year. If you lost 10 home games in a year, it was a bad year. But now you have almost as good a record as you do at home."

Still, with the long-running tradition of the franchise, hockey in Rochester is about the Americans and their sweater rather than individual players. As Gage said, "We call our jersey the flag, and because it's got the flag on it, it's never allowed to touch the floor. Every time it touched the floor, it was $100. So it was the flag, it meant something. It means something in the community and I think traditionally, as one of the best uniforms, because it does mean something . . . when you put that flag on, it represents something.

"It's hard to explain until you wear it, but the alumni talk about it and are still close. It's a great franchise and the American Hockey League, Dave Andrews and Jack Butterfield have done a great job and gone through years; you go up and down, make changes and those changes end up being the correct changes."

CHAPTER FIFTEEN

THE FUTURE

One of the main marketing points of the American Hockey League is that by in going to an AHL game, you're able to see the National Hockey League's future. It's true that many AHL players end up on NHL rosters, but that's not the only glimpse of the NHL's future you see. The league has become a bit of an experimental lab for rules for the NHL and for the game itself.

In downtown Springfield, Massachusetts, near the top of the Monarch Place building, you can see the Basketball Hall of Fame and Connecticut River down the street. Not too far away are the MassMutual Center (home of Springfield's AHL team) and the Berkshire Mountains. The tower is the home of the American Hockey League's head office. And as the league celebrates its 80th season, it's important to appreciate how much the league has grown and changed.

Just 40 years ago, the AHL had eight teams, separated by a distance of less than 1,250 mile from Nova Scotia to Virginia. In 2015–16, the league had 30 teams and spanned 4,220 miles from New Brunswick to California. The league has outlasted the World Hockey Association and the International Hockey League to become the second-oldest professional hockey league in North America, only behind the NHL, which celebrates its 100th season in 2016–17.

But the AHL has changed dramatically in recent years, putting a lot more emphasis on its relationship with the NHL and relying on an infusion of youth. The league decided its strength lay in showcasing hockey's future stars and top draft picks, and not in providing a platform for players who were depth players in NHL systems. The AHL capped the number of veterans available to skate every night.

Graham Mink played in the AHL from 2001 — he joined just after the IHL's demise — to 2013. And he saw the changes over the course of his career. "The American League made a choice when the International League folded. If they were going to survive and thrive as the premier AAA hockey league, they needed to be a development league, and they tied their business model to partnering with the NHL. Part of that, . . . they made changes and sacrifices in order to appease the NHL and keep things competitive. Otherwise, you'd have the big-budget teams that sign old guys that would just beat up 20-year-olds, and the league didn't want that," he said.

"That was a huge change, and when that occurred — and I think that was in 2004–05 where that distinction happened . . . that changed the game very quickly. You lost a lot of those older players; the teams were different after that, and it was more dominated by the younger guys than the older guys."

For Jody Gage, who has been involved with the AHL as a player, GM or team employee since 1979, the AHL's partnership with the NHL has been key. "The AHL took direction with the NHL in developing players, and that was a key move by Dave Andrews to stay close partners with the National Hockey League — which was important," Gage said.

As Derek King, who was a player-coach with Grand Rapids following a stint in the IHL and an assistant with Toronto, said, "Back then, it was all draft picks, and there wasn't a lot of free agent signings or bringing in veterans; there was no rules. It kind of got away from that. When the IHL was still on, I played in the IHL and it was all older guys like myself. I wanted to play a few more years, but I knew the

NHL was done [for me]. Now, [the AHL has] come back to where it's a development league. You have to get your draft picks in here, and you have to develop them. If you don't, you can't go out and sign players whenever you feel like it."

Todd Crocker, who calls games for the Marlies, agreed that there has been a move toward developing the younger players. "I think the structure has changed more than anything else. When there was an IHL, there were veteran guys over there and it was a different, more mature league, and the odd rookie got into it. The AHL, the majority was about development; there wasn't really a strong commitment outside of personally owned teams to win. It wasn't to win the Calder Cup. It was, this team exists so that we create assets for us to use in our lineup or trade to put into our lineup," Crocker said.

"There is a structure in the AHL, there is a need to a win, to extend your season for your prospects, to teach them how to win, to create a winning culture; these are things that go into an American Hockey League team now, and I think that's why you're seeing more NHL teams having a direct say."

Keith Jones played in the AHL briefly from 1991 to 1994. The league is a lot more prospect-heavy now compared to when he was skating. "What you see today is young players who can flat-out fly. There's fewer goons — and that part of the entertainment value was always there for the fans — if they didn't get their fill of goals scored, they could certainly get their fill with punches, as there was entertainment that way," he said. "There's less of that now. It's more of a developmental league and less of the veteran tough entertainer players that are out there for the sole purpose of prolonging their own careers but recognizing they're not getting called up to the big club."

Jones also said he'd like to see players develop even more in the minors before coming up. "You'd love to have an opportunity for all of your players to spend some time in the minors. I think young players in today's game are much more ready to play than those maybe 15 or 20 years ago. They're stronger, they're thinner and they're fast; they fit the game that's being played today. There's less time spent in the minors, but I think teams like the Los Angeles Kings, who make their players

With a greater emphasis in the AHL of developing top prospects like William Nylander, who spent ample time with the Marlies before joining the Maple Leafs, NHL franchises now focus more on growing talent, rather than filling out their rosters with veterans.
(SYRACUSE CRUNCH)

stay [in the minors] . . . that's the ideal way to go, especially if you're dealing with centermen and defensemen who take a little bit longer with the responsibilities they have in their own end."

Brian Gionta, who came up through the New Jersey Devils' system, said it was important to have a place to grow as a player before joining the National Hockey League. "It's a great development league — I think it was the IHL back then," he said with a laugh. "You look at all the guys who had success down there, and it's equated up here. I think New Jersey was one of those teams that had the model of developing guys in the minors first before taking them up, and I think it means a lot for a young player's development to find their game, find some confidence and learn to play the right way."

One of the other ways the AHL offers fans a glimpse of the future is by testing out rules that the NHL is thinking of implementing. For instance, in 2014–15, the AHL experimented with playing 3-on-3 as part of their overtime period to decide tied games.

The experiment was a success, and the NHL decided to adopt that rule for the 2015–16 season. It also was an exciting thing to see it first-hand before their NHL counterparts.

Brent Thompson, Bridgeport's head coach, likes having the AHL be the NHL's chemistry lab. "I think it's a great model," he told me. "I don't mind being the guinea pig for the NHL. It's made the game better up top. The National Hockey League has been the best it's ever been in terms of speed and pure skill and scoring; [it] seems to be coming along."

Hershey Bears' Troy Mann also likes the experimentation. "When I was an assistant, I remember when the hybrid icing rule was instituted, and this year, the overtime changes were more exciting to watch," he said with a laugh. "We experienced both ends of it, winning it, losing it, and it's exciting to have everyone on the bench."

Former Lehigh Valley Phantoms coach Terry Murray, now an assistant with the Buffalo Sabres, loved the experiment. "I love the 3-on-3. You're obviously playing your players, but everyone does get to be a part of it. You're going up and down the ice, there's a lot of skill and a lot of opportunity. The fans and I love it because you stay involved in the game. It requires coaching — am I going to put two defensemen and a forward, or three forwards going out? Do you need the points? Do you want two forwards and a D? There's a lot of decisions that need to be made. I like it that way, and come into the locker room after a big win on 3-on-3; it seems to be a lot more genuine than what comes after a shootout."

Lindsay Kramer, who covers the Syracuse Crunch, said it's been good to see the rule experimentation in the AHL. "Over the course of the years, it's pretty cool, because it goes back to innovation, not being stagnant. Some rules have been adopted by the NHL, some haven't. The overtime is a great example, the shootouts and whatnot. I like to see different things," Kramer said. "I think it's great [that] it's a league that you have a high level of hockey but also work so closely with the NHL that they're open to trying these things, and it gives credence to the bond of AHL-NHL because if this was just an independent league, they could do what they want and the league may not give it a second thought.

"When the NHL wants to start something or try something, they come here. It's clearly a partnership, and even if the fans don't like something of a specific rule, the fans know the NHL is looking. I think things need to evolve, and you see them on the ground floor first often, and almost every year there's a very cool rule that gets introduced. It's cool to see things in their embryonic form."

AHL president Dave Andrews said the experimentation also gave the league some extra attention as they tried it out. "It's good for us in some ways, probably the most attention we had all last year, and the most nationally we've had in a long time was people interested in how the [3-on-3] was going. It's good for us to be in that position. We've worked with the NHL and we provide them a good incubator for trying things, and I think we're all pretty proud of that. If you look at today's NHL rulebook, we've had a pretty big impact on what it looks like."

Sometimes, according to Andrews, some of the rules don't turn out as they hoped. "The strangest one for me, I sort of invented the puck-over-the-glass rule, which everybody hates. But it's logical. Why should the goalie be the only one penalized for shooting the puck over the glass? I took the concept to our competition committee, it was unanimously approved. I took it to our board and unanimously approved, and put in for the year. At the next annual meeting, it was unanimously taken out," he said. "And then the NHL adopted it. So there was a year where they had it and we didn't before we fell back into line. It's funny when you think about it. My sales pitch was so good, but the coaches hated it and the players hated it."

The AHL offers players a kind of a unique paradox. It gives players a chance to play, but this is not the league of their dreams — it's not the NHL, but it's the next best thing. That means spending time in its ranks requires a true passion for the game, especially considering players spend the winter months crossing North America by bus or plane, sometimes playing in front of big crowds — and sometimes not-so-big crowds.

A season that lasts from training camp in September to potentially the end of the Calder Cup playoffs in June is a tough grind.

Steve Oleksy, who worked his way up from the ECHL to play in the AHL, said loving the game is almost a requirement to last in the league. "You definitely have to love the game. It's demanding. It's not a lifestyle that is for everybody — that's why the higher you go, the guys who don't have the passion for it end up having shorter careers and get weeded out. You miss a lot of family events, a lot of holidays, and that's where you develop the fraternity-type feel when you're spending Thanksgiving and Christmas together for the guys who can't get home; it really brings people close together," Oleksy said. "It isn't a lifestyle for everybody, especially at this level. If you're not 100 percent dedicated, you're not going to have a long or successful career. It has to be your main focus in life, and if you're not passionate about it, it's a job. You get tired of it and you won't last very long."

Brian Strait, who joined Wilkes-Barre/Scranton out of Boston University before jumping to the NHL with the New York Islanders in 2012, said that the experience with the AHL really helped prepare him.

"I had a good experience in Wilkes-Barre and a lot of good relationships with good guys that I met there who I still keep in touch with all the time," he said. "Hockey's great and you love it, and you look back and see the relationships you made along the way and the life, and you know it's not going to last forever. But those people are in your life forever now, 30 years [from now] I'm going to run into them and it'll bring me right back and be a joy."

J.P. Côté said he was happy to play in the AHL, even if the NHL wasn't in the cards anymore. "I love it a lot," he said with a smile. "It's definitely fun, I'm fortunate that I've had a career path to where I'm at right now. I'm not obviously one of the 300 best players in the world, but in the next guys that might be in the NHL or AHL."

Mink said even with the grind, he was thankful to play a dozen years in the AHL. "I loved it; it was a lot of fun. I really appreciated being able to play there, I've been fortunate to have my career primarily in the American League. Obviously, playing in the NHL was my dream and where I wanted to go, but kind of given my story and where I came from, an undrafted guy out of college from Vermont to have a 12-year American League career was just — I feel fortunate to have that. I feel appreciative of that," he said. "I met a lot of great players, people, coaches, and I look back on it fondly, and wish I could play there another 10 years."

And it's not just the players who love being around the game either. Jim Sarosy works well more than the standard 40-hour workweek looking to help market his club and grow the sport in Syracuse.

"Outside of my family, every fiber of my being loves the game of hockey, and specifically the Syracuse Crunch. . . . You're earning your living by going to an ice rink every day and going around and traveling with the best athletes in the world, and both physically and socially, they have everything going for them," he said. "To see the passion of all the kids in the front office coming through, it reminds you of every day and every week why you've chosen this business. It's so refreshing, and I count my blessings and how can you not? It's cool."

Crunch owner Howard Dolgon echoed Sarosy's sentiments. "You've got to live it, you've got to love it, you've got to have a passion because you can put your money in a lot of things and do better and be safer, and [with] a lot less emotion attached to it. We have 30 teams in a great league that's the second-best in the world. I've met great friends in this league, great players and been involved with great NHL organizations. Who would have thought I've been breaking bread with Steve Yzerman and talking on the phone and sitting with him at a game and enjoying the gentleman that he is. That's such a wonderful thing," said Dolgon.

"The athletes and the hockey guys — and I've been fortunate to work with Pelé to Michael Jordan to Muhammad Ali, you name it — but there's nothing like the quality and class of hockey players. It's really amazing. It's just amazing."

According to former AHL coach Chadd Cassidy, the life isn't easy, and you have to love the game to keep playing it at that level. "I think there's a perception that the players make a ton of money — and they don't. Most of the players in this league make a pretty modest living — they're playing to try and move up and make it to the National League.

They're not out striking it rich. They're playing because they love to, and as long as they can put food on the table, they'll keep playing as long as they can.

"I think it's a very difficult life in a lot of ways. They don't have a nine-to-five job, but when you're at the pressure of having to perform every night and being under the watchful eyes of 30 NHL teams every single night, . . . you're not just competing for a job in your organization. Everyone's showcasing for every organization every night.

"The toll it takes on your body physically and mentally can be very difficult. I don't think people necessarily understand that how tough some of the trips are. It's a grinding league for players. It's very difficult."

He added that it takes a special player who loves the game to stay in the American League for a long period of time. "It's such a hard thing to go through it physically and as players get older and go on all these bus trips and their bodies start to give away, you really have to love the game. You can handle it when you're 20, 21, 22, but when you get into your mid-20s, get a lot of pro games under your belt and the wear and tear, you really find out which guys love the game and do everything they can to play as long as they can."

John Anderson said when his NHL career was ending, he wasn't sure he wanted to be in the minors, but rediscovered a love for the game with those who don't necessarily make a lot of money doing it. "I didn't know if at 33 if I could still play in the National Hockey League — but I still loved the game. But my ego was so big that I thought I could go back up there. I ended up playing five years in the minors until I was 38. My biggest fear coming down was traveling on the bus and what people would think about me. I remember coming through the airport in Indianapolis, and I was playing for the Fort Wayne Komets — I didn't even know who they were when I first joined them — and I saw my [former] teammates going through that airport and I was embarrassed to see them because I knew I was playing at the minor level," he said.

"What I found out is hockey is hockey, and hockey guys are great guys. That was one of the most fun years I had playing [in 1990–91] with Bruce Boudreau in Fort Wayne, Lonnie Loach and all the guys that I'd met there. Hockey still became hockey. Of course I was playing for $27,500 instead of $250,000 but hockey was still fun."

Wolves general manager Wendell Young also mentioned how important it is for players to appreciate what they have. "I think we all love the game. We all, and I, try to put across to the players [to] appreciate what they have. There's a million kids, a million people who want to do what we do. And really, and I try to tell them to appreciate it; we are idolized, we are this whether we ask for it or not," he said.

"People look up to pro hockey player[s] or American League; guys want to be a pro hockey player, and they all want to make it to the NHL. Some guys are high draft picks, some guys are trying to get up there and say they played. Everyone wants to get to the NHL and play pro hockey, and I carry that on every day of my life."

While the AHL is a great place to be, they'd all rather be playing elsewhere. Paul Ryan, who works for the Sound Tigers, put it succinctly: "Obviously you want to stay with the same guys all season and it sucks when they go up, but that's what they want to do. It's not that they don't want to be here, it's that they'd rather be achieving the goal of being at the highest professional league that they could be."

As the summer winds to a close, 30 NHL teams will gather their players — NHL, AHL, ECHL and other invitees — and as training camp progresses, will assign players to their respective clubs.

While most of the skaters assigned to the AHL club would rather be somewhere else, some will expect it, some will strive to get to the NHL level and others will be called on to help the others reach their goals. It begins a journey that will take them either by bus or plane for 38 road games (or in the case of the California teams, 34 games), one that lasts from just after Columbus Day to past Memorial Day, playing in 1,120 games that will be held in 30 AHL rinks, various NHL venues as well as the occasional outdoor game, before the 16 teams advance to the playoffs and eventually one team gets to hoist the Calder Cup — before the whole cycle starts again three months later.

And with more than six million fans attending AHL games each season, sometimes those coming out are those who eventually will get to play in the league. Jerry D'Amigo, who grew up just outside of Binghamton, said he remembers seeing Binghamton Senators and Rangers games as a kid at the Broome County Veterans Memorial Arena.

"All the time," he said with a grin. "Even when they were the Rangers, and also when they had an IHL team. As a kid I loved it, and I always dreamed of playing there and having my family there. And it happened."

Although he played for Toronto and Rochester, when he got to play near his hometown, he'd remember back to the day when he was in the stands, watching the skaters chasing their dreams — and coming up with one of his own. "It's just one of those things; I would remember where I sat right behind the goalie when I would come to the games," he said. "It was a good experience to have for myself, to reach that and have that goal for myself and finally reach it."

ACKNOWLEDGMENTS

This book was written over the course of eight months during the 2014–15 season, with visits to nine AHL arenas — Bridgeport, Chicago, Hartford, Hershey, Lehigh Valley, Rochester, Syracuse, Toronto and Utica — as well as NHL arenas in Buffalo, Long Island and Washington.

Special thanks are in order to all the players, coaches, broadcasters and reporters I talked to to put this special project together.

I'd like to thank the seven AHL teams who participated in the project and allowed extensive interviews and access to get a glimpse of each franchise, as well as American Hockey League president Dave Andrews and vice-president of communications Jason Chaimovitch for their support and assistance with the project from the planning stages.

For the Bridgeport Sound Tigers, I'd like to thank communications and community relations manager Paul Ryan, coach Brent Thompson and broadcaster Phil Giubileo.

With the Chicago Wolves, I'd like to thank director of public relations Lindsey Willhite, as well as owner Don Levin, general manager Wendell Young, coach John Anderson and broadcaster Jason Shaver.

In Hershey, special thanks are in order to Scott Stuccio, broadcaster and media relations manager, as well as general manager Doug Yingst and coach Troy Mann.

With Lehigh Valley, I'd like to thank Phantoms relations manager Dan Fremuth and broadcaster Bob Rotruck.

In Rochester, I'd like to thank director of public relations Rob Crean, broadcaster Don Stevens and director of strategic planning Jody Gage.

For the Syracuse Crunch, I'd like to give special thanks to chief operating officer Jim Sarosy, as well as owner Howard Dolgon, broadcaster Dan D'Uva and former director of communications and marketing Maggie Walters.

With Toronto, I'd like to thank Marlies media relations coordinator Stefano Toniutti, broadcaster Todd Crocker and director of hockey operations Brad Lynn.

I'd also like to thank Capitals coach Barry Trotz and Hurricanes coach Bill Peters for their time, as well as Sergey Kocharov, Pace Sagester and Megan Eichenberg in Washington, and Mike Sundheim and Kyle Hanlin in Carolina for arranging the interviews.

Also I'd like to thank Jesse Eisenberg with the New York Islanders, Ian Ott with the Buffalo Sabres and Carly Peters with the Minnesota Wild for their help in getting interviews arranged with NHL players for this project.

Capitals radio voice John Walton deserves a special thank you for being part of all three of my books, Comcast SportsNet's Joe Beninati for taking part in the last two. Fellow broadcasters Kenny Albert, Keith Jones, Dave Starman, Eric Lindquist and Ken Cail also deserve thanks.

I've been fortunate to speak to Tim Leone of the *Patriot-News* and Erik Erlendsson of the *Tampa Tribune* for my last two books. I appreciate Lindsay Kramer of the *Syracuse Post-Standard* and Kevin Oklobzjia of the *Rochester Democrat & Chronicle* taking time to discuss the league.

Thanks also are in order to all the current and former players and coaches I spoke with during this terrific project to undertake.

This project also wouldn't have been possible without the assistance of Jamshid Mousavinezhad and Mandy Hofmockel of *Newsday*, who allowed me to do the project, and my editor with ECW Press for my last two books, Michael Holmes, as well as John Manasso for the advice before the first book.

Lastly but most importantly, I'd like to thank my wife, Pam; daughter, Victoria; mother, Margaret; and my father, Don, all of whom helped me chase the dream of becoming a hockey writer.

Ted Starkey is a veteran sportswriter who has written for *Newsday*, the *Washington Times, The Tampa Tribune, Pittsburgh Tribune-Review*, AOL Sports, USAHockey.com and BuffaloBills.com.

Ted has written three books, *Transition Game: The Story of the 2010–11 Washington Capitals* in 2011, *Red Rising: The Washington Capitals Story* in 2012 and *Chasing the Dream: Life in the American Hockey League* in 2016.

He also has covered numerous events, such as the 2002 Salt Lake Olympics; the 2010 Vancouver Olympics; the 2010 and 2013 Stanley Cup Finals; the 2011 NHL All-Star Game; the 2010, 2013 and 2015 Calder Cup Finals; the 2011 and 2015 Winter Classics and the 2012 and 2013 AHL Outdoor Classics. He also has covered numerous NHL, AHL, NFL and MLB games for various outlets.

He attended American University in Washington, D.C., and Boston University in Boston, Massachusetts, and is a graduate of the Potomac School in McLean, Virginia.

Ted lives in Smithtown, New York, with his wife, Pam, and daughter, Victoria.